# Lyndon B. Johnson 104-124 192-208
# and American Liberalism

## A Brief Biography with Documents

Related Titles in
# THE BEDFORD SERIES IN HISTORY AND CULTURE
*Advisory Editors:* Natalie Zemon Davis, Princeton University
Ernest R. May, Harvard University

---

*The Era of Franklin D. Roosevelt, 1932–1945: A Brief History with Documents* (forthcoming)
Richard Polenberg, *Cornell University*

*Confronting Southern Poverty in the Great Depression:* THE REPORT ON ECONOMIC CONDITIONS OF THE SOUTH *with Related Documents*
Edited with an Introduction by David L. Carlton, *Vanderbilt University,* and Peter A. Coclanis, *University of North Carolina at Chapel Hill*

*American Cold War Strategy: Interpreting NSC 68*
Edited with an Introduction by Ernest R. May, *Harvard University*

*The Age of McCarthyism: A Brief History with Documents*
Ellen Schrecker, *Yeshiva University*

*American Social Classes in the 1950s: Selections from Vance Packard's* THE STATUS SEEKERS
Edited with an Introduction by Daniel Horowitz, *Smith College*

*Women's Magazines, 1940–1960: Gender Roles and the Popular Press*
Edited with an Introduction by Nancy A. Walker, *Vanderbilt University*

*Postwar Immigrant America: A Social History*
Reed Ueda, *Tufts University*

*Brown v. Board of Education: A Brief History with Documents*
Edited with an Introduction by Waldo E. Martin, *University of California, Berkeley*

*My Lai: A Brief History with Documents*
James S. Olson, *Sam Houston State University,* and Randy Roberts, *Purdue University*

THE BEDFORD SERIES IN HISTORY AND CULTURE

# Lyndon B. Johnson
# and
# American Liberalism
## A Brief Biography with Documents

**Bruce J. Schulman**

*Boston University*

BEDFORD/ST. MARTIN'S    Boston ♦ New York

*For my mother, Marianne Schulman*

**For Bedford/St. Martin's**
*President and Publisher:* Charles H. Christensen
*Associate Publisher/General Manager:* Joan E. Feinberg
*History Editor:* Niels Aaboe
*Developmental Editor:* Louise D. Townsend
*Editorial Assistant:* Richard Keaveny
*Managing Editor:* Elizabeth M. Schaaf
*Production Editor:* Anne Benaquist
*Copyeditor:* Nancy Ludlow
*Indexers:* Phil Roberts and Peggy Bieber-Roberts
*Text Design:* Claire Seng-Niemoeller
*Cover Design:* Richard Emery Design, Inc.
*Cover Art:* Photograph of Lyndon Baines Johnson courtesy of The Bettmann Archive, New York.

Library of Congress Catalog Card Number: 92–75892

Manufactured in the United States of America.

5   4   3   2   1   0
j   i   h   g   f   e

*For information, write:* Bedford/St. Martin's, 75 Arlington Street, Boston, MA 02116 (617-399-4000)

ISBN: 0–312–08351–3 (paperback)
ISBN: 0–312–10282–8 (hardcover)

### Acknowledgments

James Burnham. Reprinted from "What Is the President Wating For?" by James Burnham. © 1966 by *National Review,* Inc., 150 East 35th Street, New York, NY 10016. Reprinted by permission.

Joseph A. Califano. Reprinted by permission of the LBJ School of Public Affairs and by permission of the author.

James Farmer. Reprinted by permission of James Farmer.

Martin Luther King, Jr. "Beyond Vietnam" reprinted by arrangement with the Heirs to the Estate of Martin Luther King, Jr., c/o Joan Daves Agency as agent for the proprietor. Copyright 1967 by Martin Luther King, Jr.

*Acknowledgments and copyrights are continued at the back of the book on page 257, which constitutes an extension of the copyright page. It is a violation of the law to reproduce these selections by any means whatsoever without the written permission of the copyright holder.*

# Foreword

*The Bedford Series in History and Culture* is designed so that readers can study the past as historians do.

The historian's first task is finding the evidence. Documents, letters, memoirs, interviews, pictures, movies, novels, or poems can provide facts and clues. Then the historian questions and compares the sources. There is more to do than in a courtroom, for hearsay evidence is welcome, and the historian is usually looking for answers beyond act and motive. Different views of an event may be as important as a single verdict. How a story is told may yield as much information as what it says.

Along the way the historian seeks help from other historians and perhaps from specialists in other disciplines. Finally, it is time to write, to decide on an interpretation and how to arrange the evidence for readers.

Each book in this series contains an important historical document or group of documents, each document a witness from the past and open to interpretation in different ways. The documents are combined with some element of historical narrative—an introduction or a biographical essay, for example—that provides students with an analysis of the primary source material and important background information about the world in which it was produced.

Each book in the series focuses on a specific topic within a specific historical period. Each provides a basis for lively thought and discussion about several aspects of the topic and the historian's role. Each is short enough (and inexpensive enough) to be a reasonable one-week assignment in a college course. Whether as classroom or personal reading, each book in the series provides firsthand experience of the challenge—and fun—of discovering, recreating, and interpreting the past.

Natalie Zemon Davis
Ernest R. May

# Preface

Lyndon Baines Johnson transformed America. In achievements so grand that few politicians would have dared them and in humiliations so painful that no one, not even Johnson, could bear them, LBJ altered the way Americans worked, played, voted, lived and died. For his triumphs and his failures, Johnson has been admired, criticized, and reviled. His gigantic presence and volcanic personality have spawned vociferous debate and inspired biographies as large and monumental as Johnson himself.

This book is not one of them. While *Lyndon B. Johnson and American Liberalism* does examine Johnson's character—his dishonesty, nobility, ambition, vulgarity, generosity, greed—this account focuses less on LBJ's personal traits and more on the ways he embodied the principles, obsessions, and contradictions of his era. The analytic biography that makes up the first part of this book attempts to immerse Johnson in his times; it portrays him as an emblematic figure, indeed *the* emblematic figure in the rise and fall of postwar American liberalism. The documents that make up the second part of this book revive the voices of historical actors and assemble a wide range of contemporary opinion. Addressing the great issues of Johnson's public life—civil rights, Vietnam and American foreign policy, the Great Society, and the fate of liberal reform—Johnson, his aides, his opponents, and his interpreters all speak of LBJ's ambitions, achievements, defeats, and legacy. Collected together, they reveal the complexity of Lyndon Johnson's character and the profound and continuing impact of his tumultuous presidency.

## ACKNOWLEDGMENTS

In assembling this little book, I have incurred unusually large debts. Six distinguished historians reviewed the manuscript for the publisher. Lewis L. Gould shared his expert knowledge of Johnson's career and corrected many embarrassing errors. Paul Boyer suggested ways to deepen the historical context and slim down some of my "high calorie" prose. Laura Kalman's mastery of the historical record and of the art of biography contributed much to this book, as did Elizabeth Cobbs's incisive commentary and Philip Ethington's penetrating reading and provocative interpretations of Johnson and his milieu. David M. Kennedy examined the manuscript with his customary insight and care, displaying his uncanny knack for exposing the difficult issues I had tried to finesse and forcing me to confront them. Kennedy's obligations to this former student ended many years ago, but he has continued to support my work with candor, dedication, and grace. He sets a model as a scholar, colleague, and mentor that I have tried to emulate, without ever expecting to approach.

Mary Corey, Stephen Davis, Julie Reuben, Charles Romney, and Stewart Weaver read sections of this manuscript and contributed many useful suggestions. Robert Dallek offered the benefits of his unparalleled knowledge of Johnson and the presidency and his savvy advice about fashioning a brief interpretive essay.

Although born and bred in Texas, Lyndon Johnson spent most of his adult life in Washington, D.C. Fittingly, I completed the greater part of this book during a year-and-a-half sojourn in the nation's capital, in the hospitable surroundings of UCLA's Center for American Politics and Public Policy. I would like to thank Center Director Joel Aberbach for opening those splendid facilities to me; Washington Director Peter Skerry for welcoming me to Washington; UC Washington staff members Helen Chatalas, Caroline Hartzell, Melody Johnson, Dave Lewis, and Alverta Scott for providing a congenial setting; and especially, Program Administrator Darlene Otten, whose efforts made my stay particularly pleasant and productive.

It is commonplace for authors to acknowledge their publishers, but all too frequently (as many authors know) one can offer only perfunctory, dutiful expressions of gratitude. Not so in this case. The staff at Bedford Books, beginning with President and Publisher Chuck Christensen and History Editor Sabra Scribner, have won my admiration for their work and my sincere thanks for their consistent aid and support. Joan Feinberg, Niels Aaboe, Elizabeth Schaaf, Richard Keaveny, Karen Baart, and Nancy Ludlow all contributed to the completion of this book. Production Editor Anne Benaquist's rigorous and sensitive attention to the manuscript—her devotion to precision and clarity—rescued this book from many errors and inconsistencies. I owe particular gratitude to my developmental editor, Louise Townsend, who shepherded this book and its author through many difficult passages with enthusiasm, insight, and a sense of humor.

With patience and panache, Louise edited the biography, helped trim the documents, and guided this book through every stage of the development process.

Finally, Alice Killian read every page of the manuscript many times. Wrestling with the roughest of first drafts, her editing repeatedly turned odorous, murky mash into smooth, clear malt. In this, as in all other endeavors, she has been a loving and supportive partner.

Bruce J. Schulman

# Contents

THE BEDFORD SERIES IN HISTORY AND CULTURE

# Lyndon B. Johnson and American Liberalism

### A Brief Biography with Documents

# PART ONE

# Lyndon B. Johnson and American Liberalism

For half a century, from the New Deal of the 1930s to the Reagan Revolution of the 1980s, liberalism was the dominant political philosophy in the United States. Liberals prescribed active government as the cure for the nation's ills, and millions of Americans embraced that therapy. They turned to Washington to provide economic prosperity, international security, and some measure of social justice.

One man, Lyndon Baines Johnson (LBJ), towered over the entire era from Roosevelt to Reagan—his long legs striding through the corridors of power, his outsized, homely features facing down his opponents. In a period when Americans shared his faith in the federal government's capacity to solve the nation's problems, Johnson personified liberal, activist government. His career traced the path of modern American liberalism—a path beginning with the New Deal, culminating in the Great Society and the Vietnam War, and, finally, pointing toward the conservative backlash of the 1970s and 1980s. At a time when Americans relied on the national government for relief from economic depression, security in old age, education of their children, homes for their families, and safety from foreign menace, Lyndon Johnson became the principal champion of liberal government. He was the architect of its most important legislative achievements and, also, a major agent of its eventual demise. More than any other politician of the past five decades, Lyndon

Johnson embodied the contradictions of political liberalism in post–World War II America, orchestrated its triumphs, and endured its agonies.

In historian Robert Dallek's words, it was an age "when politics was king," and Lyndon Johnson never strayed far from the throne.[1] "Now of course you have to understand," his vice president, Hubert Humphrey, explained, "above all he was a man steeped in politics. Politics was not an avocation with him. It was it. It was *the* vocation. It was his life, it was his religion, it was his family. . . . Every time you saw him it wasn't like seeing a man; it was like seeing an institution, a whole system that just encompassed you. Johnson thought he could pick up the globe and walk off with it."[2] The man and the era fused in that passion for politics, in a vision of political office as a platform for constructive action. "Some men want power simply to strut around the world and to hear the tune of 'Hail to the Chief,' " LBJ once remarked. "Others want it simply to build prestige, to collect antiques, and to buy pretty things. Well, I wanted power to give things to people, all sorts of things to all sorts of people. . . . "[3]

Politics mattered to Lyndon Johnson because he and his fellow liberals intended widespread and dramatic action. They harbored no doubts that government could and should improve American life. They had little sense of the limits of political action, the unintended, self-defeating consequences of some well-intentioned policies. Ironically, Johnson's own presidency alerted Americans to those dangers and shook their faith in the capacity of their president and their government to meet the challenges of modern life.

Johnson's career, then, offers an unparalleled opportunity for investigating United States politics and public policy from the 1930s to the 1970s. To study LBJ is to survey his times, for Johnson was a historical lightning rod, a huge presence that attracted and absorbed the great forces of his era.

In every sense, Johnson was big—in his overweening ambition, his vulgarity, his generosity, his greed. Texas Governor John B. Connally, a friend and one-time protégé of LBJ, maintained that "there is no adjective in the dictionary to describe him. He was cruel and kind, generous and greedy, sensitive and insensitive, crafty and naive, ruthless and thoughtful, simple in many ways yet extremely complex, caring and totally not caring. . . . As a matter of fact," Connally concluded, "it would take *every* adjective in the dictionary to describe him."[4]

Johnson left huge footprints wherever he stepped, overwhelming nearly everyone who crossed his path and achieving more than nearly any other American politician. He finally retired to Texas in defeat, his leadership and his liberalism repudiated by the American people.

The pages that follow retrace those footprints and reconstruct, as best they can, the story of Lyndon Baines Johnson and American liberalism.

## NOTES

[1] Robert Dallek, conversation with the author, April 1992.

[2] Hubert H. Humphrey, quoted in Merle Miller, *Lyndon: An Oral Biography* (New York: Ballantine, 1980), xvii.

[3] Doris Kearns, *Lyndon Johnson and the American Dream* (New York: Signet, 1976), 57.

[4] John B. Connally, in Miller, *Lyndon,* xvi.

# 1

# "The Perfect Roosevelt Man": Young Lyndon Johnson, 1908–1948

Johnson City, a tiny town in the Hill Country of central Texas, primped and preened in expectation of its most famous native. Lyndon Baines Johnson—congressman, senator, now president of the United States— was coming home. He was headed not to the LBJ Ranch, the spectacular spread he had built a few miles away, but to the town itself, to the shabby six-room schoolhouse where he had begun his rise to power. Johnson had almost single-handedly brought electricity and running water to the Hill Country, secured pensions for its elderly, and obtained subsidies for its hardscrabble farmers. He built the dams, the roads, the hospitals, and the schools.

This time, Lyndon Johnson carried one last great gift—for the Hill Country, the schools, and every poor, striving child in the nation. In Johnson City he would sign the Elementary and Secondary Education Act of 1965, a massive federal aid program for education designed, as Johnson often put it, to allow every student, no matter how poor or wretched, to "get as much schooling as he could take." Franklin D. Roosevelt, Johnson's idol and mentor, had sought such a comprehensive federal education law and failed. So, too, had LBJ's predecessor, John F. Kennedy. But Lyndon had delivered. "You take it from me," he explained, "I worked harder and longer on this measure than on any measure I ever worked on since I came to Washington in 1931." A boy of modest means from a starved, desolate land, he believed education the only escape from a life of want and squalor. "Education," President Johnson instructed the audience at the signing ceremony, "is the only valid passport from poverty."[1]

Few of LBJ's hometown neighbors ever had that passport stamped or found any other safe-conduct out of poverty. The unforgiving Hill Country wrecked many a family. One sign, posted on an abandoned farm during a severe drought near the end of the nineteenth century, expressed the desolation of the region and the desperation of its people: "200 miles to nearest post office; 100 miles to wood; 20 miles to water; 6 inches to hell. God bless our home."[2]

Johnson's parents left that hard country life for Johnson City in 1913 when Lyndon turned five years old. But this metropolis, with a population of 323, offered little more comfort than the isolated farm. Without electricity or indoor plumbing, Johnson City boasted one bank with a total capital reserve of $23,000 and one "factory," a pitiful little cotton gin built out of corrugated tin. Nowhere could you buy a loaf of bread or fresh meat, and the nearest railroad bypassed the area, many miles away. "When I came to Johnson City," one neighbor remembered of those days, "I thought I had come to the end of the earth."[3]

That barren country formed the sometimes loving, sometimes ruthless man who created the compassionate Great Society and directed the cruel battle in Vietnam. It nurtured the fiery ambition that never let Johnson rest and vaulted him from the end of the earth to the most powerful office in the world. Resting just beyond the 98th meridian, the Hill Country straddled the boundary between the South and the West and divided the cotton-growing, fertile plantation region of east Texas from the arid, cowboy-and-rattlesnake country of the west. It was pure Texas and many were proud of it. Lyndon's father, Sam Ealy Johnson, Jr., had himself preserved the Alamo as a historic monument and shrine to state history. Nonetheless, Johnson City and its hilly environs stood apart from the rest of Texas; it had no oil to speak of, few wealthy men, and almost no blacks or Mexican Americans (and most Hill Country whites hoped to keep it that way). Everybody knew one another; it was a place, Lyndon's father said, where people know when you're sick and care when you die.

## FROM THE HILL COUNTRY
## TO CAPITOL HILL

From the very beginning, Lyndon Johnson stood out. For three months after his birth in 1908, his parents could not even agree on a name for their long-eared, big-nosed boy. His mother, Rebekah Baines Johnson, an unusually refined woman for the uncouth prairie, treasured poetry, revered knowledge, and detested anything dirty or shabby. She insisted on filling her children's minds, even when neighbors thought she should worry more about feeding their growling stomachs. The boy's father cared little for the farming he did near the family's cabin on the Pedernales River and still less for the real estate work he pursued after moving his young family to town. Sam Johnson's passion was politics. He wanted to name the baby for one of his political friends, but Rebekah found that too mean, too common. Finally, she agreed to name the boy for a lawyer friend, W. C. Linden, but only if she could spell it "L-Y-N-D-O-N."

The boy soon absorbed his father's passion for politics. He hid under tables or stood behind doors, straining to hear every word of his father's evening bull sessions with political friends. Sam Johnson, a six-term member of the state legislature, took his son along with him on the campaign trail and brought him onto the floor of the Texas House of Representatives in Austin. On their rounds about the district, Lyndon and his father drove from farm to farm, stopping at every isolated homestead, trading gossip, bringing news, listening to problems, and looking after Sam's constituents. For Sam Johnson believed in "the kind of government that could do things personally for people." He would spend hours helping widows and veterans apply for pensions. And, according to one of his neighbors in Johnson City, "he was always the person we went to, whenever assistance was needed."[4]

In Austin, Sam Johnson fought for the Hill Country—to pave roads, build schools, eradicate pests. Sam championed the little man—the poor dirt farmer—against the rich and powerful. He supported an eight-hour day for exploited railroad workers, boldly criticized the Ku Klux Klan, and voted to tax corporations, regulate utilities, and ensure pure food. Lyndon watched it all at close range; he imbibed his father's liberal philosophy and imitated Sam's persuasive style of getting up really close to someone, nose to nose, when he wanted to convince them of something. Lyndon surely also noticed that Sam Johnson almost always remained on the losing side; few of the liberal measures he supported ever became law.

For Lyndon Johnson's father not only fought for the dispossessed, he fought cleanly. The legislature was a full-time job for a dedicated representative like Sam Johnson, but it offered nothing like a full-time salary. Texans distrusted government so much that they ensured, even to the point of writing it into their state constitution, that the legislature met seldom, transacted its business, and got out of town quickly. Legislators earned five dollars a day for the two-month-long regular session; if they stayed longer, they received just two dollars a day. Most of Sam Johnson's colleagues did not mind the paltry pay. Lobbyists for railroads, oil companies, and other big businesses made it worth their while, buying their votes and treating them to "beefsteak, bourbon, and blondes" in Austin's saloons and brothels. But Sam Johnson never accepted a dime from a lobbyist. He did his share of drinking and whoring in the capital (in fact, he was too fond of whiskey for his own good), but he paid for them with his own money.

Sam would not get rich in Austin and could not earn enough for his family to prosper in the Hill Country. The real estate business flagged, and when Lyndon was twelve, he and his family, including his siblings, Josefa, Sam Houston, and Lucia, returned to the homestead on the Pedernales River, thirteen miles from Johnson City. Sam Johnson managed the farm successfully for a few years, but a collapse in cotton prices eventually ruined him. With cotton at forty-four cents a pound and expected to climb to fifty, Sam borrowed money to purchase equipment and rent some extra property. When the price plummeted to a meager six cents a pound, Sam lost the family farm and never climbed out of debt. He kept his home only because his brothers guaranteed the mortgage. Eventually, Sam Johnson found a menial job on a road crew and built the very highways he had fought for in the state legislature. He also worked as a bus inspector for the state railroad commission. Hill Country neighbors admired Sam's compassion and steadfastness, but they thought him foolish, a man without common sense. Thirteen-year-old Lyndon saw his father's disgrace and learned hard lessons from it.

Immediately after finishing high school in 1924, Lyndon determined to break free of his father, his mother, and the Hill Country. As he later put it, "I graduated from the Johnson City High School in a class of six. For some time I had felt that my father was not really as smart as I thought he ought to be, and I thought I could improve on a good many of my mother's approaches to life."[5] His parents insisted that he attend college, but Lyndon rebelled. With just twenty-six dollars in his pocket, he crammed his six-foot-three-inch frame into a Model T Ford with five of his school friends, several cases of canned pork and beans, plenty of home-made pickles and cornbread, and one .22 rifle. The carload of young Texans headed for California to make their fortunes in the "Golden West."

In California, Lyndon found only hard labor in dead-end jobs, and a year later he returned to Texas. After a stint working for the highway department, Lyndon changed his mind about college and decided to enroll in the only institution he could afford, Southwest Texas State Teacher's College in San Marcos. With the little money he had saved from the road crew and a seventy-five-dollar bank loan, Johnson hitchhiked to San Marcos. In college, he truly launched his political career—joining the campus government, becoming the protégé of the college president, and displaying such a propensity for grandiose boasting that some of his fellow students nick-named him "Bull Johnson."

A shortage of funds forced Johnson to interrupt his studies and spend a year earning money in Cotulla, Texas, a small town sixty miles north of the

Mexican border. Anglos composed only one-quarter of the town's three thousand residents. The rest were Mexican Americans who lived on the east side of the city, across the railroad tracks from the wealthy, white part of town. Johnson, not yet a college graduate, with a two-year elementary school teacher's credential, was about the only person the school board could lure to teach in Welhausen Ward Elementary School, a drab and dingy all-Mexican school in the poorest part of Cotulla. In fact, the twenty-year-old Johnson was hired as both a teacher and principal for the school.

There was no lunch hour in Welhausen; the hungry pupils had no lunch to eat. Recess amounted to nothing more than sending the children outside onto a dirt lot, without playground equipment or supervision. Principal Johnson's first decision was to purchase sporting equipment; his first order was to have teachers organize games at recess. Johnson soon realized that the other teachers, all Anglo women from the other side of town, could not have cared less about their poor, Mexican-American pupils. And the students had come to expect such neglect.

But Welhausen Elementary had never seen a teacher like Lyndon Johnson. He worked long hours and demanded dedication from his students. "I'd just try to run 'em under ground, just about stomp 'em," LBJ recalled, "until they got to where they could take care of themselves, which they did." Years later, one of the students remembered Johnson's year in Cotulla as "a blessing from a clear sky."[6]

For his own part, LBJ long remembered the year at Cotulla as one of the formative influences in his life: "I could never forget," he reminisced, "seeing the disappointment in their eyes and seeing the quizzical expression on their faces when they had come to school that morning, most of them without any breakfast, most of them hungry, and all the time they seemed to be asking me, 'Why don't people like me? Why do they hate me? . . . ' " "Somehow," he said on another occasion, "you never forget what poverty and hatred can do when you see its scars on the face of a young child."[7]

Johnson's students spoke little English, but he insisted they learn, punishing any student who spoke Spanish on school grounds. He organized a debating team so the children could practice language skills and personally arranged transportation because the Mexican school had no bus. Johnson was convinced, rightly so for Texas in the 1920s, that his students needed English to break free from poverty. But his rigidity on this matter betrayed a certain insensitivity to his students' culture and traditions. Decades later, President Johnson would be mystified when protesters demanded the preservation of ethnic cultures and languages and criticized his efforts to assimilate all Americans into a homogeneous national mainstream.

Johnson returned to San Marcos to finish his studies. Then, in July, 1930, a well-timed political debut launched Lyndon on the road to Washington. At a political barbecue in Henly, Texas, an eager audience waited during the speeches of numerous local candidates for the main event, an address by Pat Neff, a former governor of Texas then running for a seat on the state railroad commission. But Neff never appeared. The master of ceremonies delayed and delayed, finally asking for a surrogate to speak on Neff's behalf. Prompted by his father who knew Neff would not attend the rally, Lyndon shouted "I'll make a speech for Pat Neff," and the gangly twenty-one-year-old loped up to the platform. Introduced as "Sam Johnson's boy," he delivered what one hearer called "the goddamn most typical speech you ever heard," a spirited, arm-swinging and hollering defense of good ol' Pat Neff against his "city slickin' " opponent.[8]

Conventional as it was, young Lyndon's speech impressed Welly Hopkins, one of the earlier speakers at the rally and a candidate for the state senate. Recognizing the young Johnson's political talents, Hopkins recruited him for his campaign staff and soon allowed Johnson to manage his entire campaign.

Meanwhile, Johnson graduated from San Marcos and found a job as a teacher at Sam Houston High School in Houston. There he displayed the same insatiable energy and drove himself and his students much as he had in Cotulla and on the campaign trail, coaching the school's debate team to second place in the state tournament. A sudden telephone call in the fall of 1931 gave vent to his restless ambition. Welly Hopkins had recommended the political wonder boy to Richard Kleberg, the newly elected congressman from the fourteenth district in south Texas. Kleberg needed a congressional secretary (the title for the person who ran the congressman's office in Washington), and he asked Johnson to interview for the job. Five days later, his scant belongings packed into a cardboard suitcase, Lyndon joined Kleberg on the train to Washington. To pursue this opportunity in the nation's capital, Johnson arranged for a temporary leave of absence from Sam Houston High. His leave, his sojourn in Washington, would last thirty-eight years.

Kleberg, the proprietor of one of the largest ranches in Texas, harbored few political ambitions of his own. A basically conservative man of immense wealth, Mr. Dick, as he was called, devoted most of his attention to golf, fine dinners, and good whiskey. Kleberg enjoyed the prestige of a seat in Congress, with little concern about the actual business of the House of Representatives. For the most part, Kleberg was content to wile away his afternoons at the exclusive Burning Tree Country Club and to let his secretary run the congressional office.

As congressional secretary, Johnson immediately immersed himself in the rules and mores of the nation's capital. He moved into the Dodge Hotel—a dormitory-like boarding house with communal bathrooms that was home to many young congressional staffers—and began introducing himself even before he had finished unpacking his little suitcase. On his first night in the Dodge, Johnson took four separate showers and brushed his teeth five different times, just so that he could "accidentally" run into his fellow residents and pump them for information. Soon he was mastering the city, learning who possessed power in Congress and how they exerted it.

At the same time, he worked himself and his assistants mercilessly, answering letters from distraught constituents, doing favors for the district, interceding with federal agencies on behalf of south Texas interests. But, as responsive as Johnson's office was, it could offer slender consolation to the anguished farmers and workers whose cries for help flooded the office.

During the winter of 1932, the vise of the Great Depression—the worst economic catastrophe in the nation's history—crushed ever more Americans in its merciless grip. Banks failed, and millions pounded on closed doors as their life's savings vanished overnight. Factories shut down, lifting the unemployment rate above 30 percent, a startling statistic that recorded the misery of millions without jobs, without food, without hope.

Mailbags arrived in Johnson's office filled with desperate petitions for assistance—cries from proud Texans who had never before asked for anything from their government. Now they called for help, begging aid for their farms and their families. They were sick, jobless, homeless, and hungry. But, aside from securing military pensions for veterans of World War I, Johnson could do little. As the Depression deepened, the House and Senate readied for action. In the words of Speaker of the House William Bankhead, Congress reluctantly prepared to "abandon our preconceived notions of economic policy" and "burn some of our bridges behind us."[9] But President Herbert Hoover would take only cautious, tentative steps. He proffered only modest and outworn solutions to this new, unprecedented, and terrible crisis.

The Depression deepened during the winter of 1932–33 as Americans waited impatiently for the inauguration of the new president, Franklin Delano Roosevelt (FDR). Panic gripped the nation as thirty-eight states ordered their banks to close. Roosevelt moved quickly to restore confidence. Somehow, his comforting voice and confident manner managed to reinstill hope and courage. Johnson was among the throng crowding around FDR on inauguration day. Johnson later remembered, "People took heart when they saw that great man march up and hold on to that podium and say, 'The only thing we have to fear is fear itself.' "[10]

## THE NEW DEAL

Once in the White House, Roosevelt launched his New Deal, a bold effort to combat the Depression and relieve the suffering. The New Deal drew on the legacies of FDR's cousin Theodore Roosevelt (TR) and his one-time boss Woodrow Wilson—the two great presidents of the Progressive Era. In the early years of the twentieth century, TR, Wilson, and the Progressives had initiated a transformation of American liberalism, changing the very meaning of the term. *Liberalism* derived, of course, from a passion for liberty, a concern for freedom. Nineteenth-century liberalism, what historians now term *classical liberalism,* embraced a largely negative view of freedom. Freedom, in this sense, meant only absence of restraint, the ability to do as one pleased without undue encumberance or regulation. Classical liberals saw government as the gravest threat to freedom and believed that the government that governs least governs best.

The complexity of modern life and the forces unleashed by the industrial revolution called into question this negative definition of liberty. Small, limited government conferred only the most tenuous sort of freedom when it afforded citizens no protection against contaminated meat, adulterated drugs, unsafe factories, and price-gouging monopolists. Encountering these new realities, modern liberals recognized that real freedom required the active protection of an interventionist government. "In the present day," Theodore Roosevelt had explained, "the limitation of governmental power means the enslavement of the people." He and his fellow Progressives envisioned a larger role for government as a referee or police officer, ensuring that the economy and society operated freely and fairly.

Franklin Roosevelt inherited and extended this positive view of freedom. He cemented the alliance between liberalism and activist government that his forebear first forged. When FDR laid out what he described as the four basic freedoms in 1941, he included not only traditional liberties like freedom of speech and freedom of religion, but also freedom from want and freedom from fear. These last freedoms represented guaranteed security against economic depression and foreign aggression, freedoms that only an energetic, vigilant big government could assure.

Adopting the Progressives' zest for experimentation, FDR converted government into a "laboratory of democracy" and tested new approaches for solving social problems. His basic philosophy, he once explained, was "Try something. If it works, keep doing it. If it doesn't, try something else. But above all, try something." In his inaugural address, Roosevelt promised "bold, persistent experimentation."[11]

But FDR's New Deal far exceeded the achievements, even the imagination, of the Progressives. In fact, most of the old Progressives, those still alive and active during the 1930s, opposed the New Deal. They thought it dangerously radical. For FDR pursued four new objectives that even the most far-sighted Progressives had been unable or unwilling to accomplish.

First, the New Deal offered direct aid to the American people. Not content merely to play the role of referee or police officer, FDR provided subsidies for farmers, tuition grants for indigent students, public works jobs for the unemployed, pensions for the elderly, electricity for cold rural homes, and food for the desperate and hungry. Millions of Americans felt their government, their president, as a powerful personal force in their lives. When FDR toured the country during his 1936 reelection campaign, thousands of onlookers thanked the president as his train or motorcade passed by. "He saved my home," they yelled. "He gave me a job."

Second, the New Deal acknowledged and empowered a number of social and economic groups. As historian William Leuchtenburg has observed, "When Roosevelt took office, the country, to a very large extent, responded to the will of a single element: the white, Anglo-Saxon, Protestant property-holding class. Under the New Deal, new groups took their place in the sun."[12] Roosevelt forced business to recognize unions and negotiate in good faith with organized labor. He opened the doors of government to ethnic Americans, offering new opportunities for the children of immigrant Catholics and Jews. A few New Deal agencies also quietly earmarked benefits and positions for African American communities and institutions.

Third, FDR expanded and reorganized the executive branch of government. He made it the fountainhead and uncontested leader of American politics and policymaking. Before the 1930s, the presidency had been only one player among many. Congress initiated much of federal policy, and most Americans looked to state and local government rather than to Washington for assistance and leadership. Roosevelt changed all that; he concentrated political power in the federal government and federal power in his newly created Executive Office of the President. Of course, FDR continued to struggle with Congress and the courts, but by the end of his presidency, the major powers and responsibilities of American governance, foreign and domestic, lay in the White House and the executive agencies FDR had created.

Fourth, the New Deal transformed the American party system. The election of FDR ended almost seventy-five years of Republican party dominance. Between 1860 and 1932, only two Democrats reached the White House, Grover Cleveland (1885–89, 1893–97) and Woodrow Wilson (1913–21). Roosevelt constructed the "New Deal coalition" by joining into a massive Democratic majority all the supporters of activist government—farmers, organized labor, capital-intensive businesses, immigrants, and African Americans. This coalition reelected FDR in 1936, giving him the greatest landslide victory then recorded in U.S. history and commencing a two-decade-long era of Democratic party preeminence in American politics. Roosevelt built a devoted constituency for modern liberalism.

For young Lyndon Johnson and his beleaguered assistants in Richard Kleberg's congressional office, Roosevelt's arrival meant only longer, harder hours. In his first one hundred days, FDR created new programs for agriculture, industry, and banking; started direct relief for the destitute; and introduced jobs programs for the unemployed. He even ended Prohibition by making beer legal and available again. With the New Deal in place, there was much LBJ could do for Kleberg's constituents, and he served them with a success and ferocity unmatched by any other congressional aide. What some of Johnson's opponents would later denounce as his "clientism," the tradeoff of government financial and material aid in return for political support that lay near the core of Johnson's brand of liberal politics, first took shape in Congressman Kleberg's office in the early 1930s.

Johnson became a fixture in the offices of New Deal administrators and mastered the alphabet agencies that FDR established. He charmed everybody. Any time he visited an office, he would not only appeal to the person in charge but would chat up the secretaries, clerks, and assistants, bring them little presents on their birthdays, ask about their families, and remember every personal detail. Soon everyone in the office wanted to help him. Kleberg's south Texas district became a major beneficiary of New Deal largesse.

Congressman Kleberg barely noticed that Johnson had turned his office into one of the most effective conduits of the New Deal or that, at the same time, Lyndon was girding himself for power. Johnson quickly took over the Little Congress, the mock House of Representatives for congressional assistants. And although he abused his own staff and dominated his fellow secretaries in the Little Congress, Johnson ingratiated himself with influential older men on Capitol Hill and in the executive branch. He became, according to one colleague, a "professional son," winning the affection and patronage of some of the most powerful men in Washington.[13] He drew particularly close to two prominent Texas congressmen, Maury Maverick, a liberal reformer from San Antonio, and Sam Rayburn, the majority leader soon to become speaker of the house. Johnson worked on Maverick's campaigns: he wrote speeches, greeted citizens in San Antonio's heavily Mexican American neighborhoods, and, in a tradition typical of Texas elections, handed out five dollar bills to buy votes on election day. Maverick would remember Johnson's support, acclaim him "the brightest secretary in Washington," and help him on to bigger and better positions. Rayburn, a bachelor known for his aloofness, came to regard Kleberg's young secretary almost as his own son. Rayburn frequently dined at the Johnsons' home; Lyndon's wife made sure to serve his favorite dishes, chili and peach ice cream, prepared just the way Rayburn liked them. Bystanders were stunned to see Johnson stoop over and kiss the normally intimidating Rayburn on his bald pate.

While Johnson pursued these influential patrons, he also acquired the partner and friend who would sustain him throughout his career, his wife Claudia Alta ("Lady Bird") Taylor. Meeting Lady Bird during a brief visit to Austin in September 1934, Johnson courted her with the same audacity and restless ambition he showed in politics. Lyndon decided to marry Lady Bird as soon as they met and formally proposed just twenty-four hours later. "It would be hard to say what I thought," Lady Bird remembered years later. "I was just astonished, amazed. It was like finding yourself in the middle of a whirlwind. I wanted to stay off on the edges of it. I wasn't sure I wanted to get caught up in it as a matter of self-preservation."[14] But Lyndon Johnson pressed on, and after a two-month courtship, the two were married. According to biographer Doris Kearns, who interviewed LBJ at the end of his career and analyzed his psychology, Lady Bird "provided that totally secure and loyal center to his private life which alone could have sustained him through the exigencies of his public career. . . . "[15]

With his new family responsibilities and his burning ambition, Johnson was not content to remain a congressional secretary. He received and turned down an offer to work as a lobbyist for General Electric. Even though it would pay almost three times his salary, Johnson decided that accepting a job as a lobbyist would ruin his chances for elective office. A more favorable opportunity appeared in June 1935, when FDR established the National Youth Administration (NYA). Despite earlier efforts to put young people to work or help them to finish school, twenty-two million youngsters remained without prospects, either on relief or riding the rails. As one of FDR's closest advisers explained, "In 1935, there were still millions of kids out of work. It didn't take the Old Man long to see that those who wanted to continue school or training of some kind ought to have a chance to do it, and that's how the NYA started."[16]

Johnson decided to seek an appointment as the Texas state director of the NYA, and his friend Maury Maverick lobbied FDR on his behalf. Roosevelt thought the job too important for a boy just twenty-six years old, but when Rayburn also supported Johnson's bid, FDR assented. A few days later, Johnson was interviewed by Aubrey Williams, the liberal Alabaman whom FDR had appointed national director of the NYA. The outspoken Williams, a southerner too liberal for his native region, was immediately impressed with the young Texan who shared his zest for the New Deal. Johnson got the job.

He moved to Austin and began working seventeen-hour days, from seven in the morning until midnight, seven days a week. Johnson's office arranged schooling and training for more than twenty thousand young Texans and found work for nearly ten thousand others. Texas soon boasted the most successful NYA program in the nation. Aubrey Williams congratulated Lyndon for "a beautiful job" and sent other state directors to observe and emulate Johnson's operation.[17] The NYA also won accolades for Johnson in his home state; nearly every Texas newspaper supported the program and praised its young director.

Johnson even earned the respect and appreciation of the state's black community. Publicly, Johnson hewed to the strict segregationist line that prevailed across the South; he would not formally appoint African Americans to his advisory board. But he quietly met with African American leaders, established a separate Negro advisory board, and made sure that black youths were able to participate in NYA programs. Under Johnson's leadership, the Texas College Aid Program enrolled 24 percent of the eligible black students and only 14 percent of the eligible white students. At a time when blacks and whites never shared the same hotels or public facilities, Johnson occasionally spent the night at black colleges to observe the programs in action. Johnson carefully steered away from offending the racist sensibilities of most white Texans but did more than any other official in the South to bring New Deal benefits to African Americans.

Indeed, that same mixture of passion and political savvy guided Johnson's entire tenure at the NYA. He deeply believed in the NYA's mission and constantly goaded his staff: "Put them to work—Get them to school!" When a San Antonio businessman criticized the NYA, insisting that "all these kids need to do is get out and hustle," Johnson lit into him. "Right," Johnson replied. "Last week I saw a couple of your local kids hustling—a boy and a girl, nine or ten years old. They were hustling through a garbage can in an alley. . . . hustling" just to survive.[18] But Johnson simultaneously used his position to make political contacts across the state. Wherever he traveled, Johnson made sure to call on the mayor, the justice of the peace, the business leaders, and the school principals. He built support for the NYA and also prepared for a career in elective office.

Throughout his days at the NYA, Johnson dreamed of returning to Washington, of winning election to the U.S. Congress. State politics, the route his father had followed, offered few opportunities for a New Dealer since southern state governments looked askance on young liberals. Thus, in the 1930s, most ambitious southern liberals made an end run around their state capitals and headed directly to Washington: Leon Keyserling of South Carolina drafted the Wagner Act, the bill of rights for American unions; Abe Fortas of Tennessee led the fight for public power in the Interior Department; Alabama's Aubrey Williams headed the NYA; Mississippi's Will Alexander ran the Farm Security Administration; and, Claude Pepper of Florida won a seat in the U.S. Senate. Johnson hoped to join them, but his chances appeared slim. Once elected, Texas members of Congress pretty much held onto their seats for life, and Representative James B. Buchanan, the congressman from Johnson's home district in the Hill Country, was not about to retire.

In February 1937, Buchanan suddenly died. Johnson, just twenty-eight years old and almost unknown in his district, quickly gathered his closest advisers and decided to run for the seat. Lady Bird's father wired ten thousand dollars to finance the race, and Alvin Wirtz, a tough-minded Texas kingmaker in Lyndon's camp, devised the campaign strategy. Johnson would link his name with FDR's, pledging enthusiastic support for the popular president straight down the line. Johnson even wholeheartedly supported the president's controversial proposal to enlarge the Supreme Court, the so-called court-packing plan that most members of Congress, including many Democrats, opposed. Only one obstacle stood in Johnson's way—the chance that Buchanan's widow would announce for the seat. It would be unseemly to oppose Mrs. Buchanan. Waiting nervously for her decision, Johnson visited his ailing father in Johnson City and received from

Newly elected Congressman Johnson meets President Franklin D. Roosevelt in Galveston, Texas (1937). Between them stands Texas Governor Jimmy Allred.

Sam Johnson one last piece of political advice. "Goddammit, Lyndon, you never learn anything about politics," chastised Sam. "She's an old woman. She's too old for a fight. If she knows she'll have to fight, she won't run. Announce now—before she decides. If you do, she won't run."[19] Lyndon immediately called reporters and promised to run for the seat, whatever the widow decided. The next day, just as Sam predicted, Mrs. Buchanan bowed out.

Johnson began his campaign in earnest. Telling Lady Bird never to allow him in the house during daylight hours, he left home before dawn and seldom returned before the wee hours. He stopped at every gas station, accosted every farmer he saw, and covered the district with signs proclaiming "Franklin D. and Lyndon B." On election day, Johnson won 28 percent of the vote, edging out eight rivals for the victory. In a stroke of luck for the new congressman, President Roosevelt visited Texas right after the election. Pleased that Texas had sent a strong supporter of his embattled court plan to Congress, FDR arranged to meet his protégé, LBJ, in Galveston.

Johnson made the most of the opportunity. Knowing of the president's particular interest in naval affairs (FDR had been undersecretary of the Navy during World War I), Johnson told FDR of his own consuming passion for the Navy, an interest inspired by FDR and by his cousin

Theodore Roosevelt—and one which LBJ had invented just to please the president. Roosevelt saw through the young man on the make but liked him nonetheless. The president told Johnson to call Thomas G. Corcoran, Roosevelt's political adviser, better known as Tommy the Cork. Meanwhile, Roosevelt instructed Corcoran to help the young Texan, and Tommy the Cork arranged a seat on the powerful House Naval Affairs Committee for LBJ. Roosevelt also mentioned Johnson to Harold Ickes, the secretary of the interior, and Harry Hopkins, his top White House aide. According to Hopkins, FDR saw a lot of himself in LBJ. Hopkins remembered FDR saying that if he hadn't gone to Harvard, "that's just the kind of uninhibited young pro he'd like to be—that in the next generation the balance of power would shift south and west, and this boy could well be the first Southern President."[20]

If Roosevelt's reading of the political future proved amazingly prophetic, Congressman Johnson's assessment of the political present was equally acute. In the words of a fellow New Dealer, White House aide James Rowe, LBJ "made a hardboiled judgment that power in Washington was in the Executive Branch, not on the Hill."[21] Rather than work his way up through the House of Representatives, LBJ fell in with a circle of young New Dealers, many of them southerners like himself. They met frequently, talked politics and policy, helped each other and the president, and thoroughly enjoyed the pleasures of life in the nation's capital. And LBJ's presence automatically turned up the excitement several notches. "There was never a dull moment around him," one of the members of the circle remembered. "If Lyndon Johnson was there, a party would be livelier. The moment he walked in the door, it would take fire."[22]

Johnson used this personal magic and his close connections within the Roosevelt administration to generate favorable publicity for himself and federal projects for the Hill Country. In 1939, LBJ convinced the president to give a surprise birthday party for Sam Rayburn. On the appointed day, the guests gathered at the White House while Roosevelt sent an urgent message to Rayburn, telling him to report at once to the White House. The nervous House leader raced down Pennsylvania Avenue, rushed into the Oval Office, and heard Roosevelt warn him that "You are in real trouble and I'm the fellow to tell you." Just then, the guests jumped out and sang "Happy Birthday." Johnson organized the whole affair, right down to buying a big Stetson hat with his own money for FDR to present to Rayburn. The next day, when pictures of the party appeared in the press, Johnson stood between Rayburn and Roosevelt in all the newspaper photos. Seeing those pictures, one administration insider realized that in young Johnson he had "really met an operator."[23]

## THE BEST CONGRESSMAN
## A DISTRICT EVER HAD

Congressman Johnson worked himself and his staff relentlessly, serving the needs and answering the requests of his Hill Country constituents. Johnson's first secretary lost thirty-five pounds in a few months and quit the job, afraid he would have a nervous breakdown. His replacement did suffer a breakdown, cracking under the strain of constant fourteen-hour days. But Johnson himself never slowed down, chain-smoking, barely pausing to wolf down his meals, unfazed by a nervous rash between his fingers that burst the skin and made his hand bleed.

Just as he had promised, Congressman Johnson voted with President Roosevelt on nearly every legislative measure to reach the House between 1937 and 1941. In return for his loyalty, the Roosevelt administration satisfied Johnson's requests for aid to the impoverished Hill Country. Johnson won federal dollars to renovate schools, fight polio, and install fire alarms. He lobbied the U.S. Housing Authority to construct low-cost apartments for Austin and convinced the Works Progress Administration to erect a new building in Elgin, Texas, and finance a sewing room project for Bastrop County. Johnson's efforts amazed Tommy the Cork, a shrewd political operator in his own right. "He got more projects, and more money for his district, than anybody else," Corcoran recalled. "He was the best Congressman for a district that ever was."[24]

Johnson's main interests, his principal efforts as a member of Congress, focused on public power and rural electrification. He wanted to construct massive dams on the Lower Colorado and Pedernales rivers—gigantic public works that would provide jobs for construction workers, flood and erosion control for farmers and, most important, cheap hydroelectric power for the dark, cold Hill Country. In this effort, Johnson called upon influential allies, both the Texas contracting firms that stood to earn millions of dollars from the projects and the impassioned advocates of public power in Washington. Leading the latter group were the irascible Secretary of Interior, Harold Ickes, and his deputy, Abe Fortas. Ickes, a dedicated New Dealer, called LBJ the only real liberal in Congress from Texas. With the help of Ickes and Fortas, Johnson secured fourteen million dollars for the Lower Colorado River Authority to construct several dams around the Hill Country.

Building the dams marked only the first round in a long, tough struggle because the public power program aroused powerful enemies. Johnson and his allies wanted the government to sell hydroelectric power directly to the people of Texas—at low prices—and to run lines into the countryside where most Hill Country farmers continued to live and work without electricity. "There are plenty of rural communities throughout the whole area," LBJ declared, "where smoky lanterns are the chief means of lighting and elbow-grease is still the main motive power though this is the Twentieth Century, not the Middle Ages."[25] Private utility companies opposed such plans and demanded continued control of all electricity in the region. They wanted to collect the power generated by the dams and sell it at high prices. Moreover, as profit-making concerns, the utilities had no interest in bringing electricity to remote rural areas. It would take millions of dollars to run power lines to the isolated homesteads spread throughout the Hill Country, and there were few paying customers to cover the costs.

Still, the Roosevelt Administration fought for public power and rural electrification across the nation. In 1933, when FDR took office, ninety percent of American farms operated without electricity. Milking machines had already been invented, but farmers without power could not use them. Stores stocked refrigerators to keep milk from spoiling, but most dairies still used ice. And, in the heat of the Texas summer, many gallons of milk spoiled before they ever got to market. Towns could boast of their "Great White Ways," brightly lit districts that rattled and roared all night long, but beyond the city limits loomed darkness broken only by dim kerosene lamps. Roosevelt, Harold Ickes, and Abe Fortas determined to defeat the private utilities and electrify the American countryside.

In that battle, they found no more dedicated a soldier than Congressman Lyndon Baines Johnson. "That river belongs to the people," LBJ declared on a speaking tour of his district. "They have a right to put it to work to do their washing and ironing. They have a right to make it light their homes, pump their water, milk their cows, bring the world into their homes by radio, and to do the 1,000 other things electricity alone can do. They have a right to get that power at a decent and a fair rate, a rate based on the cost of production, rather than upon the greed and avarice of some pyramid of holding companies."[26] Johnson waged the battle for public power and rural electrification with peculiar, unusual vehemence — with a passion born of bitter memory and hard experience. According to Lady Bird, Johnson's concern stemmed "from seeing his mother have to draw up water from the well and not having a washing machine and having to scrub the floor on her hands and knees."[27] Young Lyndon was ashamed that his refined and beautiful mother always hid her swollen, ruddy hands. As a boy, he promised that he would free her of hard labor so she could have dainty, soft hands.

Johnson's efforts bore fruit. The Lower Colorado River Authority generated public power for the Hill Country and the Rural Electrification

Administration (REA) brought that electricity to the district's isolated farmers. Congressman Johnson dragged his constituents, almost single-handedly, into the modern, industrial era. So impressed with his efforts were President Roosevelt and Secretary Ickes that they offered LBJ the chairmanship of the REA. Johnson politely turned them down, citing his desire to remain in Congress, and his ambitions for higher office.

But despite his accomplishments, the impatient young Texan found the House of Representatives a frustrating place. The House contained 435 members—too many for LBJ to know, charm, manipulate—and it followed rigid rules of seniority. To move up, to win powerful committee assignments, to gain real authority took time, and Lyndon Johnson never could wait. Frustrated by his lack of power, he paid less and less attention to the business of the chamber. Although he remained attentive to the needs of his district, he rarely even appeared on the floor of the House.

During these years, Johnson came to believe that his future—and the nation's—rested more with the White House than with the Congress. And he vividly demonstrated his loyalty to FDR, even at the expense of antagonizing influential members of the House, including his fellow southerners. In 1939, the vice president of the United States, a hard-drinking, conservative Texan named John Nance Garner, prepared to enter the contest for the 1940 presidential nomination. Testifying before Congress, one of Garner's enemies, the fiery union leader John L. Lewis, attacked the "labor-baiting, poker-playing, whiskey-drinking, evil old man whose name is Garner."[28] The entire Texas delegation rallied to Garner's defense, and Sam Rayburn prepared a statement for the twenty-three Texas congressmen to approve, unanimously denouncing Lewis for his false, defamatory attacks. President Roosevelt, however, intended to squelch any such statement; he wanted to appease Lewis and, especially, to embarrass the vice president who was becoming a thorn in his side. Roosevelt's lieutenants called LBJ and, when the Texas delegation convened, Johnson refused to sign the statement. Texans stick up for Texans, LBJ's colleagues insisted, but LBJ would not budge. After all, Johnson reminded the delegation, everyone knew about Garner's drinking and gambling. To deny those charges would sound foolish. Wanting a unanimous statement, Rayburn adjourned the meeting to lobby LBJ privately. But Johnson stuck with the president against his congressional colleagues. Eventually, the delegation agreed to a bland, nonspecific statement—one that disappointed Garner and pleased FDR.

The White House appreciated Johnson's devotion. General Pa Watson, FDR's confidential assistant, called LBJ the "perfect Roosevelt man." The president and the congressman developed a rapport not so much because they shared a political ideology or a policy agenda but because both men cared more about accomplishments than principles. "Johnson could get things done," Tommy Corcoran said, "and that is what impressed Roosevelt. He was never much impressed with theory or theoreticians. He always wanted to know what you could do and had you done it and was there someone who could have done it better. Roosevelt, contrary to some, was a very down-to-earth politician, and so was Lyndon, and that's why they got along."[29] Congressman Johnson proved to be a down-to-earth politician indeed—far down, deep in the gutter, his critics would soon charge.

## MONEY AND POLITICS, TEXAS-SIZED

Young Lyndon had become the toast of New Deal Washington, "Roosevelt's man in Texas," adored by such prominent liberals as Harold Ickes, Aubrey Williams, and Maury Maverick. Roosevelt himself personally admired the junior congressman and boosted his career. But, at the same time, LBJ drew close to Herman Brown, owner and operator of the contracting firm Brown and Root, which had constructed the massive high dams on the Pedernales and Lower Colorado rivers. Congressman Johnson, of course, had brought those projects to the Texas Hill Country, carrying with them hydroelectric power and relief from devastating floods for the region's struggling farmers. But the dams had also poured millions of dollars into the coffers of Brown's firm, winning Johnson the loyalty and the grudging respect of its owner.

Only grudging respect, for Herman Brown was no New Deal liberal. He was one of the "economic royalists," the privileged and selfish few whom FDR had vehemently denounced in his 1936 election campaign. "They hate Roosevelt," the president had explained, "and I welcome their hatred."[30] A reactionary racist, Brown reviled unions and African Americans. He mocked New Deal programs as "gimme's"—handouts to the lazy, undeserving poor—even though he had received some of the biggest "gimme's" of them all.

Not surprisingly, then, Herman Brown remained wary of the young New Dealer who charmed everybody else, even his brother and partner George Brown. But their collaboration on the dams had convinced Herman that he could deal with Lyndon Johnson, that the two men could "play ball." Brown threw in his fortunes with Johnson and threw fortunes into Johnson's career, bankrolling every one of LBJ's campaigns and greasing the wheels for his rise to power. Excepting only Lyndon's relationship with FDR, no political association would so decisively shape LBJ's career as his ties to Herman Brown.

Johnson had forged his unseemly alliance with the Brown brothers during the fight for the Marshall Ford Dam. Johnson had ensured that the Lower Colorado River Authority proceeded with plans for the high dam and secured Brown and Root's highly profitable contracts. In gratitude, Herman Brown became LBJ's financial angel, promising not only his own support in future elections, but the contributions of the subcontractors, brokers, and bankers who relied on Brown and Root for their business. Johnson never again would have to borrow money from his father-in-law to finance a political campaign. As Tommy the Cork explained, "A young guy might be as wise as Solomon, as winning as Will Rogers, and as popular as Santa Claus, but if he didn't have a firm financial base his opponents could squeeze him. . . . In Lyndon's case, there was just this little road building firm, Brown and Root, run by a pair of Germans."[31]

With Johnson's assistance, the "little road building firm" became an immense government contractor. Using his influence on the House Naval Affairs Committee, Congressman Johnson persuaded the military to build a new naval air base in Corpus Christi, Texas. Brown and Root won the generous contract to build the base, then the largest contract ever awarded by the federal government. After World War II, when Brown and Root moved into the pipeline business, Lyndon helped engineer the sale of the Little and Big Inch pipelines to the Browns at a very favorable price.

Johnson's egregious relationship with Brown and Root became the stuff of legend. During the 1960 election, when LBJ ran on the same ticket with the Roman Catholic John F. Kennedy, a joke circulated about a conversation between the two candidates. "When I get to the White House," Kennedy tells his running mate, "I'm going to build a secret tunnel to the Vatican." LBJ replies, "That's all right with me, Jack, as long as Brown and Root gets the contract."[32]

Still, Johnson's arrangement with the Browns was hardly atypical. As journalist J. Ronnie Dugger has written: "What happened to Johnson has happened, in different permutations, to most American politicians, and what happened to Brown and Root was happening in different permutations (including the modern day political action committees, or PACS) to most major American corporations. Corporate business needed political services; politicians needed corporate money. So politics went into partnership with business. . . . "[33]

In 1940, this unholy union between money and politics allowed Congressman Johnson to take his first tentative steps onto the national political stage. Johnson headed the Democratic Congressional Campaign Committee, an outfit that directed campaign funds and political support to Democratic candidates facing tough congressional races. With war raging in Europe and the New Deal stalled at home, everyone expected the Democrats to lose seats in Congress. The party did drop three seats in the Senate, but over in the House, LBJ's efforts turned a seemingly certain defeat into a small gain. The strong showing made Johnson a formidable presence on Capitol Hill, where several members owed their narrow victories to Johnson's shrewd tactics and his injections of Texas money. According to Jim Rowe, Johnson's campaign work "impressed the hell out of Roosevelt."[34]

With the grateful president's backing, LBJ next turned his sights on the U.S. Senate. In April 1941, the death of Texas Senator Morris Sheppard offered an unparalleled opportunity. A special election would fill Sheppard's seat for the remaining year of his term; LBJ could thus run for the Senate without risking his seat in the House. Johnson announced his candidacy on the steps of the White House, but even with the president's imprimatur, Johnson's prospects appeared bleak. Texas was a big state and LBJ was little known outside the Hill Country. He faced a formidable list of well-known opponents, including State Attorney General Gerald Mann and Representative Martin Dies, the notorious chairman of the House Un-American Activities Committee.

The leading candidate, and LBJ's principal rival, was the popular Governor of Texas, W. Lee (Pappy) O'Daniel. A shrewd salesman, O'Daniel had made his fortune as a flour salesman; his company's slogan, "Pass the biscuits, Pappy," and his radio show had literally made Pappy's name a household word throughout the state. O'Daniel ran his Senate campaign as a cross between a religious revival and a traveling road show. It featured a hillbilly band and a bus topped with a loudspeaker in the shape of the state capitol building. At each stop, the governor would appear between musical numbers and lay out his platform: "One hundred percent approval of the Lord God Jehovah, widows, orphans, low taxes, the Ten Commandments, and the Golden Rule."[35]

His own coffers stuffed with Brown and Root dollars, LBJ mounted an impressive traveling carnival of his own. A twenty-three piece band warmed up the crowd with patriotic songs and cowboy ballads, followed by a half-hour musical pageant called "The Spirit of American Unity." Modeled after "The March of Time," a popular newscast of the era, the pageant led the audience through an emotional tour of the recent past. By the end of the show, the excited audience impatiently looked for the candidate himself. At this dramatic moment, to the strains of "God Bless America," LBJ emerged and made his stump speech. According to the pageant's producer, "This little thirty-minute show" inspired people who a few hours earlier "didn't know Lyndon from anybody and getting them involved in it and wanting to see this man that Franklin D. Roosevelt thought so much of."[36]

Johnson matched O'Daniel step-for-step in hokiness and spectacle, but at the same time sold himself as a different kind of politician—as a representative of modern, activist government against the old-fashioned, do-nothing Pappy. Johnson wrapped himself in the New Deal and promised to do things for Texas—to bring jobs, programs, and defense plants. The strategy succeeded; as election day approached, LBJ came from way behind to take a small lead in the polls.

The initial election returns showed LBJ as the winner by more than five thousand votes. Texas newspapers reported his victory. But before the counting finished, Johnson blundered and O'Daniel stole the election. Stolen elections were not unusual in southern politics, in Texas politics especially. In many areas of the state, political machines controlled the balloting and could deliver large sums of votes to the highest bidder. If your candidate fell behind, the machine could "find" a few more votes. It was crucial, however, not to report your precincts too soon; otherwise, the opposing side knew your total and could maneuver to beat it. In the 1941 Senate race, both candidates had made such arrangements with political bosses around Texas. But the overly confident and inexperienced LBJ erred and reported his total too early. O'Daniel's forces furnished just enough additional votes to tip the election. It was the first—and last— election Lyndon Johnson ever lost.

Johnson never contested the outcome of the 1941 race. In part, he believed, as he told Tommy the Cork, that "in the political business, if you're counted out, you're never a crybaby in public about it."[37] Johnson also realized that any investigation would likely turn up irregularities in his own campaign as well as in O'Daniel's.

Putting a brave face on a bitter defeat, LBJ returned to Washington and quickly wrote a note to FDR. President Roosevelt was not renowned for compassion toward defeated politicians. Usually, the president spurned losers. But FDR continued to aid his Texas protégé; on the margin of LBJ's note, Roosevelt instructed his assistant to bring Lyndon to the White House. When they met, the president teased Johnson: "Lyndon, apparently you Texans haven't learned one of the first things we learned up in New York State, and that is that when the election is over, you have to sit on the ballot boxes."[38] FDR also boosted Lyndon's career by arranging a joint appearance at the Young Democrat's Convention in

Kentucky—rewarding the young member of Congress with favorable national exposure.

Roosevelt rendered an even larger service to the defeated Texan in the months immediately following the election. In the fall of 1941, the Internal Revenue Service investigated Brown and Root for income tax evasion. Johnson, hoping to protect his financial benefactors and fearful that criminal charges against the Browns would compromise his own political prospects, interceded with the president and his top aides. The White House slowed down the investigation and hushed up the results. Brown and Root had to pay back taxes and penalties, but there were no indictments, no trials, and no unfavorable publicity.

Meanwhile, LBJ prepared for a rematch against O'Daniel. After serving out the remaining months of Sheppard's term, Pappy would face new elections for a full six-year term and Johnson was ready to take him on. The unexpected Japanese raid on Pearl Harbor on December 7, 1941 changed LBJ's plans. During the 1941 race, LBJ had promised to join the boys in the trenches if the United States entered the war. And immediately after the declaration of war, Congressman Johnson, already commissioned a lieutenant commander in the naval reserve, rose on the floor of the House and asked for a leave of absence to assume active duty. The leave granted, Lyndon turned the operation of his congressional office over to Lady Bird and set off to earn for himself a military reputation.

Along with fellow Congressman Warren Magnuson of Washington, LBJ petitioned Admiral Chester Nimitz to assign them to active duty on a military vessel. The admiral denied their request, little relishing the idea of legislators without real training on a ship headed for the war zone. Magnuson refused to take no for an answer; he used his influence in the government to secure a place aboard an aircraft carrier. Johnson, happy to avoid physical danger, never appealed the decision. He worked on labor and production problems, inspected shipyards, and served as the navy's liaison to the government of New Zealand.

Johnson realized, however, that a safe desk job would not suit a man of his intense political ambitions. He needed to see combat—to be able to call himself a battle-scarred veteran. In June 1942, while on an inspection tour of the Pacific, Johnson flew on a dangerous air raid against Japanese forces around Lae, New Guinea. Although his companions thought the young congressman crazy, LBJ climbed aboard a B-26 bomber named the *Wabash Cannonball*. A few minutes before takeoff, however, Johnson left his seat to go to the bathroom. When he returned, another man had taken his place and Johnson was forced onto another plane, the *Heckling Hare.* During the mission, the *Wabash Cannonball* was shot down; its entire crew, including the man in Johnson's seat, perished. The *Heckling Hare* was also ambushed and severely damaged by a wing of Japanese Zeroes; only the skillful evasive action of its pilot saved the crew and its celebrity guest.

Hoping to win favor with a member of Congress, General Douglas MacArthur, the commanding officer in the Pacific, awarded Johnson the Silver Star for his exploits aboard the *Heckling Hare.* No one else aboard the bomber received a medal of any kind. Johnson realized that he did not deserve the award; he admitted it in a speech soon after his return from the Pacific and even drafted a letter formally refusing the decoration. But he never sent the letter. Johnson simply could not forego the political advantage of a combat decoration. For the rest of his life, he proudly wore the Silver Star.

After his one day in combat, LBJ grew bored with navy work and hankered for a return to congressional battles and maneuvers. On July 9, 1942, FDR gave Lyndon the pretext he was seeking by calling all congressmen in the armed services back to Washington. Four of the eight representatives in the service resigned from the Congress to remain in the military; the other four, including LBJ, returned to the House. Johnson even went so far as to arrange for the secretary of the navy to send him a letter ordering him back to the House of Representatives.

Back in the Congress, LBJ continued to serve President Roosevelt. In December 1943, in one of the most daring votes of his career, Johnson opposed a bill raising the wartime price ceiling on crude oil. The Roosevelt administration, believing that it needed to hold the line on prices, opposed the increase in oil prices as injurious to the war effort. Texans, however, overwhelmingly supported the measure. Johnson was one of only two Texas congressman who defied the oil barons and voted with the president.

The oil vote dramatized the political dilemma Johnson faced during the war years. He had traveled far on Roosevelt's coattails, but FDR's liberal policies were losing popularity, especially in Texas. Johnson needed to appease Texas conservatives, to mend fences with the oil and other business interests that controlled the state. This task became particularly urgent after FDR's death and the end of World War II, as conservatives reasserted influence across the nation. In Texas, the Democratic party openly split into pro- and anti-Roosevelt factions. Both Johnson and Rayburn were targeted by conservative "Texas Regulars" in the 1944 and 1946 elections.

Mindful of his tenuous position, Johnson used his strong support for the war effort and military preparedness to win support among conservative Texans. A lucrative new industry—aircraft and aerospace—had emerged during the war and LBJ had successfully steered much of the business to Texas. He also established conservative credentials on two issues of particular importance to Texans, race and labor. Johnson voted against President Truman's civil rights program and for the Taft-Hartley law placing restrictions on organized labor.

On most economic and political matters, however, Johnson remained a New Dealer. Johnson supported continued funding for rural electrification, housing, and roads. He voted against restrictions on federal programs and opposed the two-term rule, the limit on presidential service which Republicans pushed through as a rebuff to FDR's legacy. Shifting with the political wind, LBJ edged toward the right, but he remained committed to big government. He still believed the federal government must play the leading role in American life—guaranteeing economic opportunity and international security. "If that be centralizing power in Washington," LBJ conceded, then he was for it and wanted to "make the most of it."[39]

Thus, LBJ readied for the 1948 Senate campaign by positioning himself as a modern liberal, one dedicated to activist government but more attuned to Texas interests and the rightward drift of the postwar era. He prepared for what would become one of the wildest, dirtiest, most controversial elections in U.S. history, a tale of missing ballot boxes, bought votes, and long dead Texans returning from the grave to cast one last ballot for Lyndon Johnson.

Southern elections were famous for such irregularities. Right after World War II, Herman Talmadge became governor of Georgia when his supporters discovered a cache of uncounted ballots three months after he had lost the election. As one observer described it, "They rose from the dead in Telfair County, marched in alphabetical order to the polls, cast their votes for Herman Talmadge, and went back to their last repose." In 1962, future President Jimmy Carter lost his initial bid for public office when the opposing political boss "lined up the dead, imprisoned, and other absent voters."[40]

But even in that "distinguished" company, the 1948 Texas election stood apart. Johnson mounted one of the first modern media campaigns, using scientific polling, media blitzes, and radio advertising as never before. Johnson introduced the helicopter to political campaigning; in fact, the whirlybird became the principal attraction of his public appearances. A rare sight in rural Texas, the helicopter drew huge crowds to LBJ's rallies. So unusual was the machine in 1948 that Johnson's campaign had trouble finding the high octane fuel it required and adequate space for takeoffs. The ever resourceful LBJ even turned these difficulties into a campaign ploy. At the beginning of his speech, Johnson would inform the audience that "My good pilot Joe tells me it'll be too dangerous if I take off with him because we wouldn't have enough power to clear those 30,000 volt high-tension wires over there."[41] If people started to leave his rally, Johnson reminded them of the pilot's daredevil feat to come.

When Johnson flew over towns too small for a campaign stop, he would hover above the main street and bellow through a loudspeaker, "Hello, down there, this is your Congressman, Lyndon Johnson." His staff would provide the names of people in each town, often the names of constituents who had written to his office, and Johnson would address one or two by name in each flyover—mixing old-fashioned personal campaigning and modern technology. The helicopter allowed Johnson to cover the enormous state, to visit scores of small towns in a single day, to broadcast his name and platform.

Johnson campaigned against a long list of opponents for the July Democratic primary; if no candidate won a majority of the votes, the two leaders would face off in a runoff five weeks later. The winner of the runoff would face only token opposition in the November general election and surely become the state's next senator.

Johnson's principal opponent, Texas Governor Coke Stevenson, was a master politician of the old style. As one contemporary Texan put it, "Coke Stevenson was just like Coca-Cola. He was a state-known product. Everybody knew who he was." Called "the household word of conservatism," Coke had built his reputation by starving state services—cutting schools, blocking river management programs, eliminating old age assistance and aid to the blind. Stevenson's racism was unusually vicious, even by Texas standards. He campaigned for the Senate against Washington, against government, against liberalism. According to one observer, "Coke stands for dollars and he does not stand for civilized life as it is furthered by schools, hospitals, and other institutions that must be promoted at public expense." Simply put, Coke stood for do-nothing government that left people alone. At one 1947 interview, a touring writer asked him to recall the greatest decision he had made as governor. Coke puffed on his pipe, smiled, and answered, "Never had any."[42]

Johnson, on the other hand, campaigned as an activist, someone who would use government to benefit Texans. He portrayed Stevenson as "calculatin' Coke," a cautious, outmoded, old and obsolete candidate from a bygone era. Johnson hoped that a modernizing Texas—a rapidly urbanizing, industrializing state, relying more and more on federal largesse—would reject the anti–New Deal, antigovernment conservatism of Coke Stevenson. However appealing Coke's personal style, LBJ believed Texans would not surrender the benefits his own political philosophy had conferred: rural electrification, defense jobs, hospitals, and pensions.

The primary results proved disappointing. Stevenson led with 40 percent of the vote, and LBJ fought his way into the runoff with 34 percent. Johnson had just five weeks to catch Stevenson and he relentlessly attacked the governor, slowly eroding Stevenson's lead. The runoff was so close that no victor could be pronounced. Both sides sent out poll watchers to monitor the other's supporters. Stevenson controlled east Texas, while Johnson commanded the loyalty of the powerful Parr machine in south Texas. Results trickled in as both camps sat on their ballot boxes, waiting and maneuvering.

Johnson's fortunes rested with Boss George Parr and his south Texas machine. Before 1948, Parr had always supported Coke Stevenson. But then Coke broke his promise of letting Parr hand out patronage appointments in south Texas and Parr determined to punish him. As one of Stevenson's supporters later explained, "What happened was going to happen whoever the other candidate was. The Parr machine had to demonstrate that nobody could stand up against them."[43]

Parr's territory was, in the words of one Johnson staffer, "mostly Mexican, almost totally illiterate." Parr would give voters names to vote for, and they would follow orders because Parr controlled all services and public sector jobs in the region. "Ideology had nothing whatever to do with it. Liberals, conservatives, George Parr didn't care. He just wanted to be left alone to run things the way he wanted to run them, and that's all he wanted."[44]

With both sides holding firm, counting the ballots stretched on for days. After five days, LBJ edged ahead—thanks to corrected returns from the tiny hamlet of Alice in south Texas, where LBJ received 202 votes and Stevenson only one. Johnson won the election by a razor-thin margin of 87 votes. Stevenson charged fraud and tried to block the results, but Johnson's forces held him off and the Democratic party certified LBJ as the winner of the runoff.

Stevenson then turned to the courts. Significantly, Coke avoided state court, the normal place to contest an election. Stevenson knew that the state court would impound all the ballots, not just those from south Texas; the investigation would expose his own fraud as well as Johnson's. Instead, Stevenson filed his suit in federal court and won a temporary injunction—a court order that kept Johnson's name off the November ballot and would effectively deny him the Senate seat.

Timing, not the merits of the case, now posed the major problem for LBJ. His attorneys understood that the injunction had no firm basis in law, that it would be overturned once the case was heard. But the sure and safe route to void the injunction—through the standard appeal procedure— would take too long. The November ballots would be printed without LBJ's name.

Johnson called in expert legal counsel, including Abe Fortas, often called the most brilliant legal mind ever to come out of Yale Law School. Fortas devised a typically ingenious but risky solution—a way of taking the decision to Supreme Court Justice Hugo Black for an immediate ruling. In Fortas's words, his plan "was not a conventional course of action. Lawyers like to do things by the book—B comes after A—and here we are skipping right through to Z."[45] Essentially, Fortas was offering Johnson a one-shot deal—abandon the slow-but-sure path for one risky, winner-take-all spin of the wheel.

After a long, silent moment, LBJ adopted Fortas's plan. Justice Black ruled in their favor, and Lyndon Baines Johnson was elected a United States senator.

# NOTES

[1] *Public Papers of the Presidents of the United States: Lyndon B. Johnson, 1963–1969*, 11 vols. (Washington, D.C.: Government Printing Office, 1964–1969), 1966, 417; *New York Times*, April 12, 1965, 1.

[2] Robert Dallek, *Lone Star Rising: Lyndon Johnson and His Times* (New York: Oxford University Press, 1991), 20.

[3] Robert A. Caro, *The Years of Lyndon Johnson: The Path to Power* (New York: Alfred A. Knopf, 1982), 56.

[4] Emmette Redford and Stella Gliddon, quoted in Caro, *Path to Power*, 83.

[5] Lyndon B. Johnson, *Quotations from Chairman LBJ* (New York: Simon and Schuster, 1968), 128–30.

[6] Dallek, *Lone Star Rising*, 40.

[7] J. Ronnie Dugger, *The Politician* (New York: W. W. Norton and Co., 1982), 115–16. *Papers*, 1965, 286.

[8] Welly K. Hopkins, quoted in Merle Miller, *Lyndon: An Oral Biography* (New York: Ballantine Books, 1980), 43–44; Dallek, *Lone Star Rising*, 87.

[9] *Congressional Record*, 72nd Cong., 1st sess., June 3, 1932, 75. pt. 15, 11931.

[10] Dallek, *Lone Star Rising*, 107.

[11] Samuel Rosenman, ed., *The Public Papers and Addresses of Franklin D. Roosevelt*, 13 vols. (New York: Macmillan, 1938–50), vol. 2, 11–15.

[12] William E. Leuchtenburg, *Franklin D. Roosevelt and the New Deal* (New York: Harper Colophon, 1963), 332.

[13] Caro, *Path to Power*, 271.

[14] Lady Bird Johnson, quoted in Miller, *Lyndon*, 52–53.

[15] Doris Kearns, *Lyndon Johnson and the American Dream* (New York: Signet Books, 1976), 86.

[16] Thomas G. Corcoran, quoted in Miller, *Lyndon*, 63–64.

[17] Dugger, *The Politician*, 189.

[18] Dallek, *Lone Star Rising*, 131–32.

[19] Caro, *Path to Power*, 399.

[20] Dallek, *Lone Star Rising*, 161.

[21] Ibid., 163–64.

[22] Robert A. Caro, *The Years of Lyndon Johnson: Means of Ascent* (New York: Alfred A. Knopf, 1990), 13–14.

[23] Dallek, *Lone Star Rising*, 166–67.

[24] Caro, *Path to Power*, 531.

[25] Dallek, *Lone Star Rising*, 178.

[26] Ibid., 182.

[27] Lady Bird Johnson, quoted in Miller, *Lyndon*, 11.

[28] Caro, *Path to Power*, 572.

[29] Corcoran, quoted in Miller, *Lyndon*, 94; Caro, *Path to Power*, 768.

[30] Rosenman, ed., *Public Papers and Addresses*, vol. 5, 568–69.

[31] Dallek, *Lone Star Rising*, 176.

[32] Dugger, *The Politician*, 286–87.

[33] Ibid., 273.

[34] Dallek, *Lone Star Rising*, 205.

[35] Ibid., 215.

[36] Ibid., 218

[37] Johnson, quoted by Thomas Corcoran, in Miller, *Lyndon*, 106.

[38] James H. Rowe, Jr., quoted in Miller, *Lyndon*, 106.

[39] Lyndon B. Johnson, Address to the Texas State Legislature, Austin, Texas, January 3, 1944.

[40] Numan V. Bartley, "One Grave, One Vote," *New York Times Book Review*, January 17, 1993, 28.

[41] Caro, *Means of Ascent*, 249.

[42] Dallek, *Lone Star Rising*, 315–16; Miller, *Lyndon*, 143.

[43] Callan Graham, quoted in Miller, *Lyndon*, 153.

[44] George Reedy, quoted in Miller, *Lyndon*, 152.

[45] Caro, *Means of Ascent*, 371–72.

# 2

## Democratic Leader:
## Senator Johnson,
## 1948–1960

After FDR's death, American liberalism retreated into a cocoon, entering a decade-and-a-half period of quiet yet profound metamorphosis. Old champions, like LBJ's mentors Harold Ickes and Aubrey Williams, were driven out of office. Other liberals, like Lyndon Johnson himself, drifted right to save their political skins. New leaders appeared, focused no longer on the economic catastrophe of the Great Depression but on the defense of the "free world" against the menace of international communism. When liberalism reemerged in the 1960s, it was a vastly changed creature—in outlook, style, and personnel. In fact, Lyndon Johnson was one of few public officials active in both the 1930s and the 1960s, spanning both great eras of liberal reform.

The late 1940s and 1950s proved particularly frustrating for the Democratic party, the political vessel of New Deal liberalism. During the 1948 presidential election, the party literally split apart, with conservative southern Democrats and radical supporters of former Vice President Henry Wallace bolting the party and backing their own independent candidates. In one of the great surprises of American political history, President Truman narrowly defeated Republican Governor Thomas Dewey of New York. But Truman's slim margin proved too fragile a foundation for governing the country. Truman led an unpopular and ineffective administration; his domestic agenda stalled while the nation found itself mired in a stalemated war in Korea. Worst of all, Truman's promise to root out communist sympathizers in the government backfired, as Republicans attacked "the mess in Washington" and suggested not only that Truman's government harbored communist fellow travelers but that the New Deal and liberalism itself had been nothing more than "twenty years of treason," a muted pink version of Red Communism.[1]

After Truman's retirement, the Republicans captured the White House and maintained a sizable presence in both houses of Congress throughout the 1950s. Frustrated liberals found the national mood and a popular president, the war hero Dwight David Eisenhower, arrayed against them. Democrats needed a leader to shepherd them through these years of want and wandering.

No one seemed less well fitted for the job than the new junior senator from Texas. Johnson entered the Senate along with one of the most distinguished "freshmen classes" in that body's history. Among the men sworn in with LBJ in January 1949 were Clinton Anderson of New Mexico, a former member of the president's cabinet; the flamboyant Tennessean Estes Kefauver, who would lead investigations of labor racketeering and juvenile delinquency; and Paul Douglas of Illinois, a renowned professor of economics at the University of Chicago and champion of liberal economic policies. Hubert Humphrey of Minnesota rounded out the impressive list. As reform mayor of Minneapolis, Humphrey had electrified the nation with his stirring address on civil rights to the 1948 Democratic National Convention. Humphrey had demanded that the party "get out of the shadow of state's rights and walk forthrightly into the bright sunshine of human rights."[2] His eloquence catapulted Humphrey to national prominence, drove southern Democrats out of the convention hall, and won him election to the Senate. Every one of these men possessed a national reputation when he entered the Senate and strong support from his constituents back home.

Alongside them stood "Landslide Lyndon," the gangly, six-foot-three-inch junior senator from Texas, elected by the slimmest of margins in a contested race. Johnson's narrow victory made him something of a comic figure in the back corridors of the Capitol. Many stories circulated about just how Johnson had won his seat in the upper house. In one oft-repeated joke, a passerby stumbles across a little boy crying on a street. "Son, are you hurt?" the concerned man asks the boy. "No, I'm not hurt," he replies. "Are you sick?" "No." "Are you hungry?" "No, I'm not hungry." "What's the matter then?" the passerby finally asks. "Why are you crying?" "Well," the boy answers, "yesterday my father, who's been dead for five years, came back to vote for Lyndon Johnson and he didn't come by and say hello to me."[3]

Lyndon's tenuous grip on the office meant that his liberal friends in Washington and the national Democratic party could expect little from him. Before he finished unpacking his new office, Johnson spread the word around the Senate that his first—and principal—concern was appeasing the dominant interests in his home state. Texas is "much more conservative than the national Democratic Party," he told the Senate's chief page, Bobby Baker. "I got elected by just eighty-seven votes and I ran against a caveman."[4]

During his first year in office, LBJ steered that very cautious course. "The New Deal spirit's gone from Texas," he told Baker in December 1948, and he would do nothing to risk his political future.[5] In particular, Johnson dissociated himself from organized labor and emphatically supported preferential treatment for the oil and gas industry—two positions that reflected his reading of the situation in his home state.

## SHIFTING RIGHT: COLD WAR LIBERALISM

By tilting rightward in the late 1940s, the ambitious young senator not only protected himself, he also followed a broader shift in national politics and policy. The New Deal spirit faded in Texas and across the nation in the late 1940s. FDR's few remaining reform lieutenants were chased out of Washington, and many prominent New Dealers were accused of being soft on communism.

More important, liberalism itself evolved, breaking its New Deal template in three crucial respects. First, postwar liberals developed a new attitude toward business and the economy. Economic policy had always been redistributive—taking advantages from one segment of the population and conferring them on another. In some periods, government had favored big business and the wealthy; at other times, such as during the Great Depression, national policy had attempted to uplift those at the bottom of the economic ladder. New Deal liberals had believed that government needed to restrain the worst excesses of big business, guarantee workers a fair shake, and ensure a minimum American standard of living for the poorest citizens.

World War II ended the Depression, however, removing the sense of desperation that underlay economic policy in the 1930s. The war also showed that cooperation between government, big business, and labor could enrich everyone while defeating a common foe, that economic concord could replace economic conflict. Most important, the wartime experience seemed to prove the efficacy of a new type of liberal economic policy—a way to improve the lives of ordinary Americans without offending business, to feed the hungry and shelter the homeless without asking the well-off to sacrifice.

This new liberal tool was called Keynesian economics, named for its originator, the British economist John Maynard Keynes. For American liberals after World War II, Keynes's most useful insight was that government could use fiscal policy, its powers of taxing and spending, to stimulate the economy. Washington policymakers learned from Keynes that they could heat up a slowing economy and prevent future depressions. But American Keynesians were not content with averting future downturns; they wanted to use Keynesian economics to ensure continued and continuous economic growth, to make the economic pie bigger and bigger. There would be more for everyone, rich and poor, labor and business. Postwar liberals were willing to cooperate with business and ensure economic growth; they were less interested than their New Deal predecessors in redistributing resources and restraining business abuses.

Second, American liberals developed a new view of the political process after World War II, a new vision of democracy. Public policy had become so complicated and distant that individuals had little knowledge of and less input into the nation's most important decisions. Foreign relations required either secrecy (as in the atomic bomb program) or such rapid action (as in Truman's decision to intervene in Korea) that citizens could only respond to accomplished facts, not influence the policies themselves. Even mundane domestic matters, like setting new regulations for home mortgages, were filled with arcane, technical details that no voter had the time or knowledge to master. In the 1950s political theorists believed that when the people did mobilize and masses of citizens involved themselves in the political process, they tended to act on vague, irrational principles and emotions, not on informed, sober reflection. The rise of Nazism in Germany had proved that mass participation did not necessarily mean increased democracy.

In this setting postwar liberals championed pluralist politics, a view of American democracy as a process of bargaining among groups. All sorts of organizations participated in the process: occupational associations like the American Medical Association, business groups like the Chamber of Commerce, labor unions, religious bodies, veteran's societies, and so forth. These groups could do what individuals could not: monitor issues, lobby in Washington, influence policy, and negotiate compromises. They seemed less susceptible to emotional appeals, less likely to adopt extreme positions or insist on all-out conflict.

Pluralists thus believed that the interplay of groups—the constant building and rearranging of coalitions on different issues—ensured that representative democracy would flourish, even if individual voices were not heard. Pluralism also focused government action on building consensus. Standing on principle, emphatically enunciating a particular ideology, made compromise impossible and fostered division. On the contrary, group bargaining focused on problem solving, on policy rather than pure principle. As Johnson explained to Doris Kearns late in his life, "The biggest danger to American politics is the politics of principle, which brings out the masses in irrational fights for unlimited goals. . . . Thus it is for the sake of nothing less than stability that I consider myself a consensus man."[6]

Third, and most important, postwar liberals focused their energies on the struggle against international communism. It was the Democratic administration of Harry Truman, not conservative Republicans, that launched the global struggle against communism abroad and initiated the federal loyalty and security program, an effort to root out subversives at home. Adlai Stevenson, the leading liberal Democrat of the 1950s and twice his party's candidate for president, insisted that if Americans did not fight the communists in Asia, they would have to fight them in Wichita. Lyndon Johnson opened his 1948 campaign for the Senate by warning that "Communism surges forward in a blood red tide."[7] And Hubert Humphrey cosponsored a law outlawing the Communist party in the United States.

Even opponents of Senator Joseph McCarthy and his attacks on the loyalty of American citizens espoused the anticommunist faith. They simply maintained that the most serious threat came from abroad, from Soviet Russia and its satellites, rather than from internal enemies. The most important liberal lobbying group of the 1950s, the Americans for Democratic Action (ADA), fought for what one of its leaders called the "vital center," a "middle ground" that condemned McCarthyite witch-hunts at home but also rejected any negotiations or accommodations with the Soviets.[8]

In fact, the cold war struggle against communism underlay all of these changes in liberal outlook. Constant economic growth distinguished American capitalism from Soviet communism, with its commitment to class conflict. For example, Walt Whitman Rostow, a liberal economist and key adviser to Presidents Kennedy and Johnson in the 1960s, depicted growth Keynesianism as the American alternative to Marxism; he even subtitled his award-winning 1950s study of economic growth "A Non-Communist Manifesto."[9] Pluralist politics allowed Americans to contrast American democracy with Soviet dictatorship, to champion pragmatic problem solving over crusading ideology.

These cold war innovations blunted liberalism in certain respects while sharpening it in others. Liberals muted their calls for economic justice and their attacks on the rich and powerful. Many prominent New Dealers even cozied up to the very interests they had been regulating as government officials. Franklin Delano Roosevelt had established a network of agencies and bureaus that supervised nearly every aspect of national life. Thousands of young reformers had staffed these agencies and launched pitched battles against entrenched special interests. But by the 1940s and 1950s, many regulated groups stopped fighting government action and tried instead to manipulate it to their advantage. They recruited lawyers and lobbyists with expertise in government regulation, many of whom had run New Deal agencies in the 1930s. For instance, LBJ's friend and adviser Abe Fortas, a stalwart liberal advocate of public power and stock market regulation during the New Deal, founded a law firm and began representing the banks and power companies he had once brought to heel. Eventually, many such Washington lawyers returned to public office and began to move in and out through a kind of revolving door, working alternately for the regulators and the regulated.

Politicians in office, Democrats and Republicans, also cut themselves generous pieces of the expanded public pie. They directed lucrative government contracts toward their friends and campaign contributors, supported the proposals of agency chiefs who did them favors, and even enriched themselves. No politician milked this system for personal and political profit so well as Lyndon Johnson. In the 1940s and 1950s, there were fortunes to be made in the new business of radio and television broadcasting, and the government picked the winners and losers in that industry. The Federal Communications Commission granted licenses, assigning exclusive use of a broadcast frequency to one station or another. Lyndon and Lady Bird Johnson bought a number of Texas radio and TV stations, and LBJ used his influence with the Federal Communications Commission (FCC) to win favorable treatment for his station and to prevent competitors from entering the field. Nearly penniless when he first entered public life, LBJ had become a millionaire many times over by the time he reached the White House.

Postwar liberals shied away from economic conflict, championed pain-less growth, and became increasingly comfortable in the boardrooms of big business. But at the same time, they stepped up the battle for racial justice and civil rights. With a few notable exceptions, New Dealers had paid little attention to racial discrimination in the 1930s. Many of the leading New Deal liberals were white southerners, people unable or unwilling to chal-lenge the South's brutal system of segregation. New Deal liberals re-garded the nation's racial problems as mainly regional, nearly insoluble, and hopelessly divisive. To the extent they concerned themselves at all with the plight of black and Latino Americans, they believed that poverty formed the foundation of racial injustice, that they could best address the race problem by improving the everyday lives of poor African Americans and Mexican Americans.

After World War II, however, such an approach no longer sufficed. In search of work, African Americans migrated to northern cities in large numbers; race relations had become a national, not just a sectional, problem. Black soldiers who had fought to defend democracy were not content to return to a nation that denied them the fundamental rights of citizens. Northern liberals joined the fight against segregation and discrimination. White southerners either tempered their liberalism like Lyndon Johnson or were turned out of office.

During his first term, Senator Johnson personified all the growing pains of postwar liberalism. He established his anticommunist credentials by supporting Truman's military buildup and by viciously smearing as a communist sympathizer a man he opposed for a presidential appointment. When war broke out in Korea, LBJ chaired a special committee overseeing the war effort and never failed to denounce the Soviet Union as the instigator of the conflict. "Someday, somewhere, someway, there must be a clear-cut settlement between the forces of freedom and the forces of communism," he warned in the best saber-rattling style of the early cold war. "It is foolish to talk of avoiding war."[10] At the same time, LBJ worked tirelessly for the oil and gas industry and accepted their support. And, he became the real-life master of pluralist politics, deftly building coalitions and making deals between contending interests to move legislation through the Senate.

Most important, for a man with burning national ambitions, Johnson walked a tightrope between northern liberalism and Texas conservatism. The northernization of liberalism after 1945, with its increasing focus on civil rights, gave a southern New Dealer like LBJ little political maneuvering room. If he proclaimed himself a national liberal, particularly if he stood up against segregation, he would likely lose his seat in the Senate and forfeit any chance for higher office. Yet if he aligned himself too closely with southern conservatives, he would mark himself as just another regional politician and sacrifice his hopes for national leadership. Johnson plotted out a cautious middle course. On economic matters not related to oil and gas, he joined the most liberal northern Democrats in the Congress. Senator Johnson supported aid to education, a higher minimum wage, extended rent control, public housing, and increased farm subsidies. He never compromised his bedrock liberal belief that government could and should play a leading role in American life, that government must ensure prosperity for all. When a Fort Worth businessman complained about too much government spending, too much waste and red tape, Johnson rebuffed him. "Would you scrap all our programs of veterans' benefits?" LBJ asked. Did the man find the courts, the public health service, and federal meat inspection dispensable? "Perhaps you think we can get along without any government at all," Johnson concluded. "If that is what you think, then you and I disagree fundamentally."[11]

Still, at the same time, Johnson opposed every piece of civil rights legislation in the Congress and apprenticed himself to the old guard southern senators who controlled the real authority in the upper house. Johnson wooed Richard Russell, the courtly senator from Georgia, who was widely regarded as the most powerful man in the Senate. Lyndon won a coveted seat on the Senate Armed Services Committee which Russell chaired, saw the senior senator every day, and soon befriended him. The usually brash and frantic LBJ became calm and courteous in Russell's presence. Soon the Georgian, a bachelor, was spending Sundays at the Johnsons' home and regarding Lyndon as the son he never had.

But while Johnson sought out Russell's patronage and support, he maintained a critical distance between himself and the southern leadership. He refused to join the southern caucus, the formal meetings of southern Democrats, because it would forever brand him a conservative and a merely regional politican. As Hubert Humphrey explained, "Johnson did not consider himself a southerner, and he knew he could not be its captive. He was a Texan, enjoying the benefits of southern hospitality, southern power, southern support, but who carefully avoided the liabilities of being clearly labeled a southerner."[12]

Humphrey understood this, because at the same time LBJ was courting the southern conservatives, he was reaching out to the liberal firebrand from Minnesota. Humphrey's first days in the Senate were painful ones. His political philosophy alienated the Senate's old guard, and his intemperate attack on Senator Harry Byrd of Virginia, a seeming breach of the Senate's code of honor, made him anathema to nearly every senator. One day Hubert passed a group of senior colleagues and overheard Richard Russell ask, "Can you imagine the people of Minnesota sending that damn fool down here to represent them?" Humphrey was crushed, but soon he was comforted by a visit from LBJ. Johnson urged Humphrey to become a "liberal doer," not just a "liberal talker"; he took the Minnesotan under his wing and soon made him the most effective liberal in the Senate and Johnson's personal link to northern liberalism.[13]

Johnson's political predicament and his political philosophy revolved around one thing: effectiveness. For LBJ, winning elections, passing bills, and implementing policy were the stuff of government, the purpose of liberalism. "There's nothing so useless as a dead liberal," he often said during his career and he meant it. Johnson's liberalism revolved around delivering concrete things to people, not around abstract principles. He distrusted, even despised, crusading leaders and unwavering attachment to principle, however high-minded. He was always willing to compromise, to build a consensus. For some liberals, including some of his closest advisers during the 1960s, this insistence on effectiveness would prove to be a trap. They would become so concerned with accomplishing a task, so afraid to lose influence by backing out of the process, that they would forget their basic objectives and find themselves inexorably drawn toward betraying their fundamental values. But Lyndon Johnson never felt torn between principle and expediency. Effectiveness was his basic principle, the cornerstone of his brand of liberalism. And during the 1940s and 1950s, it proved to be the secret of his success.

## "E = LBJ": THE SENATE LEADER

The United States Senate was the ideal playing field for a man of Johnson's talents, a master of face-to-face contact. He could please, tease, cajole, trade, deal, threaten—grab a man by his lapels, speak right into his face, look into his heart, and convince him that he had always wanted to vote the way LBJ was asking. He got to know all of the senators—their quirks, their worries, their styles. He could share whiskey and rude stories with some, enter scholarly policy discussions with others; he toasted their successes and mourned their losses. In 1952, the daughter of Virginia Senator Harry Byrd died, and LBJ drove out to Winchester, Virginia, for the funeral. Johnson was the only one of Byrd's colleagues to attend, and the Virginia senator deeply appreciated it. Years later, when Johnson needed Byrd's vote on a certain bill, Byrd remembered the funeral and repaid Johnson's kindness. "Mr. Johnson took to the Senate as if he'd been born there," his aide Walter Jenkins recalled. "From the first day on it was obvious it was *his* place—just the right size; he was at his best with small groups, and at that time he was one of only ninety-six senators, while in the House he had been one of 435, a group in which it was much more difficult to make his influence felt, to be effective. But with only ninety-five others—he *knew* he could manage that."[14]

Johnson managed the Senate by ruthlessly driving himself and his staff. He put his office on a twenty-four-hour day, with shifts running day and night. He himself worked from sunup until the early hours of the next day, routinely talking and chain-smoking through eighteen- or twenty-hour days, barely pausing to inhale his meals (no one ever saw LBJ eat slowly). Johnson expected similar dedication from his aides and more than one staffer broke under the pressure. But LBJ never slowed down. In the 1950s, one amazed journalist wrote that "$E = mc^2$ is Albert Einstein's world-shaking formula for energy. But in Washington, D.C., there is a simpler, more understandable formula. In that city of energetic men, energy in its purest political form is expressed in the letters E = LBJ."[15]

Early on in his Senate career, Johnson focused that energy on securing a position in the Senate's formal leadership. At the beginning of a new Congress, each party selected a floor leader (the majority leader and minority leader, respectively) and an assistant (or whip, responsible for whipping up support for a given measure or strategy). Few of Johnson's colleagues shared his ambition for these posts. The leadership required a lot of time and often tedious effort, it remained a largely ceremonial and procedural post with little authority, and it carried serious political risks. Real power in the Senate was vested in the senior members, who controlled the congressional committees and decided which bills the full body would consider. The leader had to spend so much time on his duties that he was often distracted from the concerns of his constituents and vulnerable to the charge that he did not care enough for his home state. Many a senator had accepted the honor of whip or majority leader from his colleagues and found himself turned out at the next election.

Just that fate met Senator Scott Lucas of Indiana, the Democratic majority leader, and his whip, Senator Francis Myers of Pennsylvania, in the 1950 elections. Ernest McFarland, a nondescript Arizonan, succeeded to the leadership, and Lyndon Johnson became the whip. Two years later, in November of 1952, McFarland also lost his seat. Johnson wasted no time in mounting a campaign to replace him. He even phoned the new class of freshman Democrats, just elected to the Senate, before they had a chance to celebrate their victories. One of the 1952 freshmen, John Fitzgerald Kennedy of Massachusetts, was stunned and pleased to receive a call from LBJ before the sun rose on the morning after election day. Kennedy pledged to support Johnson for the leadership, hung up the phone, and exclaimed, "The guy must never sleep."[16]

Johnson, a forty-four-year-old first-term senator, became minority leader, and in January 1955, after the Democrats narrowly recaptured control of the Senate in the 1954 midterm elections, he became the youngest majority leader in United States history. He also soon became the most successful and most powerful floor leader the Senate or the nation had ever seen. Central to Johnson's leadership was his personal style, what syndicated newspaper columnists Rowland Evans and Robert Novak called "The Treatment," his magical way of handling face-to-face encounters with individuals and small groups. Evans and Novak vividly portrayed The Treatment as "supplication, accusation, cajolery, exuberance, scorn, tears, complaint, the hint of threat. It was all of these together. Its velocity was breathtaking, and it was all in one direction.

Johnson administers The Treatment to Abe Fortas. Johnson later inscribed the photo: "For Abe, who's resisting me with all the horsepower God gave him."

Interjections from the target were rare. Johnson anticipated them before they could be spoken. He moved in close, his face a scant millimeter from his target, his eyes widening and narrowing, his eyebrows rising and falling."[17]

Once, the historian Arthur Schlesinger, Jr., a leading liberal, came to LBJ's office for an interview. Johnson hit him like a whirlwind, first giving him a concise description of every member of the Senate—each senator's political friends and enemies, drinking habits, health, pet projects, marital problems, and so forth. Then he explained how you managed these ninety-six vain and powerful persons. "Imagine a football team," he told Schlesinger in one account of the meeting, "and I'm the coach, and I'm also the quarterback. I have to call the signals, and I have to center the ball, run the ball, pass the ball." He reminded Schlesinger of all the bills he had steered through Congress in the past year, how he massaged liberal Hubert Humphrey on one, cajoled conservative Richard Russell on another, outfoxed the Republican leader on a third. Schlesinger was impressed and told a friend it was the "most informative morning I ever spent. Never got a word in edgewise." When that same man ran into Johnson, LBJ gave his version of the conversation: "I've been meeting with your friend, Arthur Schlesinger. Really had a very good meeting. We had a long talk. He's a right smart fellow. But, damn fellow talks too much."[18]

The Treatment demanded more calculation, more thought, than most observers imagined. Johnson mastered policy as well as personalities; he had statistics and memos bulging out of his pockets, details of bills and programs at the tip of his tongue, arguments for and against every measure. He also knew the Senate, speeding up votes when he knew he had a majority on the floor, delaying action when the opposition had the upper hand. In 1955, he steered an increase in the minimum wage through the Senate, the first one in six years. He also won passage of a liberal public housing bill, stunning the Republicans with a brilliant flanking maneuver. In that battle, Johnson brought to the floor a proposal by Senator John Sparkman to build 135,000 housing units, while Republican Senator Homer Capehart of Indiana introduced a more modest alternative, calling for only 70,000 units. Everyone assumed that conservative Democrats, who opposed all public housing, would vote with the Republicans and support the more conservative Capehart bill. The press predicted a major defeat for the young majority leader, and Capehart himself gleefully lorded it over Johnson. "Lyndon," he said, "this is one time I've really got you. I'm going to rub your nose in it."[19]

But Johnson outwitted everyone. He convinced five Republicans to vote for the liberal Sparkman plan and prodded conservative Democrats to go with their principles and vote against both bills. Johnson also ensured that Hubert Humphrey, a supporter of the Sparkman plan, would be on the floor for the vote. Humphrey's plane from Minnesota, delayed by bad weather, was hung up over Washington's National Airport when the Senate began voting. Johnson called the control tower, ordered a priority landing, and had police escort Humphrey from the airport to the Capitol. The Capehart bill was defeated. With their plan out of the way, Republicans who wanted some kind of public housing, had no choice but to go along with the Sparkman bill. When the votes were counted, one observer recalled, Homer Capehart "was a slumped down hulk."[20]

But Johnson did not rely exclusively on parliamentary skills and The Treatment. He thoroughly revamped and expanded the office of majority leader, giving it new scope, resources, and power. He built up the staff and relied on his assistants to keep him fully informed about every senator, every bill, and every committee hearing. He took responsibility for doling out every ceremonial assignment, every perquisite of high office, so that senators would become indebted to him. The Senate routinely sent delegations to Europe and Asia for foreign policy conferences, dedication of military cemeteries, and unveiling of statues. It appointed representatives to awards committees, historical commissions, and charitable functions. Johnson knew which members wanted and needed which assignments, and he used them to build his political base, to control the legislative process.

Most important, Johnson reorganized the Senate committee system, modifying the strict seniority rules that had long governed committee assignments and vesting new power in the majority leadership. The centerpiece of Johnson's plan was his desire to give each senator, even newly arrived freshman, at least one good committee assignment. This way, young, talented senators could begin contributing to the nation. They would no longer have to waste years on inconsequential jobs like a position on the Post Office Committee, wiling away the time until they had built sufficient seniority to move up. And these new senators would, of course, owe much gratitude to the majority leader who landed them these plums. But LBJ could not move ahead with the plan until he won the acquiescence of the senior senators. They would not only have to give up the prerogatives of seniority but surrender some of their seats on choice committees to make space for the freshmen. Afraid that even senators who approved of the general idea of a good assignment for every senator would not give up one of their own plum positions for the sake of principle, Johnson also rearranged the committee system, adding seats to the major committees so that there were more good places to spread around. As one historian has noted, Johnson's plan perfectly fit his growth-oriented 1950s liberalism; even within the Senate, he would not redistribute the wealth, but simply increase the size of the pie. Johnson won the approval of the senior members and the gratitude of the newcomers.

## BECOMING A NATIONAL FIGURE: THE LEADER AND THE ISSUES

How did Johnson use the power he had amassed in the leadership? What issues did the Senate address under his supervision? How did LBJ guide his party through eight years in the wilderness, eight years without control of the White House? Lyndon answered these questions by insisting on what he called the "politics of responsibility." That is, Johnson rejected the urging of many northern liberals that the Democrats fight Eisenhower tooth and nail, that they develop their own alternative program and dramatize their differences with Ike. Instead he promised, "We Democrats are going to take the only prudent course through which we can truly serve. It is to examine the President's program item by item and take our stand on the basis of the national interest."[21]

On the floor of the Senate, then, LBJ brooked little direct confrontation with the popular president and military hero of World War II. "There were practically no circumstances under which Johnson would countenance a 'Democratic bill'," recalled George Reedy, one of LBJ's Senate staffers. "He insisted that changes be made by striking the language of key portions of an Eisenhower bill and inserting Democratic language in its place."[22] When Republican senators wrangled over the new bills, it appeared as though they were bickering with their own leader, while the Democrats loyally supported him. As Reedy described the strategy, the public would see "a Republican President and a Democratic Senate cooperating in the service of the nation while a small group of GOP partisans were trying to throw sand in the gears."[23] Meanwhile, behind the scenes, Johnson and his House counterpart, Speaker Sam Rayburn, worked closely with the president; often the two Texans snuck into the White House through a back entrance for cocktails and conferences with Eisenhower.

LBJ thought this bipartisanship necessary and proper. He believed, as one of his closest aides put it, that "the Presidency of the United States was the one great office in the system, . . . that to attack the president was inevitably to attack the presidency."[24] But LBJ also believed bipartisanship was good politics. The Democrats could quietly substitute their legislative agenda for the Republicans', avoid open breaches with the fatherly Eisenhower, and appear as patriotic servants of the common good.

Thus, LBJ picked his battles carefully, openly breaking with the Republicans on domestic policy while mostly maintaining a bipartisan front in foreign affairs. He attacked the GOP for their lackadaisical response to the economic recession of 1954, shepherded a liberal expansion of the Social Security program through the Congress, and won victories for Democratic housing, minimum wage, and agriculture plans. He occasionally criticized the administration on international matters, but never fundamentally, and he was careful to protect himself and his party from charges that they underrated the dangers of communism.

For LBJ not only sincerely believed in the cold war struggle against the

Soviet Union, as did even the most liberal Democrats in the Senate, he also greatly feared anticommunist sentiment in the United States. He dreaded the power of firebrands like Senator Joseph McCarthy, who routinely accused liberals of treason, assassinated their characters, deprived them of their livelihoods, and ruined their lives. In 1953, while Johnson was minority leader, McCarthy's attacks reached a crescendo. Johnson despised McCarthy but would not confront him openly. "McCarthy is the sorriest Senator up here. Can't tie his own shoes," he explained to Bobby Baker. "But he's riding high now, he's got people scared some Communist will strangle 'em in their sleep, and anybody who takes him on before the fevers cool—well, you don't get in a pissin' contest with a polecat."[25] Johnson warned that a liberal attack would rally the Republicans behind McCarthy and seem to confirm his charges that the Democrats had something to hide. Lyndon would not let the Republicans victimize his fellow Democrats by making them appear soft on communism.

Johnson waited until McCarthy grew too reckless, until he began attacking more conservative persons and institutions. A cardinal rule of LBJ's political strategy was that the sponsor of a certain measure counted as much as the issue itself. If he needed a concession from organized labor to get a bill through, Johnson would get a liberal northerner with a strong pro-labor record to propose it. That would stifle opposition from the unions. To go after Joe McCarthy, he needed conservative voices with impeccable anticommunist credentials. And so, LBJ waited.

In 1954, McCarthy finally misstepped; he attacked prominent conservative senators, and worst of all, accused the U.S. Army of harboring traitors. When McCarthy began his investigations of the Army, LBJ maneuvered to have the hearings televised. He believed that the more people saw of McCarthy, his menacing appearance, and his underhanded tactics, the less they would like him. Sure enough, McCarthy discredited himself and, in a memorable exchange, the chief counsel for the Army disgraced McCarthy on national television.

At this point, LBJ moved. He named a special committee to investigate McCarthy and carefully selected the members, every one of them a conservative, most of them former judges with reputations for fairness and scrupulousness. Johnson's maneuver ensured that no one would challenge the committee's recommendation to discipline McCarthy. When the motion reached the floor of the Senate, McCarthy was censured by an overwhelming margin, sixty-seven to twenty-two. All but one of the Senate's Democrats voted for the measure (the exception was the absent senator from Massachusetts, John F. Kennedy, whose family had long supported McCarthy). McCarthy never recovered from the blow. He was finished.

Johnson's slow, cautious approach had succeeded. Many observers, then and later, agreed that LBJ had waited for the right moment, that an earlier attack would have backfired. Others thought him too slow, too moderate, too sensitive to the political winds; critics did not fail to note that it was after the 1954 elections, when Johnson had won reelection in Texas by a genuine landslide, that he decided to act.

In any case, Johnson's decisive reelection margin liberated him from some of the worries of Texas politics. It allowed him to devote less attention to shoring up his base and to expend more time and effort on national politics, national policy, and his own ambitions. Johnson self-consciously began transforming himself into a national leader. He tried to improve his public speaking and to become more effective in dealing with large audiences, be they fellow senators, reporters, or voters. While no man excelled in one-on-one encounters like LBJ, he remained awkward before bigger groups. On the campaign trail, he liked to plunge into the crowd and shake hands rather than deliver formal speeches, and while The Treatment worked with individual reporters or politicians, Johnson's aggressive style often alienated television audiences or groups of reporters at press conferences. While this mattered little in the intimate confines of the Senate, it would become a major liability during his presidency.

After his reelection, LBJ also began reaching out to northern liberals. He knew they distrusted his southern roots, his caution on civil rights, his loyalty to the oil and gas industry, and his refusal to oppose Eisenhower openly. If he was ever to win the presidency, Johnson needed to convince party liberals that he was more than a regional politician. In November 1955, Johnson delivered a major speech, outlining his vision for the country, his desire to resuscitate and expand Franklin Roosevelt's New Deal. Before a packed gymnasium in the tiny town of Whitney, Texas, LBJ outlined "A Program with a Heart," a thirteen-point agenda for liberal reform.[26] Johnson called for expanded Social Security coverage, more generous subsidies for farmers, tax breaks for the poor, water conservation, economic development for chronically depressed areas, and repeal of the poll tax—a fee for voting that disenfranchised black southerners and numerous poor whites as well. The program also included more hospitals, schools, roads, and housing, all supported by the federal government. Back in Washington, LBJ worked to implement this program. When the nation slipped into another recession in 1958, Johnson secured passage of new flood control, housing, and highway measures, and enhanced protection for the unemployed. At the same time, he also won the respect of northern liberals by blocking conservative efforts to weaken the Supreme Court.

Still, all of these measures reflected LBJ's roots as a southern New Dealer. To prove himself presidential timber, Lyndon still needed to establish himself as a leader in foreign policy and national defense and to break the bottleneck on civil rights.

The first of these proved the easiest. Late in 1957, the Soviet Union shocked the world by launching *Sputnik I,* a small, unmanned satellite, into Earth orbit. *Sputnik* alarmed the American public; many feared that the Soviets had moved ahead in the arms race, that the United States faced a scientific crisis, and that Russian missiles would soon rain down on American cities. Congressional Democrats eagerly exploited the public outcry, criticizing the Republican administration for falling behind the communists. Liberal senators demanded an investigation of the nation's seemingly second-rate space program.

In *Sputnik,* Lyndon Johnson saw a main chance for his party, his region, and himself. He knew the space issue could embarrass the Republicans. He soon realized that an expanded space program, in need of a warm-weather home, could provide remunerative, high-technology jobs for his native South and help lead that desperately poor section out of poverty. Of equal appeal to Johnson were the notoriety and popularity he could earn from handling the issue. One of his supporters even circulated a memo predicting that if LBJ milked *Sputnik* for all it was worth, he would land in the White House in 1960.

Still, LBJ moved cautiously. He made sure that the Senate hearings never became too aggressive, that the committee never accused the Eisenhower administration of serious wrongdoing or spread panic around the country. While dramatizing the seriousness of the nation's problems and acknowledging that space research had developed slowly in the United States, Johnson reassured his countrymen that the United States would soon overtake its rival. To do so, Johnson produced two landmark pieces of legislation in 1958. One created a major civilian space program by establishing the National Aeronautics and Space Administration (NASA); the other reinvigorated scientific and technical education through the National Defense Education Act (NDEA).

"A Program with a Heart," NASA, wizardry on the Senate floor—these all established Johnson's national reputation and made sure that his name entered any discussion of contenders for the presidency in 1960. But one obstacle still stood in his way: civil rights. This great issue divided the Democratic party, divided the nation, and seemed to block any southerner's path to the nation's highest office. In the words of Senator John F.

Kennedy, "The Democratic Party owed Johnson the presidential nomination but it was too close to Appomattox for Johnson to be nominated and elected."[27] With the Supreme Court assailing the South's system of segregation in its 1954 *Brown* decision, with the civil rights movement gaining steam, and with recalcitrant white southerners violently resisting change, neither LBJ, his party, nor the Congress could avoid facing this divisive question.

Johnson, of course, had never been a segregationist or a virulent racist. As congressman and NYA director he had distinguished himself by his quiet, but sincere efforts on behalf of African Americans. Johnson had long advanced the standard position of southern liberals: the government should do everything in its power to remedy the want and poverty of blacks and Latinos, but civil rights laws were out of the question. As his assistant Harry McPherson put it, Senator Johnson was "your typical Southern liberal who would have done a lot more in the field of civil rights early in his career had it been possible," but knew that any such effort meant political suicide in Texas.[28] For twenty years, from the time Johnson entered the House of Representatives in 1937 until 1957, he had voted against every civil rights proposal he faced.

But Johnson never aligned himself with the southern segregationists. When the Supreme Court handed down its decision in *Brown v. Board of Education,* three-fourths of the people in Texas opposed the Court and President Eisenhower refused to endorse the decision. Johnson, however, publically defended the Court. Two years later, southern members of Congress issued a southern manifesto promising to resist the *Brown* decision. Johnson was one of only three southern senators who refused to sign it. Senator Richard Neuberger, an Oregon Democrat, called Johnson's decision "one of the most courageous acts of political valor" he had ever seen.[29] Few others believed that, of course. They realized, as did Lyndon, that signing the southern manifesto meant kissing the presidency good-bye.

There was more at stake in the civil rights issue for Johnson than his visceral concern for the poor and oppressed or his political ambitions. For he truly believed that the issue could destroy the Democratic party and end his hopes for a new New Deal that would restore active, affirmative government. He thought that endless wrangling over race held back the South and mired it in ignorance, want, and squalor. In Harry McPherson's words, "Johnson felt about the race question much as I did, namely, that it obsessed the South and diverted it from attending to its economic and educational problems."[30] In 1957, LBJ concluded that further delay was impossible; he decided to back a federal civil rights act.

Not since the era of Reconstruction after the Civil War had Congress passed a civil rights law. In the 1940s and 1950s, six different bills had met defeat on the House and Senate floor and there seemed little hope of passing one any time soon. Senate rules allowed unlimited debate, so that a determined minority could prevent action on any bill simply by talking and talking around the clock. Conservative southerners had mastered this technique called the filibuster. They would assign teams of senators to cover shifts, reading from encyclopedias or dusty old books, relieving each other after a few hours, grinding the Senate to a halt. Shutting off a filibuster—a procedure called cloture—required the approval of two-thirds of the Senate, a number almost impossible to attain. The South had successfully buried every civil rights bill for eighty years. A civil rights act, any civil rights act, seemed impossible.

As usual, Johnson posed as the champion of compromise. He tried to fashion a bill acceptable to a broad spectrum of senators, convincing northern liberals that a compromise was better than nothing and persuading southerners to accept a weak bill now lest they face draconian measures later. After the House approved a bill, LBJ began the fight by consulting Richard Russell. Russell agreed not to filibuster against the bill if Johnson would make two changes: drop Section III, which accelerated school desegregation in the South; and add a new provision that guaranteed a jury trial to anyone accused of violating court orders in a civil rights case. Johnson now turned to the liberals. To drop Section III, he negotiated with a group of western senators. These western Democrats, though generally supportive of civil rights, had few black constituents and cared little about the issue. They cared deeply, however, about water and power development in the West and had been bitterly disappointed by the Senate's failure to approve financing for the Hell's Canyon Dam in Idaho. Johnson cut a deal, trading southern support for Hell's Canyon in return for the westerners' agreement to remove Section III from the civil rights bill.

Jury trials, then, remained the only stumbling block. Northern liberals howled about this provision. Southern juries—all-white southern juries—would never convict anyone for violating the civil rights laws. Liberals wanted federal judges, not local juries, to decide such cases. Again, LBJ looked for a compromise. He backed an amendment that would provide for jury trials in some cases, but not in others. He also had one senator insert a largely symbolic declaration guaranteeing all Americans the right to serve on federal juries, without regard to race, creed, or color. And, he persuaded two moderate liberals, both with solid civil rights measures, to introduce the changes. The jury trial amendment passed narrowly. A few days later, what Evans and Novak termed the miracle of '57 took place, and the first civil rights act in eighty years became the law of the land.[31]

The act was LBJ's baby. Nobody doubted its parentage, although opinion varied greatly on its merits. The *New York Times* called the law "incomparably the most significant domestic action of any Congress in this century." Black leader Bayard Rustin remembered it as "a weak but very important law . . . that would establish a very important precedent." A number of other black leaders thought it shamefully, ludicrously thin. Senator Paul Douglas compared it to "soup made from the shadow of a crow which had starved to death" and Eleanor Roosevelt called it "mere fakery." Even Johnson conceded that the law was largely symbolic: "I got all I could on Civil Rights in 1957," he insisted. "Next year I'll get a little more, and the year after that I'll get a little more. The difference between me and some of my northern friends is that I believe you can't force these things on the South overnight. You advance a little and consolidate; then you advance again. I think in the long run my way may prove faster than theirs."[32]

By 1958, then, Johnson had positioned himself for a run for the presidency, but he had yet to announce his candidacy or to decide in his own mind whether this was the moment to seek the office. One lingering worry was his health. In 1955, Johnson had suffered a serious heart attack—a coronary occlusion—and for two days his doctors gave him only a fifty-fifty chance of survival. Johnson rebounded quickly and soon resumed his rigorous schedule. Still, he needed more rest, had to maintain a strict diet, and hardest of all for Johnson, was ordered to quit smoking.

Another roadblock was Johnson's sense that a southerner could not win, that he could not muster the support from around the nation. During 1958 and 1959, his friends and supporters implored him to throw his hat in the ring, but LBJ balked. His closest advisers, including Lady Bird, were convinced that he would not run. Johnson decided against an open bid for the White House; he did not campaign, did not enter any of the state primary elections in the winter and spring of 1960. He wanted to appear a statesman above the fray, while the other candidates attacked each other. In the end, he figured that a deadlocked national convention, unable to decide among the other contenders, would turn to its most prominent national leader. He prepared for such an eventuality by engineering a change in the Texas election laws so that he could run for president or vice president and at the same time for reelection to the Senate. That way he could seek national office without risking his seat.

Lyndon's backroom, behind-the-scenes campaign failed miserably. It was the sort of approach that worked in the Senate (and if the Senate had

The Democratic ticket at the July 1960 National Convention in Los Angeles. Vice Presidential nominee LBJ applauds running mate John Fitzgerald Kennedy.

selected the president in 1960, LBJ certainly would have won), but not in the nation at large. By the time Johnson realized his mistake and hit the campaign trail, it was too late. John Kennedy had amassed a resounding lead and no one could stop him.

Johnson, the master politician, miscalculated badly in 1960 for many reasons. Not the least of them was that he underestimated the youthful, good-looking senator from Massachusetts. In fact, Johnson never really took him seriously. He referred to Kennedy as "the boy" and thought of both John Kennedy and his brother Bobby as mere messengers for their powerful father, Joseph Kennedy. As majority leader, LBJ often helped out young Jack because he wanted to win old Joe's gratitude and support; he never conceived of "the boy" as a serious rival. "It was the goddamnedest thing," Johnson remembered after he retired from the presidency. Kennedy "never said a word of importance in the Senate and he never did a thing. But somehow . . . he managed to create the image of himself as . . . a youthful leader who would change the face of the country. Now, I will admit that he had a good sense of humor and that he looked awfully good on the goddamned television screen . . . but his growing hold on the American people was simply a mystery to me."[33]

To Johnson's continued mystification, that television screen was coming to play an increasingly dominant role in political life and those politicians who could manipulate it for their own ends found a weapon that outperformed any of Johnson's own tactics. Johnson, the inventor of helicopter campaigning, entirely understood the triumph of style over substance, but could not translate his sense of style to the new electronic medium. The telegenic Kennedy won the Democratic presidential nomination on the first ballot. He offered the vice presidency to Johnson and LBJ accepted it. The decision surprised many of LBJ's friends. After all, Johnson would be handing over leadership of the Senate, one of the most powerful positions in the world, for an inconsequential post with little influence on anything. But LBJ realized that the number-two slot would firmly establish him as a national figure. Johnson also recognized that whichever candidate won the election, a new and younger president would aggressively pursue his own program, so that Johnson would no longer command as much authority as majority leader.

As vice president, Lyndon Johnson would stand only a heartbeat away from the presidency, but miles from any real authority. For a man who wanted most of all to be "effective," the nation's second highest office would prove a bitter, disappointing, and depressing trial.

## NOTES

[1] Numerous Republicans made this charge. Prominent among them was Senator Joseph McCarthy of Wisconsin.

[2] Hubert H. Humphrey, quoted in Alan H. Ryskind, *Hubert* (New Rochelle: Arlington House, 1968), 132.

[3] Robert Dallek, *Lone Star Rising: Lyndon Johnson and His Times* (New York: Oxford University Press, 1991), 346.

[4] J. Ronnie Dugger, *The Politician* (New York: W. W. Norton and Co., 1982), 342.

[5] Ibid., 343.

[6] Doris Kearns, *Lyndon Johnson and the American Dream* (New York: Signet Books, 1976), 160–61.

[7] Dallek, *Lone Star Rising*, 299.

[8] Arthur M. Schlesinger, Jr., popularized these terms in *The Vital Center* (Boston: Houghton Mifflin, 1949).

[9] Walt Whitman Rostow, *The Stages of Economic Growth: A Non-Communist Manifesto* (Cambridge: Cambridge University Press, 1960).

[10] Dugger, *The Politician*, 371.

[11] Dallek, *Lone Star Rising*, 371.

[12] Dugger, *The Politician*, 344.

[13] Ibid., 346. Dallek, *Lone Star Rising*, 380–81. Kearns, *Johnson and the American Dream*, 138–39.

[14] Walter Jenkins, quoted in Merle Miller, *Lyndon: An Oral Biography* (New York: Ballantine, 1980), 171 (emphasis in original).

[15] Al Toffler, "The Senate's Mr. Energy," *Pageant* (July 1958):102.

[16] Dallek, *Lone Star Rising,* 423.

[17] Rowland Evans and Robert Novak, *Lyndon B. Johnson: The Exercise of Power* (New York: Signet Books, 1966), 115–16.

[18] Ibid., 116–17. Dallek, *Lone Star Rising,* 352.

[19] Dallek, *Lone Star Rising,* 482.

[20] Ibid.

[21] Ibid., 438.

[22] Ibid., 494.

[23] Ibid., 437.

[24] Harry McPherson, quoted in Miller, *Lyndon,* 248.

[25] Dallek, *Lone Star Rising,* 453.

[26] Lyndon B. Johnson, "A Program with a Heart," (address at Whitney, Texas, November 21, 1955).

[27] Dallek, *Lone Star Rising,* 541.

[28] Ibid., 520.

[29] Ibid., 496.

[30] Ibid., 519.

[31] Evans and Novak, *Exercise of Power,* 131.

[32] Bayard Rustin, quoted in Miller, *Lyndon,* 258. Kearns, *Johnson and the American Dream,* 157. Dallek, *Lone Star Rising,* 526–27.

[33] Dallek, *Lone Star Rising,* 555–56, 559, 565.

# 3

# "Let Us Continue": LBJ and the Kennedy Legacy, 1960–1964

John Adams, the first vice president of the United States, called that post "the most insignificant office that ever the invention of man contrived or his imagination conceived."[1] Adams liked to joke about a poor, bereaved mother with two sons. One went off to sea, the other became vice president . . . and neither was heard from again. Nearly every one of Adams's successors shared his opinion. Woodrow Wilson's vice president, Thomas R. Marshall, claimed that the vice president "is like a man in a cataleptic state. He cannot speak. He cannot move. He suffers no pain. And yet he is conscious of all that goes on around him."[2]

In January 1961, the restless, ambitious Lyndon Baines Johnson occupied this despised office. He had surrendered the leadership of the Senate, one of the most powerful political positions in the country, for a negligible post. But LBJ had no intention of remaining silent and motionless. Johnson told surprised friends that "power is where power goes," that he could turn a ceremonial position into one with real authority.[3] After all, LBJ's political genius had repeatedly asserted itself in just such unlikely places. Over and over again in the past, he had accepted apparently insignificant offices—congressional secretary, director of the Democratic Congressional Campaign Committee, the senate majority leader—and built them into real bases of authority, centers for political action. When Johnson asked his Senate chauffeur to follow him to his new position, the driver balked. He said, LBJ remembered, that "he liked to drive the Majority Leader because there was a man with real power. He said the Vice President doesn't have any power at all."[4] Johnson convinced him otherwise.

Wasting no time, Johnson launched an audacious effort to transform the vice presidency—to win it real power in both the legislative and executive branches of the government. Under the Constitution, the vice president nominally serves as presiding officer of the Senate. Johnson intended to run the Senate in fact as well as in name; he convinced the new majority leader, Senator Mike Mansfield of Montana, to let him keep the plush offices he had held as Senate leader, a vast suite known as the "Taj Mahal." At LBJ's direction, Mansfield also moved to formalize Johnson's control over the day-to-day operations of the Senate by naming Vice President Johnson presiding officer of the Senate Democratic caucus. But LBJ's former colleagues rebuffed him. They would not breach years of tradition and accept a non-senator as their leader.

The vice president also met defeat at the other end of Pennsylvania Avenue. Johnson drew up an executive order for President Kennedy's signature—an order that would in effect have made him assistant president or even co-president. The document conferred upon the vice president "general supervision" over a number of areas of the national government, including control of the National Aeronautics and Space Administration. It also required that the vice president receive copies of every report, briefing paper, and top-secret document that crossed the president's desk. The president was not about to surrender so much authority; the order was never signed.

After a few months in the vice presidency, LBJ ruefully tipped his hat to the wisdom of his driver. "That's a smart man, my chauffeur," Johnson conceded as he settled into the least productive and most miserable years of his life. To a large extent, Johnson became the "cataleptic" that Thomas Marshall described. At Washington cocktail parties, political insiders wondered at the disappearance of the man who had so long towered over the town and its affairs. He rarely spoke at meetings, stayed away from Capitol Hill, and exerted little influence on his former colleagues in the Senate. "The Vice Presidency," Johnson told Doris Kearns at the end of his career, "is filled with trips around the world, chauffeurs, men saluting, people clapping, chairmanships of councils, but in the end it is nothing. I detested every minute of it."[5]

Johnson found servility to a younger man (nine years his junior) formerly in his charge particularly difficult. The role reversal made both men uncomfortable. "I spent years of my life," JFK remembered, "when I could not get consideration for a bill until I went around and begged Lyndon Johnson to let it go ahead."[6] Nonetheless, the men respected each other. Kennedy appreciated his vice president's loyalty and self-restraint, for despite their differences, Johnson never criticized the president publicly and never even made fun of him in private. Moreover, JFK recognized Johnson's political value. He had won the 1960 election by one of the narrowest margins in history, with less than fifty percent of the popular vote. JFK had carried—and needed to carry—six southern states. Without Johnson's help, the Massachusetts Catholic would have struggled in the South and would likely have lost the election. Shortly before his death, the president declared unequivocally that LBJ would remain on the ticket in 1964.

Although LBJ maintained cordial relations with John Kennedy, his relations with the president's brother, Attorney General Robert F. Kennedy (RFK), never possessed even a sheen of civility. Johnson had long detested RFK; he thought him a brash, uppity, spoiled brat. "That upstart's come too far and too fast," LBJ told one of his aides. "He skipped the grades where you learn the rules of life. He never liked me and that's nothing compared to what I think of him."[7] Johnson considered Bobby Kennedy a dirty and dishonest player. Bobby had worked for Joseph McCarthy, and LBJ believed that RFK had tried to keep him off the ticket in 1960. Vice President Johnson also thought that Attorney General Kennedy was wiretapping his phones. After LBJ became president, his distrust of RFK would intensify. Every time he tried to climb out of the Kennedy shadow and advance his own program, he would see Bobby, taking credit or finding fault.

## THE VICE PRESIDENT

President Kennedy assigned his vice president three major roles—representing the White House overseas, overseeing the space program, and, most important, chairing the President's Committee on Equal Employment Opportunity (PCEEO). Johnson's old New Deal friend, Abe Fortas, drafted an executive order banning racial discrimination by government contractors, and the PCEEO would enforce that decree. Any company or labor union doing business with the federal government would have to root out discrimination or risk losing its government contract. Fortas's directive significantly strengthened civil rights protections for employees of federal contractors. Previously, an African American worker would have to lodge a complaint and prove that the employer had practiced racial discrimination. Under the new authority, employers had to demonstrate actual efforts to combat racist practices; they were obligated to take affirmative action to remedy racial discrimination.

Vice President Johnson devoted many hours to the PCEEO, turning it into something of a national racial conciliation and mediation service. Rarely did the committee threaten cancellation of a company's contract;

Johnson and his associates instead prodded and cajoled offending parties, negotiating settlements, and defusing tensions. "Let's make it fashionable to end discrimination," Johnson said, explaining the PCEEO's mission to his staff.[8]

But LBJ never felt entirely comfortable about this position. In part, his uneasiness was personal. As head of the Justice Department, Robert Kennedy superintended the administration's civil rights policy and Bobby frequently interfered in the committee's work, simultaneously limiting LBJ's freedom of action and rebuking him for not producing more dramatic results. But Johnson's mixed feelings about the PCEEO also reflected political and policy differences with President Kennedy. As a northern liberal, JFK was confident of the support of the civil rights community, but wary of enraging white southern Democrats. He could afford caution on civil rights. Johnson, on the other hand, finally free of the demands of Texas politics, thought the time was ripe for decisive action on the race question. To prove himself a national leader, he had to show boldness on the civil rights front.

In the spring of 1963, as the Kennedy administration prepared to submit civil rights legislation to the Congress, Vice President Johnson broke his usual silence in high-level meetings and pressed JFK to introduce a tough, no-holds-barred bill that would end segregation in the South once and for all. Johnson lobbied the reluctant president to take the case directly to the people, going over the heads of the Congress, to build support for the measure. Kennedy demurred, but in May LBJ traveled to the Civil War battlefield at Gettysburg and demanded an end to vacillation and compromise on civil rights. "We do not answer those who lie beneath this soil," LBJ paraphrased a famous speech by civil rights leader Martin Luther King, Jr., "when we reply to the Negro by asking 'Patience.' "[9]

Vice President Johnson also served as the administration's goodwill ambassador to foreign lands. During his two-and-a-half years as Kennedy's understudy, LBJ made eleven separate trips outside the United States, far more than any previous vice president. Indeed, away from Washington, out of JFK's shadow, and amid the cheers of admiring crowds, Johnson regained some of the confidence, ebullience, and swagger for which he had been famous as majority leader. He insisted on royal treatment, wiring his special requirements ahead to every stop, including a special oversized bed for his six-foot-three-inch frame and several cases of Cutty Sark, the Scotch whiskey he preferred.

Two of these overseas tours made lasting impressions on LBJ. The first, a 1961 mission to Vietnam, convinced Johnson that the fate of all Asia depended on American leadership in the region. "In large measure," Johnson informed JFK in a confidential report, "the greatest danger that Southeast Asia offers to nations like the United States is not the momentary threat of communism itself. Rather, that danger stems from hunger, ignorance, poverty and disease."[10] In fact, LBJ saw in Vietnam the problems of rural America in the 1920s and 1930s and was convinced that the same solution—a beneficent U.S. government—would work in the Mekong River Valley of Vietnam just as well as it had in the Lower Colorado River Valley of central Texas. "I felt a special rapport with those Asians," Johnson remembered. "I know how desperately they needed our help and I wanted to give it. I wanted them to have all the dams and all the projects they could handle."[11]

This sentimentality, while obscuring LBJ's understanding of Vietnam's distinctive culture, history, and problems, did not confuse Johnson about the real weaknesses of the American position in Southeast Asia. "The fundamental decision required of the United States," he wrote President Kennedy, "is whether we are to attempt to meet the challenge of Communist expansion in Southeast Asia by a major effort in support of the forces of freedom in the area or throw in the towel. This decision must be made in a full realization of the very heavy and continuing costs involved in terms of money, of effort, and of United States prestige. It must be made with the knowledge that at some point we may be faced with the further decision of whether we commit major United States forces to the area or cut our losses and withdraw should our efforts fail."[12] That point would be reached four years later, and that "further decision" would fall on President Lyndon Johnson's shoulders.

Johnson's second important overseas mission as vice president followed a few months later when the Soviet Union sealed off the borders between East and West Germany and stunned the world by constructing, almost overnight, a wall between East and West Berlin. President Kennedy dispatched LBJ to Berlin to reassure its frightened and bewildered citizens. At first, Johnson had tried to evade the assignment; he thought he would become the scapegoat for Kennedy's failure to prevent the erection of the Berlin Wall, that he would become the symbol for the administration's failure. The trip, however, proved a great personal and political success. Johnson received a hero's welcome, pledging "our lives, our fortunes, and our sacred honor" to defend the liberty of West Berlin.[13]

Such triumphant moments came seldom to Vice President Johnson. For the most part, LBJ's years as Kennedy's second in command were filled with disappointment and frustration. For a man who cared most of all about getting things done, the impotence of the office proved unbearable.

## YEARS OF FRUSTRATION:
## JFK AND THE LIBERAL AGENDA

During the Kennedy administration, Vice President Johnson was not alone in his frustration and disappointment. President Kennedy shared it. It is commonplace to portray the 1960 election as a turning point in American history. Kennedy's narrow victory seemed to end eight years of conservative Republicanism and social quiescence, ushering in a decade of liberal Democratic presidents, social reform, radical protest, and political turmoil. Kennedy's charisma—his youth, charm, and eloquence—contrasted sharply with the plodding, avuncular style of Dwight D. Eisenhower. And JFK promised the nation a "New Frontier," an ambitious agenda of liberal government action abroad and at home.

But JFK never delivered it. From the start of his presidency, Kennedy was preoccupied with foreign affairs. In his inaugural address, he promised to "pay any price, bear any burden" to repel communist aggression and defend the forces of freedom around the globe. International events immediately—and repeatedly—commanded the young president's attention: the abortive Bay of Pigs invasion, the establishment of the Peace Corps, the erection of the Berlin Wall, the Cuban missile crisis, and the dispatch of sixteen thousand military advisers to Vietnam.

Kennedy's domestic advisers did develop a slew of new programs, but, with only a few exceptions, the president could not get Congress to enact them. The principal objectives of Kennedy's domestic agenda—federal aid to education, the New Economics, and civil rights legislation—stalled on Capitol Hill. *New York Times* reporter Tom Wicker described Kennedy's inability to manage the Congress as one of the "great ironies of American politics"; he wondered why "JFK, the immensely popular president, could not reach his legislative goals." The stubborn opposition surprised Kennedy himself. "When I was a Congressman," the thwarted president mused, "I never realized how important Congress was. Now I do."[14]

In his defense, JFK's failure on aid to education was not unexpected; FDR and Truman had similarly tried and failed to secure such legislation. As we have seen, only LBJ's opportunistic handling of the Sputnik crisis had allowed even a basic federal aid-to-education package to pass during the Eisenhower years. Major federal education programs had foundered repeatedly upon the rocky intransigence of "three Rs"—not reading, 'riting, and 'rithmetic—but race, region, and religion. Northerners envisioned federal aid as a lever to force desegregation, intending to withhold federal funds from southern schools that lagged behind on integration. Not surprisingly, southern legislators opposed any such linkage between education and the race issue. Different regions of the country also clashed over the formula for allocating federal money. Wealthier, more populous states wanted the states to receive funds according to the size of their populations. Poor, rural states in the South and West demanded apportionment on the basis of income, a scheme that benefited them.

Religion—the third R—proved the most difficult roadblock for President Kennedy. The Roman Catholic Church wanted students in its parochial schools to be eligible for federal assistance, a position supported by many legislators from heavily Catholic areas. On the other hand, many Americans opposed public support for private schools. The controversy particularly vexed JFK. As a Roman Catholic, he was careful about not appearing to favor his co-religionists and opposed funding for parochial schools. Federal aid once again died in the Congress.

Kennedy had no more success with his economic program. The president openly endorsed the so-called New Economics—the teachings of British economist John Maynard Keynes as they had been adapted by American scholars during the 1940s and 1950s. Of course, Presidents Roosevelt, Truman, and Eisenhower had all pursued Keynesian fiscal strategies; they had used the federal government's taxing and spending powers to stimulate sluggish economies and help the nation out of economic downturns. But they had done so reluctantly, often unconsciously. At most, Keynesianism had been a justification for policies they adopted for other reasons.

Kennedy, on the other hand, gradually became a true believer—the first American president to pledge firm allegiance to the New Economics. He appointed the nation's most prominent Keynesian economists to his administration, including Walter Heller, John Kenneth Galbraith, and James Tobin. Anxious to employ their economic tools, these men were not content to wait for the next slide in economic performance. They planned to ride herd over the nation's economy, applying the whip hand of tax cuts and spending increases if business activity slowed, pulling on the reins by raising taxes and cutting spending if the economy overheated and inflation threatened. In 1963, fearing an economic slowdown, Kennedy and his Keynesians decided to propose an economic stimulus program. Galbraith, then serving as ambassador to India, lobbied for vast increases in federal spending. Government spending, he argued, would inject money directly into the economy—the most effective kind of stimulus—and would spread the benefits around more evenly. Cutting taxes would disproportionately benefit business and wealthier Americans and only indirectly fuel the economy (since the cut returned money to private citizens, some of whom would save it or invest it abroad rather than invest it in the American economy). But Kennedy opted for the more politically palatable course. In August 1963, he asked Congress for the largest tax cut in U.S. history.

Although Kennedy chose the more popular fiscal strategy, he still could not win congressional approval for his plan. Fiscal conservatives, doubtful about the New Economics, would not willingly unbalance the budget to fuel the economy. Key members of Congress refused to cut taxes unless Kennedy trimmed his spending requests to the bone and kept the budget in balance. The Senate Finance Committee buried JFK's tax reduction plan.

On taxes and aid to education, Kennedy hoped eventually to break the legislative logjam. But concerning civil rights, the most important domestic issue of the era, JFK was completely stymied. For the first two-and-a-half years of his administration, Kennedy had moved very cautiously on the race issue. In the early months of his presidency, Kennedy sent sixteen separate messages to the Congress defining his legislative agenda. None of them mentioned civil rights. He created the President's Committee on Equal Employment Opportunity and appointed a large number of African Americans to important positions in the government, including Thurgood Marshall, the first black federal judge since Reconstruction. But he also named four southern segregationists to the federal bench. Kennedy wanted to end racial discrimination in the South, but he had decided to watch and wait.

In the spring of 1963, dramatic confrontations between civil rights protesters and white authorities in Alabama forced the president's hand. In Birmingham, Martin Luther King, Jr., and the nonviolent demonstration he headed met the massive resistance of white racists led by Eugene "Bull" Connor, the city's infamous police commissioner. A virulent racist itching for a fight, Connor met the marchers with vicious dogs, fire hoses, and electric cattle prods. Watching the horrifying violence on television, the nation rallied behind the brutalized civil rights workers. Meanwhile, Alabama whites remained intransigent. The state's segregationist governor, George C. Wallace, defied court orders to enroll black students at the University of Alabama, forcing President Kennedy to send federal troops to Tuscaloosa. In the wake of these confrontations, Kennedy committed himself unambiguously to the civil rights cause. "We face a moral crisis," he told the nation on June 11, 1963. "It is time to act in Congress."[15]

Two months later, the march on Washington further stirred the country. Martin Luther King, Jr., delivered his "I Have a Dream" speech and millions of Americans agreed with civil rights lobbyist Joseph Rauh that "the March was an expression of all that's best in America." Rauh realized, however, that the noble words of King, which had moved the nation, had not turned any votes in Congress. "Three months later, when Kennedy was killed," Rauh remembered, "the bill was absolutely bogged down."[16]

So, too, was most of Kennedy's New Frontier. The 1963 session of Congress had been one of the longest in U.S. history, and one of the least productive. Congress scaled back Kennedy's requests for foreign aid and area redevelopment; killed his proposals for education, health care, and reorganizing the executive branch of the government; and bottled up the tax cut and civil rights bills. The stalemate so unnerved Walter Lippmann, the nation's most influential newspaper columnist, that he wondered whether the system "as it now operates is not a grave danger to the Republic."[17]

By the autumn of 1963, Kennedy had decided not to press his full agenda. He opted to defer most of his domestic policy initiatives until his second term and to concentrate on winning reelection. He journeyed to Dallas in November, intending to meet with state Democratic leaders and to solidify his support in Texas and the Southwest. But as his motorcade passed through the city, Kennedy was gunned down in his open car. He died a few hours later. The Secret Service rushed Vice President Johnson to Love Field, where the President's plane, *Air Force 1,* sat on the runway. Mrs. Kennedy boarded the plane along with the body of her slain husband. She was followed by a federal judge who administered the oath of office and swore in fifty-five-year-old Lyndon Baines Johnson as the thirty-sixth president of the United States.

## "LET US CONTINUE": THE TRANSITION

"Every President," LBJ wrote in his memoirs, "has to establish with the various sectors of the country what I call the 'right to govern.' Just being elected does not guarantee him that right. Every President has to inspire the confidence of the people."[18] For a president who had never won election, who had inherited the office in the wake of a shocking national tragedy, this challenge was all the more difficult. "I took the oath," Johnson told Doris Kearns. "I became president. But for millions of Americans I was still illegitimate, a naked man with no presidential covering, a pretender to the throne, an illegal usurper. And then there was Texas, my home, the home of both the murderer and the murderer of the murderer. And then there were the bigots and the dividers and the

After the assassination of John F. Kennedy in November 1963, Johnson is sworn in as president of the United States aboard *Air Force 1*. Jacqueline Kennedy looks on.

Eastern intellectuals, who were waiting to knock me down before I could even begin to stand up. The whole thing was almost unbearable."[19]

Johnson assumed the Kennedy mantle, declaring himself the "dutiful executor" of his predecessor's legacy. He shouldered a heavy burden, for the shock of the assassination instantly elevated Kennedy, an uncertain leader only beginning to establish himself, into an unparalleled martyr, the symbol of all that was grand in the nation. Only 49.7 percent of the electorate had cast their ballots for JFK in 1960, but after the assassination, 65 percent claimed that they had voted for him. Even opponents of the slain president, a national poll revealed, overwhelmingly mourned his death as "the loss of someone close and dear."[20]

Five days after the assassination, Johnson made his first presidential address to the American people (see Document 1). Significantly, he made the speech not from the Oval Office of the White House, but before a joint session of Congress, in the place where he had started his career. Johnson began by expressing the collective grief of the nation but did not content himself with honoring the fallen hero. Committing himself to vigorous action on behalf of the Kennedy agenda, Johnson promised to complete the slain leader's work, and he made it clear that the most immediate tasks were on Capitol Hill. He asked for enactment of the Kennedy tax bill and most emphatically for civil rights legislation: "We have talked long enough in this country about equal rights. We have talked for one hundred years or more. It is time now to write the next chapter, and to write it in the books of law."[21]

President Johnson had reassured the American people with his promise to "continue"; he accepted his duty as custodian of the Kennedy legacy. But he made it clear that his would be no caretaker administration. When one adviser warned him against risking too much prestige and power to implement Kennedy's legislative program, LBJ paused, raised his eyebrows, and replied, "Well, then what the hell's the presidency for?"[22]

Johnson immediately went on what his exhausted assistants called the "two-shift day."[23] Rising at six-thirty, LBJ would work furiously until about two o'clock, when he left the Oval Office and took a walk or a swim. Then he would change into his pajamas for a catnap, usually on the long couch in the private sitting room adjoining his office. At four, he was showered and dressed, ready for a "new day's work." The second shift would end after midnight, sometimes lasting until two in the morning if affairs were especially pressing.

Johnson spent many of those long hours on the telephone — barking out orders, cajoling members of Congress, flattering VIPs. He had the Army Signal Corps install scores of special POTUS lines (an acronym for "President of the United States") so that he could communicate instantly with officials around the government. Once the president called a White House staffer and was annoyed to find him away from his desk. "Where the hell is he?" LBJ demanded. "He's in the bathroom, Mr. President," the man's secretary sheepishly replied. "Isn't there a phone in there?" Johnson asked and ordered that one be hooked up right away. The aide returned to his office, called the president immediately, but ignored the order to install the phone in the bathroom. The very next day, the president called again while the aide was similarly employed. "I told you to put a phone in that toilet," he screamed at the hapless secretary.[24] A few minutes later, two Signal Corps technicians arrived and installed a phone in the restroom. In fact, Johnson spent so many hours on the phone that the sculptor commissioned to do a statue of LBJ could not get him to stay put and stay off the phone long enough to capture him in stasis. She finally — and aptly — sculpted a piece of Johnson running, the receiver of a telephone in one ear, the base cradled in his hand.

Johnson immediately began placing his own distinctive, earthy stamp on the White House. When special assistant Jack Valenti cluttered up the president's schedule with "brief visits" from prominent citizens, Johnson warned him that there was no such thing as a brief visit. "Hell," LBJ complained, "by the time a man scratches his ass, clears his throat, and tells me how smart he is, we've already wasted fifteen minutes."[25] Occasionally, Johnson would interrupt a high-level meeting for a swimming break; he would lead the assembled staff (and sometimes reporters or guests) down to the White House pool, strip naked, and dive in. He expected others to do the same. When using the bathroom, when showering in the morning, when receiving a massage at night—at all of those intimate and possibly embarrassing moments—he expected staff members to follow him into bedroom and bathroom and continue their conversations as if still in an office.

Johnson sometimes used this earthiness to humiliate and dominate his associates. For LBJ and his cronies, politics was an entirely masculine world, and a macho one. Even though feminism was emerging in the early 1960s, most politicians, even most liberals, gave it scant attention. It certainly never changed their view of public life as a struggle for precedence among bull males. Johnson invariably described meeting political defeat as having one's pecker cut off and derided JFK's reputation as a playboy by boasting that he had "slept with more women by accident than Kennedy ever had on purpose."[26]

Johnson, of course, was no lone wolf in this male world. He relied heavily on his devoted wife, working her as hard as any member of his staff. Renowned for her energy and organizational skills, Lady Bird led the Johnson administration's drive for beautification of the nation's highways and scenic preservation in Washington, D.C. But the Johnson family, every one of them carrying the initials LBJ—Lady Bird, daughters Lucy Baines and Lynda Bird—sublimated their own needs to the ambitions of the leader. As one of Lady Bird's friends remembered the first lady, "She was not a complaining type female. If he came in at three o'clock and said, 'We're going to Texas at four,' she didn't say, 'Oh, I've got this to do or that to do,' or 'I haven't packed.' She just got up and did it. And was on that plane at four."[27]

Like the first family, the entire White House quickly converted into a vast machine geared to the immediate needs of one large personality. When LBJ announced his intention to lose weight, the staff immediately stocked the White House kitchen with 150 pounds of cottage cheese, 275 containers of yogurt, and 15 cases of Melba toast. A special courier aircraft flew in ten pounds of his favorite diet candy from San Antonio. When the president traveled to the LBJ Ranch in Texas for rest and relaxation, he liked to drive guests around the vast homestead while sipping scotch and soda out of a paper cup. After draining his cup, LBJ

Johnson family members gather around their leader. Flanking LBJ are wife Lady Bird and daughters Lynda Bird and Lucy Baines.

would slow down and stick his hand holding the empty cup outside the driver's side window. Then, one of the Secret Service agents trailing the president's Lincoln would jump out of his car and hand LBJ another round. When Johnson denied one such story, his pious outrage rang hollow with the public and prompted the first of many questions about his credibility.

Even as he stamped the White House as his own, Johnson carefully honored the Kennedy legacy. In contrast to his disconcertingly familiar behavior with his own aides, he remained deeply respectful of JFK's cabinet and top officials. He needed Kennedy's aides, needed the image of continuity; and with very few exceptions, Kennedy's appointees stayed on and served the new president. Indeed, LBJ drew especially close to Kennedy's Labor Secretary Willard Wirtz and particularly valued his foreign policy team, Secretary of State Dean Rusk, National Security Adviser McGeorge Bundy, and Secretary of Defense Robert McNamara. Johnson admired Rusk's professionalism and loyalty (he valued it all the more since Bobby Kennedy disliked Rusk), but relied most heavily on McNamara. In fact, LBJ had been impressed with the computer-punching whiz kid from the first time they met, at JFK's initial cabinet meeting in 1961. "A man in this new cabinet to tie to is that young fellow McNamara," then-Vice-President Johnson told a friend after that first meeting. "If I were president I would put in my whole stack with him."[28]

With the White House geared up for two shifts and the Kennedy men on board, LBJ prepared to revive the stalled Kennedy agenda. In many ways, the moment perfectly suited Johnson's talents. The shocked and sorrowful country cried out for unity and healing, and Lyndon Johnson had spent his whole life fashioning consensus, bringing bitter rivals to compromise through sheer force of will. The liberal agenda had been formulated; it just needed congressional approval. The assassination placed LBJ—an unparalleled legislative tactician and savvy horse trader—in the White House and allowed him to use the president's tragic death to ram through Johnson's legislative program. Few legislators dared oppose the last, best hope of the martyred Kennedy, especially with Lyndon Johnson twisting their arms. Moreover, 1964 was a time of relative quiet in foreign policy. Despite two small-scale crises in Latin America (see Chapter 6) and the deteriorating situation in Vietnam, Johnson was able to hold the line on international affairs—to continue the Kennedy foreign policies while devoting himself to domestic politics. His first State of the Union Address, delivered on January 8, 1964, dealt almost exclusively with problems and prospects at home—the first State of the Union to do so since the beginning of the cold war.

In that speech, Johnson asked the Congress to "carry forward the plans and programs of John Fitzgerald Kennedy." But it was left to Lyndon Johnson to formulate those plans and to execute them. "Everything I had ever learned in the history books taught me that martyrs have to die for causes," LBJ recalled later. "John Kennedy had died. But his 'cause' was not really clear. That was my job. I had to take the dead man's program and turn it into a martyr's cause."[29]

Johnson launched the legislative battle immediately and intensively. On economic policy, he pushed the tax bill through the Congress in record time. He went beyond it, however, by linking that economic stimulus—one that would promote growth and particularly benefit the middle class and wealthier citizens—with an ambitious program to eliminate poverty in America.

The program grew out of research and planning that JFK had ordered in the last year of his administration. During the 1960s, Kennedy had become alarmed at the problem of persistent, structural poverty—the sort of tenacious deprivation that even healthy national economic growth could not alleviate. Campaigning in West Virginia, Kennedy—a man born into riches and privilege—was shocked by the appalling conditions he faced. A *New Yorker* magazine article on Michael Harrington's controversial book *The Other America* hardened JFK's determination to develop a major piece of antipoverty legislation. Harrington's book had identified an economic underworld of poor schools, substandard medical care, and dead-end jobs. Soaring national growth could not reach the denizens of this shadow economy, where illness and hunger remained unchecked, where unemployment and underemployment ran rampant, where deficient education offered few prospects of escape. In December 1962, Kennedy assigned Walter Heller, chairman of the Council of Economic Advisers, to assemble the facts and figures on the poverty problem in the United States.

Heller and other JFK staffers put together an antipoverty proposal and won the president's approval to include it in their 1964 legislative proposals. With so many other measures backed up in the Congress, they decided not to publicize the program or push it hard until after the 1964 elections. Heller and his associates planned a modest effort at first—a sort of pilot program that would target a few selected cities around the country. After the assassination, a downcast Heller approached the new president and informed him about the poverty plans. He little expected LBJ to approve a new venture, especially one so potentially expensive and controversial. But Johnson's reaction stunned and pleased the economist. "That's my kind of program," the old New Dealer told Heller. "Go ahead. Give it the highest priority. Push ahead full tilt."[30]

Johnson expanded JFK's antipoverty efforts, made them his own, and put them into effect. He rejected the idea of an introductory pilot venture. To win congressional approval, LBJ believed the plan had to be "big and bold and hit the whole nation with real impact."[31] A month after taking office, LBJ announced a billion-dollar initiative in his State of the Union Address: "This administration today, here and now, declares unconditional war on poverty in America."[32]

Waging an all-out "war on poverty" entailed serious political risks; it had little appeal for the business community and the well-to-do, who worried about the costs of such a battle. And it particularly antagonized those working Americans just above the poverty line—men and women who struggled long and hard to make ends meet and resented benefits directed toward those less fortunate than they were. Johnson understood these dangers and strove to overcome them. Using government to fight poverty had been the centerpiece of his political program from the time he

LBJ promises rapid progress to civil rights leaders in January 1964. Pictured are Roy Wilkins, executive director of the NAACP; James Farmer, national director of the Congress of Racial Equality; Rev. Martin Luther King, Jr., head of the Southern Christian Leadership Conference; and Whitney Young of the National Urban League.

arrived in Washington as Dick Kleberg's secretary; he knew what poverty did to a person and to a region, and he believed that eradicating it would help all Americans. He also thought that the crisis of the assassination had opened a window for decisive action—a narrow interval where he should act, and act boldly.

Johnson then pulled out all the stops for the poverty program. He won the support of business not only by linking the program to the tax cuts and continued growth but also by making other cuts in the budget and insisting on economies throughout the government. He convinced business that helping the poor would increase everyone's wealth; education and job training would create better workers, money in people's pockets would mean more sales of food and clothing. He preached also that failure to eradicate poverty and discrimination would bring a harvest of hate and disorder. In the spring of 1964, both the Kennedy tax bill and the War on Poverty program, known as the Economic Opportunity Act of 1964, passed Congress.

But of all the holdover measures from the Kennedy administration, LBJ devoted the greatest effort to civil rights. In the wake of Kennedy's death, a number of civil rights leaders feared that LBJ, the master Senate compromiser, would dilute the bill as he had the Civil Rights Act of 1957. But LBJ quickly assured the nation that he would accept no compromises this time around. During the first two weeks of his presidency, he met with the principal leaders of the civil rights movement—Whitney Young, James Farmer, A. Philip Randolph and Martin Luther King, Jr.—and warned them to lace up their sneakers because he was going to move so fast on civil rights that they would have trouble keeping up with him. In his memoirs, LBJ explained, "John Nance Garner, a great legislative technician as well as a good poker player, once told me that there comes a time in every leader's career when he has to put in all his stack. I decided to shove in all my stack" on the Civil Rights Act of 1964.[33]

But even with LBJ's formidable skills and the nation's grief for the martyred Kennedy, genuine civil rights legislation had little chance of passage. Even the most optimistic observers thought the bill would have to be watered down to avoid a southern filibuster in the Senate. In particular, the parts of the bill guaranteeing equal opportunity in employment and providing equal access to public accommodations—banning whites-only lunch counters, railway cars, hotels, and restaurants—seemed likely to be deleted or weakened.

The bill encountered only slight opposition in the House of Representatives. There, Representative Howard Smith of Virginia, a wily southern conservative, attempted to derail the bill with a mischievous maneuver. The bill prohibited discrimination based on race, color, or creed; Smith proposed an amendment including sex discrimination among the list of outlawed offenses. Smith hoped that a number of legislators who supported a civil rights bill for racial minorities would oppose the law if it also included women. Supporters of the bill had wanted to concentrate on racial discrimination, but they were obliged to include Smith's amendment. Still, the sex discrimination provision did not prevent the House from passing the amended bill.

Attention turned to the pivotal battleground—the Senate of the United States. Unlike the House, where debate was limited, the Senate operated under its own arcane set of rules, which provided for unlimited debate. Southern senators had often used this technique to kill civil rights bills. The only way to stop a filibuster—to "invoke cloture"—was to win the approval of two-thirds of the Senate, getting sixty-seven of the one hundred senators to agree to shut off debate. Despite hundreds of previous attempts, the Senate had never successfully invoked cloture and broken a southern filibuster on civil rights. The only way to pass any kind of civil rights bill had been to get the southerners to agree to a compromise, as LBJ had done in 1957.

This time, however, President Johnson had shoved in his stack; there would be no deal. He would go for cloture. A weary Richard Russell assembled the southern conservatives to mount a filibuster against his old protégé. Russell would fight to the end to preserve what he called the "southern way of life," but he feared Johnson. "The way that fellow operates," Russell winced, "he'll probably get the whole bill, every last bit of it."[34] Russell tried to delay action on the bill, to bottle it up in committee. He believed that if he could postpone debate until the middle of the summer, when the 1964 election campaign would heat up, he would win the battle. The White House, concentrating on the election and anxious to avoid such a divisive issue during the campaign, would be forced to withdraw the bill. But the civil rights forces—led by Minnesota Senator Hubert Humphrey in constant contact with the White House—forced the issue to the floor. The southerners retreated to their last ditch strategy of the filibuster.

But could LBJ and his lieutenants obtain the necessary sixty-seven votes? To do so, they needed the votes of the Republicans, so they assiduously courted the Republican leader, Senator Everett Dirksen of Illinois. Dirksen, like many of his fellow Republicans, had some sympathy for the civil rights cause, but generally opposed government regulation. He especially disliked a law that would tell private businesses whom they could or could not exclude and worried that equal employment provisions in the law might lead to hiring quotas. To win Republican backing, Hubert Humphrey declared on the Senate floor that the bill banned discrimination against anyone, that quotas of any kind would be prohibited. At the same time, Johnson's allies agreed to several minor amendments that Dirksen wanted.

The administration went all out to please Dirksen. Johnson awarded federal projects to Dirksen's home state and judgeships to Dirksen's cronies. The president praised the senator and posed for joint photographs with him. Finally, on June 10, 1964, Dirksen threw the Republicans behind cloture, paving the way for the enactment of the Civil Rights Act of 1964. Three weeks later, LBJ signed the landmark measure, which historian Allen Matusow (see Document 4) called "the great liberal achievement of the decade." Almost overnight, the law eliminated segregation in southern public accommodations; "separate, but equal" facilities retreated into the past. A southern president—a product of that cruel and unjust system and long a political captive of it—had helped to dismantle Jim Crow.

# PRESIDENT IN HIS OWN RIGHT

A few months after grasping the reins of the presidency, Johnson had calmed the nation and spurred a stubborn Congress into action. He had revived JFK's stalled program, broken the back of Jim Crow segregation in the South, and declared war on poverty. Johnson shrewdly and ruthlessly exploited the nation's grief over its fallen hero, so that a dead Kennedy, martyred by an assassin's bullet, proved far more effective than the living one could ever have hoped to be.

Writing in the liberal magazine *The New Republic,* columnist Richard Strout wondered at Johnson's energy and achievements. "LBJ has been hurling himself about Washington like an elemental force," Strout marveled. "To be plain about it, he has won our admiration." Johnson isn't JFK, the journalist conceded. "But so what? . . . [Johnson is] impulsive, emotional, sentimental, sensitive, bumptious, corny, prolix, able and Texan. He's also on the right side of some fine things, and is pushing them with skilled and ferocious energy."[35] *New York Times* columnist James Reston echoed these accolades: "Both the period of mourning for Kennedy and of experimentation for Johnson are over. Washington is now a little girl settling down with the old boyfriend. The mad and wonderful infatuation with the handsome young stranger from Boston is over—something she always knew wouldn't last—so she is adjusting to reality. . . . The lovers of style are not too happy," Reston concluded in the spring of 1964, "but the lovers of substance are not complaining."[36]

After the horror at Dallas, Johnson had earned the confidence of his fellow Americans, but he had not won their affection or their votes. In Johnson's mind, only one obstacle stood in his way—one person who made it impossible for him to emerge from JFK's shadow—the president's brother Robert F. Kennedy. Kennedy's younger brother became the repository for the dreams and ambitions of all the devoted Kennedyites who mourned JFK's death and missed his polish, good looks, and charm. Many former Kennedy officials suggested that LBJ select Bobby as his vice presidential nominee. These appeals enraged Johnson. He became nearly obsessed with what he called the "Bobby Problem." He wanted a Johnson administration—not an interlude between two Kennedys. "I'd waited for my turn. Bobby should've waited for his," a still embittered LBJ told Doris Kearns after leaving office. "But he and the Kennedy people wanted it now. A tidal wave of letters and memos about how great a vice president Bobby would be swept over me. But no matter what, I simply couldn't let it happen. With Bobby on the ticket, I'd never know if I could be elected on my own."[37] Johnson summoned RFK to the White House and told him he would not be on the ticket.

Johnson was intent not only on outdoing John Kennedy by winning a decisive majority in 1964, he wanted to win by the largest margin in American history—to exceed even the 60.8 percent of the popular vote his mentor FDR had won in 1936. A landslide would place LBJ in the pantheon of great leaders; it would furnish him with the mandate to build his own new New Deal.

The Republican party assisted LBJ by nominating the leader of its extreme conservative wing—Senator Barry Goldwater of Arizona. "In your heart, you know he's right," declared Goldwater's slogan. To which, most Americans replied, "Yes, far right," or as one Democratic riposte put it, "In your guts, you know he's nuts." Goldwater's saber-rattling rhetoric on foreign affairs (including a seeming recklessness about using nuclear weapons), his opposition to the Civil Rights Act of 1964, and his antipathy to all government programs frightened and alienated not only Democrats but also many moderates within the Republican party. In 1964, the United States was not ready for Barry Goldwater; he seemed headed for certain defeat.

Only one thing about Goldwater's candidacy worried the Johnson camp: the race issue. Johnson understood that his leadership on civil rights might cost the Democrats white votes. On the night after Johnson signed the Civil Rights Act of 1964, his top adviser, Bill Moyers, had found the president strangely melancholy. Arrayed in front of him were the early editions of the next day's newspapers, every one of them proclaiming his triumph on civil rights. Moyers asked the president what was wrong and LBJ replied, "I think we just delivered the South to the Republican Party for my lifetime and yours."[38] The prediction proved all too true; in November 1964, LBJ, a son of the South, lost five southern states. Between 1968 and 1992, only one Democratic candidate won a majority of the votes in the South. White southerners never forgave LBJ—or his party—for dismantling segregation.

Johnson also feared that resentment against the civil rights revolution would take hold outside the South. During the spring of 1964, George Wallace, the segregationist governor of Alabama, announced himself a candidate for president and entered the Democratic primaries in Indiana, Maryland, and Wisconsin. He campaigned against civil rights, appealing to white resentment over the protests of African Americans and the government's attention to their grievances. Few observers believed that Wallace's racist tactics—so popular in his native region—would win votes outside the South. But Wallace showed surprising strength, winning a quarter of the votes in the primary elections he contested. Wallace's support was centered in the staunchly Democratic working-class communities of northern cities—among white ethnic blue-collar workers, like the Polish-American steelworkers of Gary, Indiana. Franklin Roosevelt had built the liberal coalition by tying together the votes of African Americans and blue-collar whites; now the race issue threatened to break it apart. One political consultant noticed this phenomenon and gave it a name: "white backlash."

Johnson confronted white backlash in two ways. In the South, his advisers warned him to avoid the issue of civil rights as much as possible. Many southerners continued to draw their livelihoods from the land so that LBJ could pursue the "agricultural strategy," highlighting Republican opposition to the farm programs that had so much benefited southern farmers, hinting that defecting to the GOP over civil rights could cost them the agricultural subsidies they so much depended on. But, in New Orleans in October 1964, LBJ put aside this cautious approach and gave the most memorable speech of the 1964 campaign. Throwing aside the text of his standard stump speech, he began to extemporize. "Whatever your views are," he warned the crowd in the grand ballroom of the Jung Hotel, "we have a Constitution and we have got a Bill of Rights and we've got the law of the land." Emphatically raising his right arm, LBJ continued as his audience sat bolt upright. "And I signed it, and I am going to enforce it. . . . I'm not going to let them build up the hate and try to buy my people by appealing to their prejudice."[39]

The jovial, carnival atmosphere of a campaign speech had vanished, the room was silent, and LBJ continued with a homily. He unfolded a story of a frustrated southern senator who wanted to do great things for the South, wanted to uplift the impoverished region, but every time he proposed something the opposition stirred up the race issue and thwarted his plans. At the end of his career, this old campaigner expressed the wish to return home and, as LBJ described it, "give them one more Democratic speech. The poor old state, they haven't heard a Democratic speech in thirty years. All they hear at election time is 'Nigra, Nigra, Nigra!' "[40] The moral of Johnson's story was clear—those days were over.

Johnson confronted racial backlash in his native South by attacking the issue head-on in New Orleans; on the national level, however, he tried to derail it, undercutting it with a strategy of his own. The Johnson campaign termed this tactic "frontlash"; if backlash referred to previously loyal Democrats who deserted their party over civil rights, frontlash was an appeal to Republicans who found Barry Goldwater too difficult to stomach. Johnson cast his campaign as a big tent under which all Americans could join. Rather than alienate the Republican rank and file with a partisan campaign, Johnson ran as president of all the people, practicing, in his

At the LBJ Ranch, President Johnson and Vice President-elect Hubert H. Humphrey celebrate their landslide victory in the 1964 election with some Texas barbecue.

words, a "politics of consensus that would make it as easy as possible for lifelong Republicans to switch their votes in November to the Democratic column."[41] Johnson sought to unite all elements of American society behind him and his liberal agenda—business and labor, black and white, rural and urban. He refused to see these groups as fundamentally in conflict; he believed they shared the same objectives, that they all wanted what he could and would provide them. "The farmer in Iowa, the fisherman in Massachusetts, the worker in Seattle, the rancher in Texas," Johnson explained during the campaign, "have the same hopes and harbor the same fears. . . . This is the real voice of America. It is one of the great tasks of political leadership to make people aware of this voice, aware that they share a fundamental unity of interest, purpose, and belief."[42]

Johnson campaigned furiously, ending his campaign in Austin. On the night before the election day, he told supporters, "It seems to me tonight that I have spent my whole life getting ready for this moment."[43] Johnson won a monumental landslide. His 61.1 percent of the popular vote eclipsed even FDR's 1936 victory, and on his coattails LBJ carried in the most liberal Congress since the Great Depression. "It was a night I shall never forget. Millions upon millions of people, each one marking my name on their ballot, each one wanting me as their President. . . . "[44]

No longer merely Kennedy's successor, LBJ had been elected president in his own right. He had won the largest mandate ever—and he planned to use it—to achieve the liberal goals Kennedy, Truman, and FDR had sought but never fully accomplished. Johnson would complete the New Deal and the New Frontier, but he would go beyond them, ushering in his own liberal reconstruction of America. He planned to build "The Great Society."

# NOTES

[1] Rowland Evans and Robert Novak, *Lyndon B. Johnson: The Exercise of Power* (New York: Signet Books, 1966), 298.

[2] Ibid., 323.

[3] Doris Kearns, *Lyndon Johnson and the American Dream* (New York: Signet Books, 1976), 168.

[4] Evans and Novak, *Exercise of Power,* 349.

[5] Kearns, *Johnson and the American Dream,* 171.

[6] Arthur M. Schlesinger, Jr., *A Thousand Days* (Boston: Houghton Mifflin, 1965), 646.

[7] Eric F. Goldman, *The Tragedy of Lyndon Johnson* (New York: Dell, 1969), 92–93.

[8] Evans and Novak, *Exercise of Power,* 336.

[9] Godfrey Hodgson, *America in Our Time* (New York: Vintage, 1976), 171.

[10] Johnson to John F. Kennedy, memorandum, May 23, 1961, reprinted in William S. White, *The Professional* (New York: Crest Books, 1964), 152–54.

[11] Kearns, *Johnson and the American Dream,* 175.

[12] Johnson to Kennedy, memorandum, May 23, 1961.

[13] Evans and Novak, *Exercise of Power,* 343–44.

[14] Tom Wicker, *JFK and LBJ* (New York: Pelican Books, 1969), 23.

[15] Hodgson, *America in Our Time,* 156–57.

[16] Ibid., 160.

[17] Walter Lippmann, quoted in Lyndon B. Johnson, *The Vantage Point* (New York: Popular Library, 1971), 34.

[18] Johnson, *Vantage Point,* 18–19.

[19] Kearns, *Johnson and the American Dream,* 177.

[20] Hodgson, *America in Our Time,* 5.

[21] See Document 1.

[22] Laura Kalman, *Abe Fortas: A Biography* (New Haven: Yale University Press, 1990), 212.

[23] Eric F. Goldman, *The Tragedy of Lyndon Johnson* (New York: Dell, 1969), 22.

[24] Joseph A. Califano, Jr., *The Triumph and Tragedy of Lyndon Johnson* (New York: Simon and Schuster, 1991), 25–26.

[25] Jack Valenti, *A Very Human President* (New York: Pocket Books, 1977), 136.

[26] Robert Dallek, *Lone Star Rising: Lyndon Johnson and His Times* (New York: Oxford University Press, 1991), 189.

[27] Ashton Gonella, quoted in Merle Miller, *Lyndon: An Oral Biography* (New York: Ballantine, 1980), 428.

[28] White, *The Professional*, 23.

[29] Kearns, *Johnson and the American Dream*, 185.

[30] Johnson, *Vantage Point*, 71. Hodgson, *America in Our Time*, 173.

[31] Johnson, *Vantage Point*, 74.

[32] *Public Papers of the Presidents of the United States: Lyndon B. Johnson, 1963–1969*, 11 vols. (Washington, D.C.: Government Printing Office, 1964–1969), 1963–1964, vol. 1, 114.

[33] Johnson, *Vantage Point*, 37.

[34] Evans and Novak, *Exercise of Power*, 401.

[35] "TRB from Washington," *The New Republic*, May 2, 1964.

[36] *New York Times*, March 22, 1964.

[37] Kearns, *Johnson and the American Dream*, 209.

[38] Califano, *Triumph and Tragedy*, 55.

[39] *Papers*, 1963–1964, vol. 1, 1286. Goldman, *Tragedy*, 290.

[40] *Papers*, 1963–1964, vol. 1, 1286.

[41] Johnson, *Vantage Point*, 103.

[42] Wicker, *JFK and LBJ*, 235.

[43] Evans and Novak, *Exercise of Power*, 505.

[44] Kearns, *Johnson and the American Dream*, 219.

# 4

# The Great Society

Some presidents preside calmly over the nation's affairs. Having fought hard to reach the White House, they are content to enjoy the prestige and power of the office, merely discharging whatever business crosses their desk. Calvin Coolidge, for example, based his presidency on the conviction that "three-quarters of the problems of the world would disappear if people would just sit down and be still."

Lyndon Johnson was not that kind of president. His personal ambition—a desire to become nothing less than the nation's greatest president, to accomplish more even than FDR, to shower benefits on all the nation's people and win their love—merged with his political creed—his liberal faith that a government could and should do good things for its people. Johnson would act.

Activism lay at the core of Johnson's personal and political philosophy. He scorned those who stressed the deficiencies of public action, the limits of liberal reform. He pooh-poohed both those who criticized the harmful and sometimes even self-defeating consequences of government programs, and those who thought the political system incapable of producing genuine change, who saw it as so mired in compromise and contingency that nothing worthwhile could ever be accomplished. Johnson believed in his own and in the system's ability to achieve what others had never before envisioned. "Politics," LBJ wrote, "goes beyond the art of the possible. It is the art of making possible what seems impossible." Lady Bird captured his attitude in simpler terms: "Lyndon," she explained, "believes that anything can be solved, and quickly."[1]

New Deal and postwar liberalism had shaped Johnson's mindset. "I had first run for public office in 1937 under the slogan 'He gets things done,' " LBJ recalled. "I built my record in the House and Senate on the same philosophy. Now, as President, watching the pendulum move, I believed that I could—for a while, at least—really get things done."[2]

"For a while, at least"—Johnson harbored no illusions about the permanence of his power or the durability of his electoral mandate. He had decided to spend his political capital rather than husband it, to convert his popularity at the polls into a massive new domestic program, to drive ahead full tilt on every aspect of his agenda. In January 1965, he called together representatives of every department in his administration and ordered them to move quickly. "I was just elected President by the biggest popular margin in the history of the country—16 million votes," he explained to the assembled officials. "Just by the way people naturally think and because Barry Goldwater had simply scared hell out of them, I've already lost about three of those sixteen. After a fight with Congress or something else, I'll lose another couple of million. I could be down to eight million in a couple of months." According to domestic policy adviser Joseph Califano, "LBJ knew that the sympathy generated by John Kennedy's assassination and huge margin of his own presidential victory in 1964 gave him a unique opportunity to change America, if he could move fast enough. He was always conscious that his days were numbered and that his political capital, however enormous as he began his presidency, was limited."[3]

## JOHNSONIAN LIBERALISM

As he commenced his own term in the White House, Johnson determined to spend his mandate on a legislative agenda of unparalleled scope. He would provide something for everyone: health care for the old; new facilities and programs for the schools; food stamps for the hungry; parks and wilderness preservation for environmentalists; improved transport for commuters; civil rights for racial minorities; labor standards for farm workers; tax incentives for business; job training for the unemployed; financial support for artists, museums, and orchestras; and, an expanded, reorganized federal government to deliver these services. "I could see and almost touch," he later told Doris Kearns, "my youthful dream of improving life for more people and in more ways than any other political leader, including FDR."[4]

Roosevelt's New Deal offered Johnson a model to emulate and to surpass. At a ceremony celebrating the anniversary of FDR's birth, Johnson honored the "cherished memory" of his former mentor and cited him as the inspiration for his war on poverty. "The meek and the humble and the lowly share this life and this earth with us all. We must never forget them. President Roosevelt never did." But President Johnson was not satisfied with wrapping himself in the legacy of FDR. "We cannot be content in the 1960s," he instructed the nation, "with the answers of the 1930s."[5]

Johnson was right. Franklin Roosevelt had launched his New Deal amidst the greatest economic catastrophe in U.S. history. Nearly every American faced hardship and ruin—banks failed, businesses closed, farmers lost their land, workers lost their jobs. Everyone had a direct stake in FDR's efforts at recovery, reform, and relief. In fact, New Deal measures mostly benefited those perched above the very lowest rungs on the social and economic ladder. The very bottom—racial minorities, tenant farmers, unskilled workers—received less.

Johnson, on the other hand, unveiled his Great Society during an era of affluence, a time when most Americans lived comfortably. Although LBJ included something for everyone in his reform package, he concentrated on the unfortunate, on those "who have been forgotten and passed over and passed by." At the FDR birthday festivities, he noted, "We are not faced with depression," but insisted that "in our richness we not forget the poor. . . . " The people he most wanted to help, he told Joe Califano, "are the ones who've never held real jobs and aren't equipped to handle them. . . . They have no motivation to reach for something better because the sum total of their lives is losing." Roosevelt had offered a "New Deal" to the American people, Harry Truman a "Fair Deal." During the early months of 1964, LBJ spoke repeatedly about providing a "Better Deal."[6]

Johnson also departed from the tenets of postwar liberalism. He never challenged the emphasis on economic growth, on an ever-expanding economic pie as a bulwark against recessions and a source of widespread prosperity. Johnson subscribed as zealously and as sincerely to the New Economics as had JFK. He had lobbied for the Kennedy tax cut as a way to "generate jobs and income at a pace that will provide an escape from poverty for many of our least fortunate families."[7] But his own experience in central Texas and the tutelage of his advisers about the intractability of poverty among the nation's most wretched citizens convinced Johnson that the Keynesian tools of postwar liberalism were insufficient. "General prosperity and growth," his 1964 economic report declared, "leave untouched many of the roots of human poverty." Johnson recognized that the popular growth-centered strategies of the 1950s and early 1960s had neither recognized nor addressed the problems of those at the very bottom of the social and economic ladder, those whose voices Johnson believed would become insistent, desperate, even dangerous if his government failed them. As he pieced his program together, LBJ stressed the need to "build a society where progress is the servant of the neediest," not one "where old values and new visions are buried under unbridled growth."[8]

Through the early days of his presidency, then, Johnson searched for a vivid idea that would explain his domestic agenda, a slogan that would encapsulate it. He tried out "Better Deal," but that too much evoked his ties to FDR and too little emphasized LBJ's own distinctive contributions. Finally, the president's speechwriter unearthed the phrase "Great Society," and Johnson began inserting it into his speeches. The slogan suggested new objectives for an age of abundance—a time when securing prosperity no longer remained the principal task of government; when, instead, government must begin ministering to the social, spiritual, and aesthetic needs of the nation, as well as to its diplomatic and economic needs.

On May 22, 1964, in Ann Arbor, Michigan, Lyndon Johnson offered his vision of the Great Society (see Document 2). The speech and the objectives it promulgated were extraordinary—not in their highfalutin' rhetoric, which nearly every president occasionally indulged in, but in the ambitions that underlay it. Johnson promised to complete the liberal agenda of Roosevelt, Truman, and Kennedy, "to guarantee abundance and liberty for all." But he also carved out a new, broader program for American liberals. He envisioned affirmative government guaranteeing not only opportunity and prosperity, but also beauty, learning, and community—a richer quality of life as well as a decent standard of living.

Central to the Great Society, at the core of Johnsonian liberalism, rested liberal universalism—belief in the fundamental unity and sameness of all mankind. For universalists, every person possessed the same intrinsic worth, deserved the same opportunities, shared the same basic aspirations. In LBJ's terms, they had the same hopes and harbored the same fears. The hungry Mexican students in Cotulla, disfranchised black southerners, Appalachian miners, Detroit autoworkers, and Vietnamese peasants all needed and wanted the same things, things LBJ and activist government could provide them.

Lyndon Johnson saw building consensus as the central task of his presidency. He wanted to unify Americans behind his leadership, to demonstrate their basic community of interests. The Great Society melded a war on poverty with the aspirations of more affluent Americans, the concerns of the wretched with those of the fortunate. Critics saw LBJ's emphasis on consensus as evidence of caution and compromise, an unwillingness to challenge the powers that be, to redistribute power and wealth, to benefit some Americans at others' expense. Many Americans thought the interests of business and labor, blacks and whites, rich and poor, to be fundamentally in conflict—that you could not aid one without hurting the other. They viewed Johnson's invocation of unity as timid appeals to the least common denominator. But LBJ refused to see the interests of rich and poor as competitive or incompatible; he genuinely believed that he could forge a broad consensus and that only a broad consensus could ensure action.

Johnson particularly labored to enlist the business community behind his program. Confident that liberals would back him, LBJ feared conservative recalcitrance, especially from business-oriented Republicans who opposed aid to the poor and government regulation. In his experience, conservatives and business interests had long posed the major threat to liberal reform—they had foiled FDR. Johnson campaigned tirelessly to consolidate business behind his liberal Democratic administration. Indeed, one pundit concluded that "the greatest political event of 1964 . . . has been the inclusion of a glittering cross-section of the national corporate community within the Democratic Party."[9] Johnson's close friend and crony Abe Fortas began constructing links with business leaders, offering them favors and tax breaks in return for support of Johnson's social welfare programs.

Johnson himself proselytized business leaders at the White House, lecturing them about their common interests with the poor ("They get hungry like you and me. They have feelings like you and me," he told a group of executives) and their special interest in supporting his programs. Johnson persuaded corporate chieftains that aiding the dispossessed would provide better-trained and better-educated workers for their factories, create more consumers for their products, and defuse the seething discontent that threatened the stability of their cities and businesses. "Doing something about poverty is economical in the long run," Johnson maintained. "You don't have to be loose with a dollar to prove you are a liberal—or callous to prove you are conservative."[10]

To win over business leaders and secure conservative votes in Congress, LBJ stressed government economies. He believed that Republicans and conservative Democrats had derailed previous liberal presidents by attacking activist programs as wasteful, reckless spending of the public's money. In pushing for the Kennedy program in 1964, LBJ had combined budget cuts with his call for new programs. Johnson became obsessive about appearing to cut every unnecessary expenditure. In a public relations gesture that even his closest associates thought corny, LBJ turned off the lights at the White House whenever the residence was not in use—he bragged about how this saved several thousand dollars a month. Two years later, a top aide suggested that the lights be turned on again,

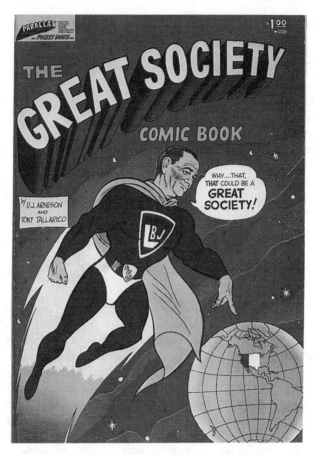

*The Great Society Comic Book* pokes gentle fun at the furious
pace and vaulting ambition of Johnson's legislative program.
Here "Super LBJ" soars over his Great Society.

that the magnificent facade of the president's residence added grandeur to
the nation's capital and prestige to the presidency, but LBJ would have
none of it. He was serious about the savings.

The concern for economy, however, went far beyond trivial public
relations gestures. Johnson believed that profligate government spending
aroused unnecessary opposition to liberal programs. He told his cabinet,
"Congress and the American people will provide the budgetary means to
build the Great Society only if we take positive steps to show that we are
spending only where we legitimately need to spend."[11] Johnson proposed
to launch the greatest domestic reform program in American history. He
announced his ambitions in the most grandiose of terms—he would wage

a war on poverty, build a great society, and provide education and health care for all—and he would do it on the cheap. This would prove an impossible feat, especially when he determined to fight a major war in Vietnam at the same time.

But in 1964 and 1965, Johnson's main concern was not financing the Great Society in the long run or delivering big results for a small investment. He concentrated on winning congressional approval for his program. Without support from the House and Senate, he could not even lay the foundations for his Great Society. Franklin Roosevelt, Truman, and Kennedy had all proposed great things, but every one of them had been stymied on Capitol Hill. The New Deal stalled during Roosevelt's second term, the New Frontier lay comatose in the Congress until LBJ revived it. All of these presidents had ended up in an adversarial relationship with the Congress. But LBJ was determined, above all, to avoid that mistake. Johnson's principal, and overriding, goal was to stir Congress into action, to pass his legislation.

## CHIEF LEGISLATOR

Lyndon Johnson revolutionized the relationship between the legislative and executive branches. He immersed himself and his staff in all the details of legislation, in his own words, "from the cradle to the grave, from the moment a bill is introduced to the moment it is officially enrolled as the law of the land."[12] Johnson worked so closely with the Congress that many observers thought him like the prime minister in a parliamentary system, as much the chief legislator making the laws as the executive implementing them, a part of the legislative branch rather than a separate entity. Johnson frequently visited the Capitol and met constantly with congressional leaders. "There is but one way for a President to deal with the Congress," he believed, "and that is continuously, incessantly, and without interruption. If it's really going to work, the relationship between the President and the Congress has got to be almost incestuous. He's got to know them even better than they know themselves."[13] LBJ had spent thirty-two years on Capitol Hill; understanding of its folkways and reverence for its traditions lay deep in the marrow of his bones.

He ordered his staff to give congressional relations the highest priority. "You are going to get a lot of phone calls," LBJ warned a White House adviser. "People are going to court you and flatter you because you have access to the president. You are going to find yourself a social lion and a fellow with more charm than you ever thought you had and you will be all this because of the job you hold." But, LBJ commanded, "the most important people you will talk to are senators and congressmen. You treat them as if they were president. Answer their calls immediately."[14]

Whenever Congress was in session, Johnson breakfasted once every week with the legislative leadership. As they feasted on eggs, thick farm-style bacon, toasted homemade bread, and links of the special deer sausage LBJ flew in from Texas, the president worked through a large poster board set on an easel. The poster mapped out all the pending legislation in the House and Senate, plotting its path through the various committees down into a bowl drawn on the bottom of the chart to represent final passage of the law. As they ate, LBJ applied The Treatment, cajoling, flattering, and persuading the leaders to move his bills forward. The chart accompanied Johnson to his cabinet meetings and conferences with influential citizens; during 1965, it seemed to follow him everywhere.

Johnson's legislative strategy rested, as it had during his days as majority leader, on his sure and certain knowledge of every legislator's needs, inclinations, problems, and convictions. When aides told him that they "thought" they had lined up a particular representative's support, LBJ exploded: "Don't ever think about those things. Know, know, know! You've got to know you've got him, and there's only one way you know." Johnson looked into his open hand and closed his fingers into a fist. "And that's when you've got his pecker right here." The president opened his desk drawer, acted as if he were dropping something, emphatically slammed the drawer shut, and smiled.[15]

President Johnson began the Eighty-ninth Congress, the 1965 legislative session, with a commanding Democratic majority, 295 out of 435 votes in the House. For the first time in decades, the wide margin ensured a sympathetic majority for liberal measures. Even without the support of conservative southern Democrats, the administration could count on enough votes to enact its reform agenda. The fat majority gave little comfort to Lyndon Johnson and no rest to his overworked staff; it only encouraged LBJ to propose ever more ambitious programs. As one of his congressional liaisons put it, "When we have a fat Congress as we did in the Eighty-ninth, then we can hike up our demands to fit the situation." When the votes were not "razor thin," he explained, then the administration had not pushed far enough.[16]

As soon as the new Congress convened in January 1965, LBJ revamped the committee system in the House of Representatives. Johnson understood that opposition forces, even in a minority, could frustrate his program by bottling it up in the Rules, Appropriations, and Ways and

Means committees. The three most powerful panels in the House, these committees had long remained conservative strongholds. Johnson convinced the House to curtail the Rules Committee's power to delay Congressional action and to add new members to Appropriations and Ways and Means, enabling LBJ to stock the committee with loyal allies. A few days after these reforms took effect, LBJ assessed the situation on Capitol Hill. "It could be better," he conceded, "but not on this side of Heaven."[17]

The battlefield readied, Johnson attacked along familiar lines. As his first priority, he set out to complete the old liberal agenda—to secure federal aid to education, medical care for the elderly, and reorganization of the executive branch. Previous Democratic presidents had fought unsuccessfully for these measures, which, in Johnson's words, "had been crying for action since Franklin Roosevelt's time."[18]

Johnson smashed through the legislative logjam on education, steering the Elementary and Secondary Education Act of 1965 (ESEA) through the rapids of the three "Rs." Race no longer threw up a stumbling block because the Civil Rights Act of 1964 had already stripped all federal funds from any segregated institution. But region and religion, while less acute problems for LBJ than for his Roman Catholic predecessor, remained in the way.

The administration finally hit on a strategy to break the impasse. Johnson framed the ESEA not only as a schools program, but as an antipoverty program. Education, Johnson's own experience had taught him, offered a passport out of poverty. Statistics confirmed the president's personal conviction; the more education an American possessed, the greater his or her income. Title I of the ESEA, the heart of the bill, allocated a billion dollars for "compensatory education," programs specially dedicated to improve education for poor children. The government distributed the funds on the basis of the number of poor children in a district rather than on how poor the area was, evading the region problem. And since it targeted pupils directly, poor students in parochial schools were eligible for some aid even though their schools were not. With his own first-grade teacher by his side, Johnson signed the law in his old Johnson City schoolhouse on April 11, 1965. "As a former teacher," he declared, "I have great expectations of what this law will mean for all of our young people. As President of the United States, I believe no law I have signed or will ever sign means more to the future of America."[19]

Medicare followed three months later. Like aid to education, health care for the elderly had long sunk deep into the congressional quagmire. In 1935, FDR's Council on Economic Security had endorsed such a plan. A decade later, President Harry S. Truman appeared before a joint session of Congress, campaigning in vain for a national medical program. Over the ensuing two decades, the need for Medicare intensified: the number of elderly Americans more than doubled and their medical costs exploded. Fearful of government competition, private insurance companies opposed the program as did the American Medical Association, the influential lobby for doctors who thought government regulation might limit their earnings and interfere with their practices. But LBJ negotiated a compromise with the AMA and propelled the long-awaited program through the Congress. In a clever piece of political theater, LBJ flew to Harry Truman's Missouri home to sign the law. Truman deeply appreciated the gesture. "You have done me a great honor in coming here today," he told the assembled crowd, "and you have made me a very, very happy man." President Johnson paid tribute to his predecessor and touted the benefits of a law he claimed would extend the healing miracles of modern medicine to all elderly Americans, that would provide "care for the sick and serenity for the fearful."[20] No one noted that Medicare fell far short of the comprehensive medical insurance Harry Truman had proposed or that a certain Texas congressman named Lyndon Johnson had actually opposed Truman's program in the 1940s.

Johnson also won congressional approval for expanding and revamping the executive branch—creating new cabinet-level departments of Transportation and of Housing and Urban Affairs. The transportation measure pitted LBJ and his domestic policy czar Joseph Califano against Senator John McClellan of Arkansas, chairman of the committee considering the proposal for a new department. McClellan stonewalled the measure, initially refusing even to discuss the bill with Califano. Eventually, the two men negotiated a compromise and an elated Califano returned to the White House and reported to the president. Johnson was not pleased. "Open your fly," Johnson commanded his astounded assistant. "Unzip your fly because there's nothing there. John McClellan just cut it off with a razor so sharp you didn't even notice it." Johnson grabbed the phone and immediately rang up the Arkansas senator on his POTUS line. "John, I'm calling about Joe Califano. You cut his pecker off and put it in your desk drawer. Now I'm sending him back up there to get it from you."[21] Johnson eventually worked out a new arrangement, and the Transportation Department passed the Senate.

By the middle of 1965, as Johnson later remembered, "the books were closing on our campaign to take action against the most pressing problems inherited from the past—the 'old agenda.' "[22] Congressional leaders urged him to slow down—the members were exhausted, tired of Johnson's steamroller and resistant to new programs. But LBJ never let up; he believed that the minute Congress caught its breath, the moment he stopped asking it to enact new programs, Congress would start investigating, criticizing, and reconsidering the old ones. And LBJ did not like anyone looking over his shoulder.

No president matched Johnson's skills as chief legislator. Despite the far-reaching and controversial nature of his program, LBJ won congressional approval for 58 percent of his proposals in 1964, 69 percent in 1965, and 56 percent in 1966, compared, for example, with 37 percent for Eisenhower in 1957 and just 27 percent for JFK in 1963. In the early days of LBJ's presidency, Republicans complained about the "Xerox Congress" or the "three-B Congress—bullied, badgered, and brainwashed," but they found themselves powerless against Johnson's legislative juggernaut.[23] When the "Great 89th," the Congress which LBJ swept into office with his 1964 landslide, completed its work in the autumn of 1966, it left behind the most productive law-making record in American history. Lawrence O'Brien, LBJ's chief congressional liaison, and domestic policy chief Joseph Califano proudly produced a summary of the legislative achievements (see the box).

The list was staggering. For LBJ not only secured the civil rights, health, education, and welfare measures commonly associated with the Great Society, but a host of other reforms. Less noted than Medicare or the war on poverty, many of these proved to have broader and more durable effects. The Immigration Act of 1965 eliminated the odious quota system which first became law amidst an outburst of racist nativism in the 1920s. The national origins system, as it was called, had severely limited immigration from eastern and southern Europe and all but banned arrivals from Asia. Declaring the limits "incompatible with our basic American tradition," Johnson outlawed ethnic quotas and opened the doors to a steady stream of arrivals from Asia.[24] The act made possible the large migrations of Koreans, Filipinos, Japanese, and Vietnamese to the United States that have contributed so much to the nation's economic and cultural life and so dramatically transformed the nation's western states.

Johnson pressed for restrictions on government wiretapping and surveillance and signed an act granting scholars, investigators, and private citizens access to government files. Although he privately taped many of his own phone conversations and allowed the FBI to continue electronic eavesdropping, Johnson ordered other government agencies to halt bugging and urged the Congress to limit the practice.

LBJ also stepped up government regulation of the environment. He signed major federal initiatives restricting water and air pollution, initiated with Lady Bird's help a national highway beautification program, and added

# Accomplishments of the 89th Congress

*Johnson's aides regarded the following legislation as landmark achievements:*

THE FIRST SESSION

1. Medicare
2. Elementary and Secondary Education
3. Higher Education
4. Farm Bill
5. Department of Housing and Urban Development
6. Omnibus Housing Act (including rent supplements, and low and moderate income housing)
7. Social Security Increases
8. Voting Rights
9. Immigration Bill
10. Older Americans Act
11. Heart Disease, Cancer, and Stroke Research and Facilities
12. Law Enforcement Assistance Act
13. National Crime Commission
14. Drug Controls
15. Mental Health Research and Facilities
16. Health Professions Education
17. Medical Library Facilities
18. Vocational Rehabilitation
19. Inter-American Bank Fund Increases
20. Stepping Up the War Against Poverty
21. Arts and Humanities Foundation
22. Appalachia
23. Highway Beautification
24. Air Pollution (auto exhausts and research)
25. Water Pollution Control (water quality standards)
26. High-speed Ground Transportation
27. Extension and Strengthening of MDTA
28. Presidential Disability and Succession
29. Child Health Medical Assistance
30. Regional Development

THE SECOND SESSION

1. The Department of Transportation
2. Truth in Packaging
3. Demonstration Cities
4. Funds for Rent Supplements
5. Funds for Teacher Corps

**Accomplishments of the 89th Congress** *(continued)*

6. Asian Development Bank
7. Water Pollution (Clean Rivers)
8. Food for Peace
9. March Anti-inflation package
10. Narcotics Rehabilitation
11. Child Safety
12. Vietnam Supplemental
13. Foreign Aid Extension
14. Traffic Safety
15. Highway Safety
16. Public Health Service Reorganization
17. Community Relations Service Reorganization
18. Water Pollution Control Administration Reorganization
19. Mine Safety
20. Allied Health Professions Training
21. International Education
22. Child Nutrition
23. Bail Reform
24. Civil Procedure Reforms
25. Tire Safety
26. Protection for Savers (increase in Federal Insurance for savings accounts)
27. The GI Bill
28. Minimum Wage Increase
29. Urban Mass Transit
30. Elementary and Higher Education Funds

*Source:* Lawrence F. O'Brien and Joseph A. Califano, Jr., "Final Report to President Lyndon B. Johnson on the 89th Congress," *Public Papers of the Presidents of the United States: Lyndon B. Johnson,* 1966, Vol. 2 (Washington, Government Printing Office, 1967), 1193–94.

more land to the national wildlife refuges, wilderness, and national park systems than any president of the era. At the end of his administration, the chairman of the National Geographic Society called LBJ "our greatest conservation president."[25]

Johnson had spent a lifetime working to pass laws; for him, the major struggle of political life, the principal task of presidential liberalism, was obtaining congressional approval for a broad-scale liberal program. No other president—not JFK, not even FDR, had done that so well. With a stroke of a pen, he set aside land as wilderness, opened the nation's doors to Asian immigrants, or increased the minimum wage. But, in most cases, signing a law was not enough to produce effective action. Making law was only the first step in making policy—programs needed to be implemented and administered as well as enacted by the Congress. Johnson thought that if he could just plant the seeds for his Great Society, it would slowly but surely grow into a vast, powerful, impregnable oak. But he proved better at planting than at watering and nurturing. As one Johnson-watcher put it, "Pass the bill now, worry about its effects and implementation later—this was the White House strategy. . . . The standard of success was the passage of the law—and not only within the administration, but in the press and among the public. By this standard, the Great Society was on its way to becoming the most successful domestic program in history."[26]

## THE NOT-SO-GREAT SOCIETY: IMPLEMENTING LBJ'S PROGRAM

Unfortunately, the very compromises and concessions needed to prevail on Capitol Hill hampered the programs after they won legislative approval. For example, Title I of the Elementary and Secondary Education Act, the marrow of LBJ's education program, allocated one billion federal dollars in compensatory education funds for poor students. Before Title I, local communities had always controlled and financed education in the United States. Local control not only created vast inequities between wealthier and poorer neighborhoods, but perpetuated them, since without good schools, residents of poor areas were unlikely to break free of poverty.

The Johnson administration designed Title I to end this depressing cycle of ignorance and want. The law's rationale was simple: children from poor families lacked the advantages of their better-off classmates and tended to fall behind academically. Schools could compensate for this problem by devoting more attention and resources to the poor than to the nonpoor; needy students would improve in the classroom and stay in school longer. Better education would eventually translate into higher incomes and break the cycle of poverty.

To pass the bill, however, the Johnson administration needed the support of local school districts, of the educational establishment in place. So the ESEA granted local districts the primary responsibility for conceiving and implementing the compensatory program. In the Senate hearings on the bill, LBJ's nemesis, Robert Kennedy, challenged this provision. He asked whether local schools bore responsibility for the educational deficiencies of the poor in the first place—whether it made sense to trust the very people who created the inequities with the funds to remedy them. LBJ's commissioner of education admitted the potential problem but pledged that local school officials would change their attitudes and work for reform.

Robert Kennedy's fears proved justified. The government allocated money to a district based on the number of poor students enrolled in it, but the districts selected which schools, students, and programs received the funds. Most districts pocketed the money and continued business-as-usual. Fresno, California, used its Title I allocation to buy an educational TV system for all students; Camden, New Jersey, subsidized physical education classes for pupils regardless of income. In fact, a 1977 study revealed that few Title I dollars actually benefited poor students; most of the funds supported programs for the middle class and well-to-do. As historian Allen Matusow explained (see Document 4), "President Johnson always believed that Title I was an anti-poverty program. The local school districts made sure it was not."

Similarly, Johnson compromised on Medicare to win the acquiescence of doctors, on the highway beautification bill to conciliate business interests, and on the food stamp program to satisfy southern planters. By amending Great Society bills, Johnson won over stubborn lawmakers, but in the process he diluted his programs and complicated their execution.

If LBJ had dedicated his insatiable energies to implementing the Great Society, he might have overcome weaknesses in the statutes. But Johnson displayed little interest in administrating the agencies he created. This oversight surprised many of LBJ's closest confidants. As a young congressman, Johnson had seen executive branch officials sabotage FDR's initiatives by delaying and obfuscating the president's orders. In fact, one of LBJ's favorite political stories, an anecdote he repeated over and over again to impress on his staff the need for implementing his directives, concerned a visit to a tiny east Texas town during World War II. Purchasing some gasoline, LBJ handed over the Office of Price Administration (OPA) coupons needed to purchase gasoline under wartime rationing rules. The puzzled attendant looked cockeyed at Johnson and then realized where the strange coupons had come from. "Oh, the O, P and A," he exclaimed. "Well, we didn't put that in down here." Johnson understood that laws alone accomplished little good "if you didn't put 'em in," but he found implementing them easier said than done.[27]

Johnson stinted on administration in part because he concentrated on legislative battles and because the war in Vietnam increasingly dominated his attention. But to a large extent, the problem was built into the nature of the presidency. Executive branch officials, from the lowliest bureaucrat to the president himself, papered over the problems and failures of their agencies. They believed that once Congress heard about miscues or failures, it would cut a program, rather than applaud an honest assessment and let the administration try again. "Of course, I understand the difficulties of bureaucracy," LBJ told an aide when informed of deficiencies in one Great Society program. "But what you don't understand is that the President's real trouble is with the Congress, not the bureaucracy. . . . If we went around beating our breasts and admitting difficulties in our programs, then the Congress would immediately slash all our funds for next year and then where would we be? Better to send in the reports as they are, even knowing the situation is more complicated than it appears, and then work from within to make things better and correct the problems."[28] Constantly jockeying with Congress, LBJ mainly ignored the challenges of "putting in" the Great Society programs.

No component of the Great Society aroused higher expectations in the Congress and the country than the war on poverty; none occasioned so much controversy and disappointment when it was put into effect. In 1964, the newly created Office of Economic Opportunity (OEO) led to a multipronged attack on poverty. Head Start, an early education program for preschoolers, began in 1965. Its objective was to prepare underprivileged children for first grade, equipping them with basic academic and social skills, so that they would perform better in the early grades and be more likely to remain in school. Head Start ultimately proved a modest success, although during the Johnson years, it registered few results.

Another OEO program, the Job Corps, targeted young adults; its mission was to train young people to obtain and hold jobs. The Corps reached into the nation's grimmest urban neighborhoods and plucked out mostly young men, ages sixteen to twenty-one. To provide job training, the OEO hired some of the most successful business corporations in the country—IBM, RCA, Litton Industries. In 1965, three hundred thousand youngsters applied for the ten thousand Job Corps slots. The programs' first year, however, proved a nightmare for the Johnson administration. Recruits found themselves hundreds of miles from home, isolated in remote training facilities, separated into single-sex camps. Troubles abounded—a stabbing, a food riot, charges of burglary and assault. By the summer of 1966, the camps had settled down, and the Corps got on with its work. To its credit, the program accepted desperate youths, without education or skills. But Job Corps training had little impact; graduates earned about the same income after the program as they had before, and 28 percent of them remained unemployed.

The most celebrated and controversial skirmish of the war on poverty involved the Community Action Program (CAP). Attacking persistent urban poverty head on, CAP encouraged poor neighborhoods to form their own community action agencies. These agencies would mobilize all parts of the community "to promote fundamental change in the interests of the poor." As OEO chief Sargent Shriver testified before the Congress, the War on Poverty aimed not only at individuals: "It embraces entire neighborhoods, communities, cities, and states. It is an attempt to change institutions as well as people. It must deal with the culture of poverty as well as the individual victims."[29]

Shriver's remarks revealed a new understanding of poverty, especially of the hard-core poor in inner cities, that was taking shape in the Johnson administration during the mid-1960s. Policymakers gradually developed the conception of a "culture of poverty" in the nation's slum communities. Adherents of this view no longer conceived of the urban poor as "rich people without money," essentially like everyone else but lacking resources, skills, and job opportunities. Instead they argued that the hard-core poor possessed a distinctive cultural profile, a way of life passed on from generation to generation, characterized by unstable families, high rates of illegitimacy, low levels of voting and political participation, poor self-esteem, and traumatic childhood experiences. For some liberal policymakers, like LBJ himself, the new concept of a culture of poverty barely altered their outlook; it merely offered an additional rationale for concerted federal effort to ameliorate conditions in the nation's inner cities. For other, more radical observers, it proved that traditional transfer programs must give way to community action projects that actively empowered the poor and involved them in managing their own communities.

The CAP staff contained many people of that more aggressive stripe — young idealists committed as much to stirring up the poor as to helping them. Initially, LBJ paid them little attention. Johnson gave Sargent Shriver one, and only one, piece of advice: "Keep out crooks, communists, and cocksuckers."[30]

Allowed so much free rein, the Community Action Program not only financed neighborhood development projects, but also insisted on including the poor in designing and running local programs. Convinced that the urban poor needed power as well as resources to transform their communities, CAP administrators wanted the needy to form, in the words of the program's Community Action workbook, "autonomous and self-managed organizations which are competent to exert political influence on behalf of their own self-interest."[31] Unlike federal aid to education, which granted power and money to local school boards, community action would circumvent municipal officials and local elites, directly empowering and funding the poor to rebuild their own neighborhoods. For that reason, inserted into the Economic Opportunity Act was the so-called maximum feasible participation doctrine, a clause requiring that community action agencies be developed, conducted, and administered with the maximum feasible participation of residents of the area—including the poor.

The "maximum feasible participation" directive set up an irreconcilable conflict between national and local authorities. The federalist character of the American political system—the strange division of powers among federal, state, and local governments—has always offered local actors an unusually large bag of tricks for frustrating national policy. This obstructionism was peculiarly in evidence during the War on Poverty. City governments resented the strictures and proceeded to ignore them. They designed community action projects without representatives of the impoverished communities, with little attention to the special needs of blighted neighborhoods. But the OEO meant business: it rejected these plans, held up the funds, and sent city leaders back to the drawing board. It forced them to include minorities and poor people on the boards of their community agencies and to devise projects more responsive to the problems of slum neighborhoods. The conflicts took LBJ and his top aides by surprise. Neither the Congress nor the president seemed to understand the full implications of the maximum feasible participation clause. Congress, which approved the doctrine, certainly opposed any such disruptive influences on local power structures. And President Johnson acceded to it because he feared southern whites might otherwise freeze blacks out of the program. Johnson never envisioned that the overwhelmingly Democratic mayors of northern cities would rage against a program funneling federal dollars into their towns.

The Community Action Program quickly became a political liability. Bowing to the complaints from mayors and other local officials, the Johnson administration retreated. Shriver reined in the idealists on his staff and community action agencies returned to the control of city officials concerned mainly with white middle-class constituencies. When the program came up for renewal in 1967, its ambitious agenda had vanished. Sniffing the pork barrel, ravenous mayors had become its biggest supporters.

Certainly, LBJ bore a great deal of responsibility for CAP's failure; he did not run a tight ship. But the gravest problem of CAP and of the Great

Society in general was what one administration official called "a tendency to oversell and underperform."[32] Johnson launched new programs with extravagant claims, but he put up neither the monetary muscle nor the clear administrative strategy to put them through.

Domestic policy chief Joseph Califano reflected on the administrative failures of the Great Society in similar terms: "Johnson's extravagant rhetoric announcing new programs belied the modest funds he requested to begin them." Johnson thus alienated both conservatives who "believed that he was hiding his real intentions just to get a foot in the door" and liberals who thought "he wasn't asking for enough to smash the door open."[33]

## ASSESSING THE GREAT SOCIETY

Since the 1960s, many voices have debated the success of the Great Society and the reasons for its shortcomings. For thirty years, Johnson's program has remained the standard of liberal public policy in the United States, in both indictments and defenses of modern American liberalism.

Johnson himself took pride in his record. In his memoirs, Johnson pointed to the steep drop in the number of people living below the official poverty line during his term in office, a drop caused by the expanding wartime economy as well as the social programs of the Great Society (see Document 5). "We started something in motion with the attack on poverty," LBJ insisted. "Its effects were felt in education, law, medicine, and social welfare, in business and industry, in civil and philanthropic life, and in religion. . . . Of course, we had not lifted everyone out of poverty," Johnson conceded. "There would be setbacks and frustrations and disappointments ahead. But no one would ever again be able to ignore the poverty in our midst, and I believe that is enough to assure the final outcome and to change the way of life for millions of our fellow human beings."[34]

Johnson's poverty warriors shared their chief's assessment. Joseph Califano claimed that Johnson "converted the hopes and aspirations of all kinds of Americans into a political force that brought out much of the good in each of us. . . . Whatever historians of the Great Society say twenty years later, they must admit that we tried, and I believe they will conclude that America is a better place because we did" (see Document 3). Other liberals agreed that the Great Society moved the nation in the right direction but complained that Johnson did not move fast or far enough, did not give programs enough time, and did not allocate enough money.

Conservatives, on the other hand, viewed the Great Society as big government run amok—too much intervention, too much waste, and too much bureaucratic red tape. Writing in 1968, conservative commentator Ernest Van Den Haag denounced the "welfare mess" as a "wasteful hodgepodge" of programs which only trapped and humiliated the poor.[35] During the 1970s and 1980s, for reasons explored in the chapters ahead, this conservative critique of the Great Society gained political force. Nearly two decades after LBJ launched his program, Ronald Reagan used the Great Society as a whipping boy for his resurgent conservative platform. The first annual report of Reagan's Council of Economic Advisers, published in January 1982, listed "reducing the role of the Federal Government in all its dimensions" as Reagan's top priority and blamed all the nation's woes on government "meddling." The report rejected "paternalism" in welfare policies, suggesting that antipoverty programs only aggravated the distress of the needy and trapped them in a cycle of poverty and dependence.[36]

Indeed, Reaganite calls for dismantling the welfare system rested on arguments that Great Society programs had actually harmed the impoverished—encouraging illegitimacy, welfare dependence, and hopelessness. "With the coming of the Great Society," President Reagan declared in 1982, "government began eating away at the underpinnings of the private enterprise system. The big taxers and big spenders in the Congress had started a binge that would slowly change the nature of our society and, even worse, it threatened the character of our people. . . . By the time the full weight of Great Society programs was felt, economic progress for America's poor had come to a tragic halt."[37]

During the 1960s, however, the principal critique of the Great Society came not from conservatives, but from radicals, from the student New Left, the Black Power movement, and various social protest groups. Ultimately, Johnsonian liberalism proved too timid to challenge the powers that be (see Document 4). Johnson could not, would not, see that the interests of rich and poor, business and labor, must sometimes collide; he could not win everyone's cooperation without compromising the effectiveness of his programs.

In 1971, in retirement at the LBJ ranch, Johnson reflected bitterly on the fate of his beloved Great Society. "I figured when my legislative program passed the Congress," he told Doris Kearns, "that the Great Society had the chance to grow into a beautiful woman. And I figured her growth and development would be as natural and inevitable as any small child's. . . . And when she grew up, I figured she'd be so big and beautiful that the American people couldn't help but fall in love with her, and once they did, they'd want to keep her around forever, making her a permanent part of American life, more permanent even than the New Deal." Instead, he saw his successor Richard Nixon starving his program to death: "She's getting thinner and uglier all the time; now her bones are beginning to stick out and her wrinkles are beginning to show. Soon she'll be so ugly that the American people will refuse to look at her; they'll stick her in a closet to hide her away and there she'll die. And when she dies, I, too, will die."[38]

Poignant words, but deceptive ones, for it was Lyndon Johnson himself, more than his aides or opponents or successors, who neglected the Great Society and stunted its growth. Early in his presidency, LBJ made two political mistakes, two fateful errors that ultimately stifled his beloved "child." First, he underestimated the expense of the two-front war in Vietnam. Deciding that he had no choice but to escalate the war in Southeast Asia, Johnson determined to pursue the war and the Great Society simultaneously. Strongly in his mind remained the examples of Woodrow Wilson and FDR who had abandoned domestic reform to lead the nation into war. Johnson believed he could protect the Great Society only by downplaying the expense of his two-front war; he covered up the costs of the Asian struggle, economized on every domestic program, and delayed a tax increase as long as possible. This strategy failed. Eventually, he had to scale back the Great Society to fight the war that took up more and more of his time and energy. "That bitch of a war," Johnson later admitted, "killed the lady I really loved—the Great Society."[39]

Second, he did not anticipate the insidious political current that would further undermine LBJ's liberal program—racial backlash. Even though Great Society programs mainly benefited middle-class whites—aid to education, Medicare, farm subsidies, expanded Social Security—Johnson spoke repeatedly and passionately about eradicating poverty. The special attention to the poor, combined with the ongoing civil rights revolution, convinced many Americans that Johnson and his fellow liberals lavished too many benefits on African Americans and other racial minorities. This perception stirred up simmering racial antagonisms, a backlash against civil rights and the poverty war which stoked white discontent against liberal government. As one of Johnson's cabinet members warned in 1966, "Many people think the Great Society programs are mainly designed to help the very poor and they don't believe that this Administration has much interest in the middle-class, middle income family. There must be a way to make these people see that every American has an enormous stake in what we're doing."[40]

Johnson feared the white backlash; he worried particularly about losing the backbone of the liberal coalition, the blue-collar, white ethnics of the northeast and midwest who had provided electoral support for every Democratic president since FDR. The Civil Rights Act of 1964 had already sacrificed the votes of white southerners. Now the heart of the New Deal coalition complained about Johnson's poverty program and the intensifying demands of African Americans for power and equality. These constituencies had supported the early civil rights movement—what they saw as largely southern battles for legal equality. When African Americans turned their eyes toward informal discrimination in northern cities and the federal courts began to order the integration of schools in the North, however, the fears and hatreds of people who had voted for FDR, JFK, and LBJ exploded. Liberalism's electoral base began melting in the heat and fury of those racial confrontations.

# NOTES

[1] Lyndon B. Johnson, *The Vantage Point* (New York: Popular Library, 1971), 71, 461. Eric F. Goldman, *The Tragedy of Lyndon Johnson* (New York: Dell, 1969), 423.

[2] Johnson, *Vantage Point,* 71.

[3] Joseph A. Califano, Sr., *The Triumph and Tragedy of Lyndon Johnson* (New York: Simon and Schuster, 1991), 11. Doris Kearns, *Lyndon Johnson and the American Dream* (New York: Signet Books, 1976), 226.

[4] Kearns, *Johnson and the American Dream,* 296.

[5] *Public Papers of the Presidents of the United States: Lyndon B. Johnson, 1963–1969,* 11 vols. (Washington, D.C.: Government Printing Office, 1964–1969), 1963–1964, vol. 1, 250.

[6] Ibid. Califano, *Triumph and Tragedy,* 75. Goldman, *Tragedy,* 448–49.

[7] *Papers,* 1964, vol. 1, 164.

[8] Document 2. See also *Economic Report of the President* (Washington, D.C.: Government Printing Office, 1964).

[9] David T. Bazelon, "Big Business and the Democrats," in Marvin Gettleman and David Mermelstein, eds., *The Great Society Reader* (New York: Vintage, 1967), 142.

[10] Goldman, *Tragedy,* 218.

[11] *Papers,* 1963–1964, vol. 2, 1604.

[12] Kearns, *Johnson and the American Dream,* 236–37.

[13] Ibid.

[14] Jack Valenti, *A Very Human President* (New York: Pocket Books, 1977), 138–39.

[15] Califano, *Triumph and Tragedy,* 110.

[16] Henry Hall Wilson, quoted in Kearns, *Johnson and the American Dream,* 246.

[17] Goldman, *Tragedy,* 337.

[18] Johnson, *Vantage Point,* 324.

[19] *Papers,* 1965, vol. 1, 412–14.

[20] *Papers,* 1965, vol. 2, 811–14.

[21] Califano, *Triumph and Tragedy,* 125–26.

[22] Johnson, *Vantage Point,* 322.

[23] Goldman, *Tragedy,* 395.

[24] *Papers,* 1965, vol. 1, 37.

[25] Califano, *Triumph and Tragedy,* 338.

[26] Kearns, *Johnson and the American Dream,* 228–29.

[27] Valenti, *A Very Human President*, 80–81.

[28] Kearns, *Johnson and the American Dream*, 304–05.

[29] U.S. House, *Examination of the War on Poverty Program*, Hearings Before the Subcommittee on the War on Poverty Program, Committee on Education and Labor, 89th Cong., 1st sess., April 12–30, 1965, 16–18.

[30] Allen J. Matusow, *The Unraveling of America* (New York: Harper and Row, 1984), 243.

[31] Ibid., 247.

[32] Daniel Patrick Moynihan, *Maximum Feasible Misunderstanding* (New York: The Free Press, 1969), 100.

[33] Califano, *Triumph and Tragedy*, 148.

[34] Johnson, *Vantage Point*, 87.

[35] Ernest Van den Haag, "Ending the Welfare Mess," *National Review*, December 17, 1968, 1260–63.

[36] *Economic Report of the President*, 1982, (Washington, D.C.: GPO), passim.

[37] Ronald Reagan, remarks before the National Black Republican Council, September 14, 1982, *The Weekly Compilation of Presidential Documents*, vol. 18, 1154.

[38] Kearns, *Johnson and the American Dream*, 300.

[39] Ibid., 263.

[40] Vaughan Davis Bornet, *The Presidency of Lyndon B. Johnson* (Lawrence: University Press of Kansas, 1983), 350.

# 5

## Shall We Overcome?
## LBJ and the Civil Rights Revolution

The civil rights revolution set in motion powerful centrifugal forces, tearing apart not only Lyndon Johnson's political party and his constituency for activist government, but the nation itself. The black struggle for freedom forced unexpected, and sometimes unwelcome, changes in the habits and expectations of all Americans, in business, social life, and politics. Racial conflict threatened to break the country, as one government report put it, into "two Americas, one black, one white—separate and unequal."[1]

Already by the middle of LBJ's presidency, many observers dismissed Johnson's liberal portrait of racial equality as a naive and damaging fancy. Yet LBJ retained faith in national unity and in his ability to forge it. "For our beautiful America is not a planetary system with many atmospheres, and many calendars, and many temperatures," he told a White House conference in 1966. "It is one large island of earth inhabited by mortal men of many races, and many faiths, and many colors of skin." Then, repeating the credo of universalism he still cherished, Johnson concluded, "They all cry the same way. They all laugh the same way. . . . We shall either move this Nation towards civil peace and towards social justice for all of its citizens, or for none."[2]

But not even Lyndon Johnson, with all his cajoling and bargaining and persuading, could move his country in different directions at the same time. The unmet demands of the civil rights movement—the rising expectations and mounting frustrations of black Americans—pushed for accelerated reform while the resistance of white Americans to further change hardened. The fraying social fabric threatened Johnson's presidency, his party's supremacy, and his political philosophy. "The black revolt, of itself," British journalist Godfrey Hodgson noted, "implied a crisis for the Presidency as an institution. For it was now up to the President, far more than to the Congress or to any other agency, public or private, more even than to the courts, that Americans looked for the carrying out of their ideals. Where the fulfillment of these ideals demanded a course of action that would come into conflict with so many habits, assumptions, interests and emotions then the resentment must backfire upon the presidency."[3]

Wary of such backlash after the 1964 election, Johnson's advisers asked LBJ to move more cautiously on civil rights, to avoid further controversy. But Johnson had already stepped into that minefield. He could not turn back from a confrontation that bled the nation and threatened war in its very streets. "More has been done than men thought possible just a short time ago," Johnson reminded the 1966 White House conference on civil rights, "in stripping away legal barriers—in opening political opportunity—in attacking the lack of skills and jobs, and education and housing that are really the taproots of poverty. In all of these efforts we have made mistakes," LBJ conceded. "But I came here tonight—at the end of a long day—to tell you that we are moving and we shall not turn back."[4]

Fear of social unrest, as much as Johnson's own passion for achievement and appreciation, moved LBJ to press ahead on civil rights. He saw himself, according to domestic policy chief Joseph Califano, in a race against the clock. "He was always in a hurry," Califano wrote in his memoirs, "because he feared that, once black Americans sense the prospect of a better life, their acceptance of discrimination would turn to impatience. . . . " Johnson also raced "against time with the Congress and the affluent majority of Americans. . . . He was always conscious that his days were numbered and that his political capital, however enormous as he began his presidency, was limited."[5]

Johnson worried about the race issue because even at the height of his popularity—after the successful passage of the Civil Rights Act of 1964, during his successful campaign against Barry Goldwater—he had barely contained the nation's racial tensions. A civil rights dispute had almost wrecked LBJ's crowning moment, his nomination as the party's presidential standard-bearer at the 1964 Democratic National Convention. Held in Atlantic City, New Jersey, home of the annual Miss America pageant, the elaborately scripted convention resembled the coronation of a beauty queen. Gigantic portraits of the president bedecked the convention center and Broadway star Carol Channing crooned "Hello, Lyndon, well hello, Lyndon" to the tune of the title song from the hit musical *Hello, Dolly!*

But a dispute over civil rights threatened Johnson's beautifully orchestrated shining moment and almost busted the convention apart on national television. In Mississippi, where African Americans were still denied the right to vote, the white supremacist Democratic party regulars had, as usual, selected a lily-white delegation to represent the state on the convention floor. In response, local civil rights activists had held their own counterelections, open to all Mississippians regardless of race. This Mississippi Freedom Democratic party (MFDP) sent its own delegation to Atlantic City and demanded that the convention seat it as the authentic representatives of the citizens of Mississippi.

Johnson desperately needed a compromise. He feared a divisive and embarrassing credentials fight on national television. Worse yet, he realized that the battle would either force the defection of the South, if he did seat the MFDP, or the antagonism of liberal and civil rights forces, if he rejected the freedom delegation's challenge. Johnson named Hubert Humphrey, long a hero in civil rights circles, as his running mate and deputized him to negotiate a settlement. Eventually, Johnson and Humphrey offered the MFDP (also known as the Freedom Party) two at-large seats in the convention and honorary, nonvoting places for the other sixty-six delegates. Most important, the Democratic party would ban segregated delegations from all future conventions.

Having fashioned a deal, Johnson pulled out all the stops to make it happen. He won the South's acceptance of the measure, and brought on board many civil rights champions, including Bayard Rustin, Martin Luther King, Jr., and the Freedom party's own legal counsel, the famed civil rights lawyer Joseph Rauh. All of them urged the MFDP to accept the compromise.

The MFDP, however, proved immune to the Johnson Treatment. Members of the Freedom party, indeed all Mississippi civil rights workers, daily risked their lives in the struggle. In the year before the convention challenge, several Mississippi activists had been slain, hundreds brutally beaten, and more than thirty homes and churches had been bombed. "We've been treated like beasts in Mississippi," one MFDP delegate reminded the advocates of compromise. "They shot us down like animals. We risked our lives comin' here. . . . Politics must be corrupt if it don't care none about the people down there." During the convention itself, white supremacists set fire to the MFDP headquarters in Tupelo. Fannie Lou Hamer, one of the MFDP's leaders, spoke for her colleagues when she rejected Johnson's offer. "No compromise," Hamer insisted, herself the victim of a brutal, disfiguring beating at the hands of Mississippi policemen who had been acquitted of misconduct by an all-white jury. "We didn't come all this way for no two seats."[6]

Although the MFDP rejected the plan, the offer of compromise and the support of prominent civil rights figures proved sufficient to hold the convention together. When the MFDP marched onto the convention floor without credentials, the delegates all but ignored them. Johnson had, for the moment, contained the racial tensions in his party. In November, the white South repaid him by defecting to Barry Goldwater and the Republicans.

Meanwhile, for many civil rights activists, including thousands of black and white college students who had traveled to Mississippi to take part in a "Freedom Summer" of protests and community organizing, Atlantic City dramatized the ultimate bankruptcy of liberal reform. The MFDP had come bearing a just grievance, had won promises of progress from prominent liberals, and had been turned away. Disheartened activists felt betrayed; they decided that it was foolish to rely on government action or presidential leadership and determined in the future to empower themselves and transform their own communities. They moved toward a radical critique of the American system of government; they began forging a "New Left."

Johnson felt the rising wind; early in 1965 he launched the Great Society and simultaneously instructed his attorney general to prepare legislation concerning the voting rights of African Americans. Still, he hoped for, and planned on an interregnum. He envisioned introducing the voting rights bill in the spring of 1966, giving the nation a breather from racial conflict, a quiet period of adjustment to the Civil Rights Act of 1964 while he concentrated on other matters. Then, and only then, would he prod the nation one step further down the road to racial equality.

## "WE SHALL OVERCOME": THE VOTING RIGHTS ACT OF 1965

The black struggle for freedom would not wait for Lyndon Johnson's schedule. In January 1965, local organizers invited Martin Luther King, Jr., to Selma, Alabama, to rejuvenate a frustrated voter registration campaign. Although blacks made up 58 percent of the county's population, they made up only 2 percent of its registered voters. A sheaf of infamous southern practices, from unfair tests and restrictive taxes to overt discrimination, barred black voters from the polls. Those who attempted to register—knowing they had little chance of successfully running the gamut of arcane regulations—could count on losing their jobs, their homes, their health, sometimes even their lives. White mobs threatened any black citizen who even considered attempting to register.

Undaunted, Selma activists had launched a registration campaign in 1962, but white authorities only stiffened the restrictive requirements for registration and stepped up their intimidation of black activists. The local sheriff—a rotund, crude, and violent man named James G. Clark—reveled in victimizing civil rights workers. He wore a gold-braided sheriff's cap, commanded a two-hundred-volunteer mounted posse, and ostentatiously brandished a night stick and a burnished pistol. In the seven weeks after Dr. King's arrival, Sheriff Clark and his posse had broken up peaceful demonstrations with electric cattle prods and bullwhips. They had arrested two thousand men, women, and children, including King. On February 18, 1965, Clark summoned heavily armed Alabama state troopers to accompany his own mounted patrolmen as they disbursed an unarmed protest. During the clash, a young Selma African American, Jimmie Lee Jackson, was shot to death.

In response, King called a protest march from Selma to Montgomery, the state capital located some fifty miles away. Alabama Governor George Wallace decreed the demonstration illegal and ordered his state troopers to block the marchers. As they crossed a bridge a few miles outside of Selma, the Alabama State Police and Sheriff Clark's posse ordered the demonstrators to turn around. When they refused, troops and the posse charged the protesters, chasing the choking, bloodied marchers through clouds of tear gas. The assault, on March 7, 1965, which became known as "Bloody Sunday," wounded forty marchers. Two days later, four Selma whites accosted the Reverend James Reeb, a Unitarian minister from Boston, and two companions as they walked home from dinner. Screaming "Hey, nigger-lovers!" the mob attacked the ministers with wooden planks, crashing a thick board across Reeb's skull. The minister died two days later.

The violence, much of it covered by the national media, awakened the indignation of the country. Thousands of Americans across the nation joined rallies in support of King and the Selma marchers. They pressed Johnson to send federal troops to Alabama to protect the marchers. In Selma, Martin Luther King, Jr., blamed the federal government directly for the crisis. "Jimmie Lee Jackson," King asserted, "was murdered by the timidity of the federal government that . . . cannot protect the rights of its own citizens seeking the right to vote."[7] In Washington, protesters staged a sleep-in surrounding the White House, taunting the president with cries of "LBJ just you wait/See what happens in 68" and singing "We Shall Overcome," the black spiritual that had become, in one scholar's words, the "mighty battle hymn of the civil rights crusade."[8]

Johnson dispatched two of his aides to meet with the demonstrators and hunkered down within the White House. For his part, LBJ little comprehended the militant students surrounding his gates, little appreciated the direct-action tactics practiced by the protesters outside the White House and even by Martin Luther King, Jr., in Selma. He simply did not understand their style of politics; he thought civil rights workers should be "in Washington, working on their Senators, getting a voting bill passed," not marching from Selma to Montgomery.[9] He believed in the legislative process—in the ability of president and Congress to produce meaningful reform—that the battle-scarred veterans of the southern civil rights struggle and their increasingly frustrated northern brethren had already abandoned.

Johnson heard the hoots and hollers outside his door, but waited. No president liked to send federal troops into a state unless the state's governor had requested them; tradition dictated against it. And Johnson feared that any such move would only strengthen the segregationists' hand—turning Governor Wallace and Sheriff Clark into heroic underdogs and intensifying the violence.

Then, surprisingly, Wallace miscalculated. Anxious for the limelight, the governor requested a meeting with LBJ, suggesting that he could not handle the situation alone. Two days later, Wallace convened a special joint session of the Alabama legislature to condemn the marchers and complain about the costs of supervising the march. He telegraphed the president, asking for federal funds and for nonmilitary support to protect the demonstrators.

Wallace's grandstanding gave Johnson the opening he needed—an official gubernatorial request for federal assistance. Johnson ignored the governor's request for funds and civilian authorities and immediately called up sufficient military force to "assure the rights of American citizens . . . to walk peaceably and safely without injury or loss of life from Selma to Montgomery, Alabama."[10] The march took place without incident, although violence continued in Selma.

Roused to action by the crisis in Alabama, Johnson converted the moment into a truly effective change in policy. Convening a joint session of the Congress not at the normal noon hour, but during prime time to capture the television audience, Johnson addressed the nation on the subject of the "American Promise" (see Document 6). The speech began with the business at hand—a promise to introduce a tough voting rights bill, one that would overcome the "systematic and ingenious discrimination" that had denied the ballot to black southerners. And he demanded immediate action: "This time, on this issue, there must be no delay, no hesitation and no compromise with our purpose."

Then, in his most memorable peroration, LBJ moved beyond his usual legislative exhortation and exercised moral and political leadership. "But even if we pass this bill," he warned, "the battle will not be over. What happened in Selma is part of a larger movement which reaches into every section and State of America. It is the effort of American Negroes to secure for themselves the full blessings of American life. Their cause must be our cause too," LBJ asserted. "Because it is not just Negroes, but really it is all of us, who must overcome the crippling legacy of bigotry and injustice."[11]

With those words, the president paused, raised his long arms into the air and intoned the solemn and heroic invocation of the civil rights movement itself: "And we . . . shall . . . overcome!" The audience remained silent, stunned. A southern congressman murmured "Goddamn," and the room exploded into thunderous applause.[12] Watching on television in Alabama, Dr. King began to cry; he had never expected the president of the United States to align himself so clearly with the civil rights cause.

Johnson immediately joined the legislative battle for his voting rights bill. He worked closely with Everett Dirksen, the Republican Senate leader, so that Republican votes would be available to invoke cloture and end a southern filibuster. He instructed the Justice Department to draft a truly effective bill—with an automatic triggering device that would void all local restrictions in any county that kept minority voters off the rolls and dispatch federal inspectors to offending counties to register all adult citizens. To prevent southern states from constantly creating new restrictions, forcing the administration to void them again and again, the law required offending counties to gain "preclearance" from the federal government for any change in election laws.

On August 6, 1965, Johnson signed the law in the Capitol rotunda. The very next day, the Justice Department identified southern jurisdictions in violation of the law and sent federal registrars into Alabama, Louisiana, and Mississippi. Barriers that had denied blacks the ballot crumbled; in two years, the percentage of Mississippi blacks registered to vote rose from 7 percent to 60 percent. Over the next decade and a half, Atlanta, Charlotte, and Birmingham elected black mayors; African Americans won seats in southern state legislatures and in the Congress. With the Voting Rights Act, Johnson, whose advocacy of civil rights had cost his party the votes of white southerners, brought millions of black voters into voting booths, and into the Democratic fold.

Johnson also outpaced his predecessors in appointing African Americans to influential posts in the national government. He named the first black cabinet officer (Robert Weaver as secretary of Housing and Urban Development), the first black military adviser (Major Hugh Robinson as army aide to the president), the first minority appointee to the Federal

Reserve Board (Andrew Brimmer), and the first black Justice of the Supreme Court (Thurgood Marshall). Johnson also opened federal employment to thousands of African Americans, many of whom found the first taste of middle-class security through white-collar government jobs.

But even as he removed the formal, legal barriers to racial equality, Johnson worried that "rights are not enough." On the very day he signed the Voting Rights Act, LBJ warned that people "must be able to use those rights in their personal pursuit of happiness." The nation still had to address the "wounds and the weaknesses, the outward walls and inward scars" that continued to prey on victims of discrimination. "For centuries of oppression and hatred," Johnson asserted, "have already taken their painful toll. It can be seen throughout our land in men without skills, in children without fathers, in families that are imprisoned in slums and in poverty."[13]

# FIRE IN THE STREETS

South Central Los Angeles, a ghetto community of three hundred thousand, was just such a place. Beneath its calm surface of small homes with well-manicured lawns on tree-lined streets simmered an unsavory stew of the nation's most indigestible social problems: substandard segregated schools, high unemployment, almost no job opportunities for young black men, and poor transportation systems. Because major discount chain stores refused to locate in the area, residents had to pay high prices at small local establishments. Although 98 percent of South Central's residents were black, all but five of the more than two hundred police officers assigned to the area were white. In Watts, the neighborhood at the center of the sprawling ghetto, 40 percent of the families were headed by women, 40 percent of the people lived in poverty.

On August 12, 1965, most Americans had never heard of Watts. President Johnson, fresh from his voting rights triumph, set off that night for a weekend of relaxation at the LBJ Ranch. The night before, Los Angeles police had arrested a young black man for drunk driving; a crowd gathered, the police summoned reinforcements. Almost instantaneously, a thousand people poured onto the street pounding the cops with rocks and shouting, "Burn, Baby, Burn!," the slogan of a local radio disc jockey. On August 13, the disturbance exploded into a full-fledged riot — with looting and burning all over South Central Los Angeles. Four days later, the National Guard arrived and began reasserting control of the streets. When it was all over, six nights of blood and fury had left thirty-four dead, almost a thousand injured, and property damage estimated at more than $45 million. Martin Luther King, Jr., flew to Los Angeles and preached nonviolence, but the people on the city's streets ignored him. The hope and triumph of Selma and the Voting Rights Act, and the promise of King's eloquent dreams, withered in the fury of Watts.

The news from Los Angeles shattered Johnson. He would not believe it. He saw Watts as a personal blow—wondering why the rioters were doing this to him, why they were not grateful for all he had done to aid African Americans. "How is it possible after all we've accomplished," Johnson cried plaintively. "Is the world topsy-turvy?"[14]

A man who insisted on full, immediate information about the most trivial details, who normally never traveled without a phone by his side, refused the desperate calls of his aides. "He just wouldn't accept it," Joe Califano remembered. "He refused to look at the cable from Los Angeles describing the situation. He refused to take the calls from the generals who were requesting government planes to fly in the National Guard. I tried to reach him a dozen times. We needed decisions from him. But he simply wouldn't respond."[15] Finally, the president issued a statement, calling the riot "tragic and shocking" and warning that neither "old wrongs or new fears can justify arson and murder."[16]

Local authorities dismissed the riots as the "senseless violence" of a handful of alienated "riff-raff," but closer studies proved otherwise.[17] Thirty thousand people had participated in the looting, another sixty thousand had joined them in the streets, celebrating the destruction. The typical rioter was not stuck at the very bottom of the social ladder but was more educated than the typical nonrioter and more likely to be holding a job. Watts announced the coming of age of a new generation of northern blacks, proud of their race, intolerant of discrimination, and impatient for change. Rage propelled the rioters, but theirs was not senseless violence; its targets were whites, especially white policemen with a particularly brutal record of intimidation in Los Angeles and white merchants who controlled most commerce in black neighborhoods. Looters generally spared black-owned businesses. "What happened," one Los Angeles civil rights worker concluded,

> was that people had sat here and watched all the concern about black people "over there" [in the South]. And there wasn't a damn soul paying one bit of attention to what was going on in Watts. So the black people in Watts just spontaneously rose up one day and said: "Fuck it! we're hungry. Our schools stink. We're getting the shit beaten out of us. We've tried the integration route. . . . Now we've got to go another way.[18]

Watts not only depressed Johnson, it handcuffed him ideologically. He condemned the violence, really believing that evil acts of the past did not justify evil acts of the present. He worried that Watts would impede the Great Society; that not only would the riots stimulate racial backlash and stoke conservative opposition to his program but also that he could not appear to appease rioters by increasing social services in the cities. He needed to pursue relief for the cities without seeming to reward rioting. Still, Johnson determined to forge a Great Society in the cities and he harbored sympathy for the rioters, sharing the sentiments of Vice President Humphrey that if he had seen rats gnawing at his children's feet, he, too, would riot. White House counsel Harry McPherson called these feelings the "ambivalence of the liberal."[19]

But ambivalence satisfied no one. Militant northern blacks not only rejected the means of Johnsonian liberalism, the reliance on laws and presidential leadership, but its ends. The riots accompanied a new, more defiant stage in the black struggle for freedom as attention shifted from the largely southern struggle to remove legal barriers to northern cities where more informal, insidious racial wounds festered (see Document 7). "The Civil rights movement," civil rights leader Bayard Rustin explained in 1965, "is evolving from a protest movement into a full-fledged social movement. . . . It is now concerned not merely with removing barriers to full opportunity but with achieving the fact of equality."[20] Across the nation, more radical voices preached black nationalism, advising African Americans to fend for themselves, to foresake liberal reform through a corrupt, racist political system and seek power for and over their own communities. Even Martin Luther King, Jr., applauded the new militance. "I am not sad that black Americans are in rebellion," King reflected in 1968, "this was not only inevitable but eminently desirable . . . Justice for black people will not flow into society merely from court decisions nor from fountains of political oratory."[21]

Johnson understood the growing impatience of black America. In his memoirs, he noted that "Jim Crow was on his way out in the South, but in many ways the Northern style of discrimination—subtle, unpublicized, and deep-rooted—was even tougher to break. All too often the same Northern whites who were perfectly willing to grant the Negro his formal rights as a citizen were unwilling to grant the social acceptance and compassion that would make the formal rights meaningful."[22] As racial conflict intensified in the late 1960s, many white supporters of civil rights fell by the wayside, finding the northern movement too close to home, too radical, too threatening.

At the same time, Watts unleashed a pattern of fury that rekindled every summer of Johnson's presidency. The worst outbreaks flared in 1967 in Newark, New Jersey, and Detroit, Michigan. In Newark, the violence so overwhelmed the frightened and ill-equipped National Guards that they launched what one observer called a "counter-riot," firing indiscriminately at people in the streets, even engaging in firefights with the local police.[23] Newark's police chief watched open-mouthed with horror as the Guard fired into a housing project, killing three unsuspecting women. The governor of New Jersey had to withdraw the Guard to end the blood bath.

Johnson responded to the turmoil the only way he knew how—with more programs for the cities, more black appointments to government positions, more legislation. But his efforts could not soothe the seething discontent in the nation's cities. They only provoked backlash among whites and distrust among blacks. "The long history of Negro-white relations," LBJ reflected, "had entered a new and more bewildering stage. New problems of racial discrimination came to the forefront: the problems of poverty, slums, inadequate schooling, unemployment, and substandard housing. These problems could not be solved entirely by laws, crusades, or marches."[24]

## A NEW AND BEWILDERING STAGE:
## TOWARD AFFIRMATIVE ACTION

If laws, crusades, and marches could not do it, what would? If overt racial discrimination no longer posed a major problem, what did? During the summer of 1965, the Johnson administration grappled with this new and bewildering stage of the racial struggle—attempting to develop a new understanding of race relations and a new set of solutions for the nation's complicated civil rights problems. In June 1965, before Watts, before the Voting Rights Act had proceeded through the Congress, President Johnson unveiled a new course of action, a new diagnosis of the problems of black America. At Howard University, one of the nation's foremost black colleges, LBJ delivered the commencement address before an audience of fourteen thousand (see Document 8). Hailing the imminent enactment of the Voting Rights Act, Johnson stunned his listeners by admitting that "freedom is not enough. You do not wipe away the scars of centuries by saying, 'Now you are free to go where you want, do as you desire, choose the leaders you please.'" Adopting a memorable metaphor, Johnson insisted that "you do not take a person who for years has been hobbled by chains and liberate him, bring him up to the starting line of a race and then say, 'You are free to compete with all the others,' and still believe you have been completely fair." Taking words out of the mouths of militant civil rights leaders, Johnson announced "the next and more profound stage of the battle for civil rights. We seek not just freedom but opportunity—not just equity but human ability—not just equality as a right and a theory but equality as a fact and a result."

The Howard University speech introduced new thinking about race relations and the nature of black poverty. It suggested major shifts in civil rights laws and government antipoverty programs. It committed the federal government not merely to providing equal opportunity—to removing formal barriers against black achievement—but to taking direct, positive steps, "affirmative action," to bring black Americans into the mainstream of American business, education, and politics.

"Negro poverty," Johnson asserted, differed fundamentally from white poverty. "Many of its causes and many of its cures are the same," LBJ averred. "But there are differences—deep, corrosive, obstinate differences—radiating painful roots into the community, and into the family, and the nature of the individual."[25] The early war on poverty had dismissed any such racial differences—conceiving the struggles of urban blacks as not so much a racial problem as an economic problem, part of the same poverty amidst plenty that affected Appalachia or the elderly. At Howard University, LBJ depicted black poverty as a special and especially desperate problem.

Johnson carefully denied any racial or biological basis for these differences; "They are solely and simply the consequence of ancient brutality, past injustice, and present prejudice," he declared.[26] This legacy of oppression had created distinctive conditions, distinguishing African Americans from other migrant groups that had started off in city slums and pulled themselves into suburban, middle-class prosperity. It poisoned black communities, allowing a self-perpetuating "culture of poverty" to fester, feeding a cycle of family breakdown, criminality, and continued want.

To some extent, this revised portrait of poverty flowed from demographic shifts in the population of poor people. Over time, as rural Americans fled farms and fields for the nation's cities, poverty became increasingly an urban phenomenon. Meanwhile, Medicare and expanded Social Security benefits gradually eliminated poverty among the elderly, which had long constituted the nation's largest population of impoverished. Since elderly and female-headed households made up most of the hardcore poor—the impoverished groups who did not benefit from general upturns in the national economy—a side effect of improved benefits for the elderly was to concentrate poverty warriors' attention on female-headed households in dealing with chronic, persistent deprivation. Watts and the other civil disorders accelerated this trend, turning ghetto conditions into a burning political obsession even before black female-headed households replaced the elderly as the nation's most intractable socioeconomic problem.

Demographic, political, and ideological shifts conspired to racialize poverty—to reframe it as a black problem. Liberals no longer depicted destitution as an enemy that threatened all Americans, no longer phrased freedom from want as a universal right, a privilege of every American. Denizens of black ghettos still cried and laughed like everyone else, but they felt, thought, and lived differently; they belonged to a distinctive "culture of poverty."[27] The universalism—the denial of difference between rich and poor, black and white—that had undergirded liberalism appeared inadequate to the present moment; it seemed obsolete in the face of urban America's desperate hardships. With the Howard University speech, LBJ tentatively stepped toward a new vision.

Johnson himself only imperfectly understood the novelty of his own pronouncements. His Howard University speech adopted nearly verbatim the analysis and recommendations of one of his advisers, Assistant Secretary of Labor Daniel Patrick Moynihan. Moynihan, a former Harvard professor and one of the principal architects of the war on poverty, had prepared a report for circulation within the administration entitled *The Negro Family: The Case for National Action*. The Moynihan report, as it came to be known, advanced two main arguments. First, it found the roots of black poverty, of unemployment and ghetto life, in the breakdown of the black family. The absence of stable, male-headed households and the preponderance of female-headed, single-parent families created a self-perpetuating cycle of poverty and despair. In Moynihan's words, the black family had fallen into a "pathological matriarchal situation which is beginning to feed on itself."[28] Traditional social programs, which funneled jobs, economic growth, or money into a ghetto, pruned the buds and branches of black poverty but ignored the problem's deep roots in family structure.

Second, Moynihan blamed the disintegration of the black family on the profound, even crippling, legacy of slavery. According to Moynihan, the torments of bondage exerted continuing psychological and social effects on black America, in particular weakening the authority of black men. These inherited disadvantages loomed so pervasively, Moynihan warned his colleagues, that "If you were ever going to have anything like an equal Negro community you are going to have to give them unequal treatment."[29] Moynihan's analysis of the special nature of black poverty, and his call for affirmative national action to produce genuine equality of condition, found their way straight into LBJ's Howard University speech.

Before Watts, neither Johnson's call for a new phase in civil rights policy nor Moynihan's background report aroused much concern. After the riot, however, the controversial report became public, not through official publication but through a series of leaks and rumors. Journalists Rowland Evans and Robert Novak published an incendiary column, describing Moynihan's proposed programs for black neighborhoods as ransom money to forestall further riots. "The implied message of the Moynihan report," Evans and Novak reported, "is that ending discrimination is not nearly enough for the Negro. But what is enough? . . . The phrase 'preferential treatment' implies a solution far afield from the American dream. The white majority," the columnists concluded ominously, and prophetically, "would never accept it."[30]

Neither, it turned out, would the civil rights community or liberal circles among Moynihan's former academic colleagues. Or rather, they accepted the need for accelerated government action to promote genuine racial equality but rejected Moynihan's diagnosis and prescription. They accused Moynihan of blaming the victims of bigotry rather than their oppressors, of ignoring and patronizing the real achievements of black culture. African American leaders understood the Moynihan report as a serious insult. One critic claimed that it proved that the war on poverty really amounted to a war on the poor: "The militants of the new 'war' look for the enemy and find him all too often in the personal attributes of the poor." These critics asserted that Moynihan and LBJ found black families "disintegrated" and their communities "unstable" because they expected them to resemble white, middle-class families; they admitted only one "normal" standard for everyone.[31]

Radical writers and activists condemned Johnson and his fellow liberals for their assimilationist stance. For even though LBJ had tempered his universalist vision so as to view black poverty as a unique phenomenon, he still maintained faith in assimilation, in admitting everyone into what he called the "promise of America."[32] For nearly half a century, liberals like LBJ had attempted to erase distinctions between people — to portray the assertion of difference as invidious. Appeals to the "minimum American standard of living" or the "basic rights of every American" expressed this commitment, however well or poorly realized it was in fact. But during the late 1960s, many New Left intellectuals, stimulated by the rise of black nationalism, challenged this universalist philosophy, supplanting it with a renewed emphasis on cultural diversity. These radical critics charged that while Johnson and other liberals spoke about national unity and a common destiny, they really sought to whiten everyone, to stamp out cultural differences, to enforce conformity to a dominant white, male, middle-class system of values. The Moynihan report became exhibit number one in this indictment. It labeled black family structure deviant and black behavior pathological, it sought racial equality on exclusively white terms, and it did not respect the integrity and legitimacy of African American values and mores as a distinctive culture.

At the same time, white and black radicals increasingly rejected Johnson's portrait of the Great Society, viewing his liberal vision of the American dream as a cruel deception. Leftist critics of the Johnson administration saw the Moynihan report, along with the escalating war in Vietnam, as evidence of liberalism's fatal flaw, its unwillingness and inability to foment genuine, fundamental social change. The outcry over the Moynihan report whittled away Johnson's constituency on the left, just as Watts and white backlash were eroding support for civil rights on the right.

Amid the storm of racial tension, Johnson continued to pilot his program, pushing ahead through a narrowing channel of rocks and shoals. "I can think of nothing more dangerous, more divisive, or more self-destructive than the effort to prey on what is called 'white backlash,' " he asserted. But LBJ simultaneously denounced rioting and the black militants who hailed the uprisings as first seeds of a racial revolution: "The leaders of those disorders are just as bigoted in their own way as those who now seek to exploit white backlash."[33] Amid rising fears of crime and disorder, Johnson reluctantly supported an anticrime bill, which contained elements he opposed. And after Newark and Detroit, he became vociferous in his condemnation of rioters. "Let there be no mistake about it," he told the nation in a televised address, "the looting, arson, plunder and pillage which have occurred are not part of civil rights protest. . . . That is crime—and crime must be dealt with forcefully, and swiftly, and certainly—under law."[34]

But while LBJ pledged to restore law and order, he refused to "settle for order that is imposed by the muzzle of a gun." He insisted that "the only genuine, long-range solution for what has happened lies in an attack—mounted at every level—upon the conditions that breed despair and violence." He excoriated the Congress for slowing his Great Society program, chastising the legislature for finding the money to save baby calves from worms when it refused funds to save baby boys and girls from "rats which prowl in dark alleys and tenements."[35]

The Johnson administration pressed ahead with its new stage in civil rights policy, even as its leader became preoccupied with the fighting in Vietnam and in the nation's cities. In 1966 and 1967, LBJ introduced new legislation in the Congress. The proposed Civil Rights Acts of 1966 and 1967 focused on open housing, guaranteeing qualified renters and buyers freedom from discrimination and access to any neighborhood without regard to race. But the Congress, less liberal after the 1966 elections because white backlash had increased Republican and conservative Democratic strength, balked. The coalition of Republicans and northern Democrats that coalesced to force integration on the recalcitrant South frayed in the face of an open-housing law targeted at northern landlords and homeowners. Revitalized, the Republicans saw the bill as a potent campaign issue — warning that "LBJ's bureaucrats" would surround the country and force owners to sell to African Americans.[36] Still, Johnson pushed hard, and in early 1968, competing versions of the bill meandered through the House and Senate, with no indication that their differences could be reconciled, that a real law would emerge.

Then, in April 1968, a white ex-convict assassinated Martin Luther King, Jr., in Memphis, Tennessee. "The President wants you to know his prayers are with you," LBJ's assistant told King's father in Georgia on the morning after the murder. "Oh, no," Daddy King replied. "My prayers are with the President."[37] The elder King spoke prophetically. As news of the murder spread, riots erupted in 130 cities. Forty-six people died and twenty-six hundred fires ignited, causing over $100 million in damage. The government deployed one hundred and thirty thousand troops to quiet the streets. The worst violence occurred in Washington, D.C. Just a mile from the White House, on 14th Street NW, one man captured the rage of America when he warned, "This is it, baby. The shit is going to hit the fan. We ought to burn this place down."[38] In the aftermath of the assassination, the House immediately adopted the Senate's version of the open-housing law without amendment. Johnson signed it the following day. Later, Johnson reflected that Martin Luther King, Jr., had bought the law, for which LBJ had worked more than two years, with his life.

The Open Housing Act marked the last great legislative triumph of LBJ's civil rights policy. But new legislation did not so much blaze the trail from nondiscrimination to affirmative action as did expanded, transformed enforcement of the laws. The Equal Employment Opportunity Commission (EEOC), the agency established to administer the civil rights acts, opened its doors in July 1965. The EEOC began its life as a reactive pussycat; it could not move proactively to ensure broad compliance with the laws; it could only respond to complaints filed by individuals. If it suspected an institution of discrimination, it could only wait passively for someone to complain. This case-by-case, "retail" style of enforcement declawed the EEOC. The process proved so cumbersome that by 1967 the EEOC faced a severe backlog; it was taking more than two years to investigate complaints even though the Civil Rights Act required that the agency resolve all complaints within sixty days. The EEOC idly slogged through its enormous caseload as racial violence and the pressure for constructive action intensified.

In 1966 and 1967, the administration tried to toughen the enfeebled EEOC, but the legislation it proposed stalled on Capitol Hill. Instead, the EEOC expanded its powers without statutory authority, interpreting its mandate very broadly and hoping that the courts would uphold its loose interpretation of existing law. Specifically, the EEOC shifted from an intent-based to a results-based measure of discrimination. Initially, the commission deferred action unless it could prove a party guilty of conscious, intentional racial discrimination. If a school, business, union, or public facility excluded minorities or women, the EEOC refused to intervene unless the offending institution had clearly intended that result. In the late 1960s, however, the EEOC changed tacks; it interpreted "constructive effects of discrimination" as sufficient cause for redress even if no one could prove the racial imbalance intentional. The EEOC, for example, would void admission standards that effectively barred nearly all women or minorities from an organization whether or not the requirements had been designed to do so. The Commission then moved from a "retail" to a "wholesale" mode of enforcement, setting integration targets and guidelines for businesses, labor unions, and schools. It advised organizations to recruit underrepresented minorities, to initiate affirmative action programs lest they be investigated by the EEOC and cited for violations of the civil rights laws.[39]

The EEOC's interventionist, proactive stance reflected the new direction outlined by the Moynihan report and the Howard University address. The concern with unequal results regardless of intent signaled a commitment not only to equality of opportunity but to greater equality of condition. It required heightened attention to group-based rights and remedies, a shift away from the government's traditional focus on individual complaints and individual liberties. This marked a new phase in the evolution of American liberalism. The federal government would not merely redress the grievances of specific women or minorities, people who had been victims of overt discrimination; it would assure the fair representation of those groups, as groups, in all arenas of American life. This shift implied broader, more vigilant government action on all fronts—not merely police officers prohibiting certain proscribed acts but an armada of statisticians, analysts, and bureaucrats requiring specific procedures and decisions.

The Supreme Court under Chief Justice Earl Warren ratified and accelerated this growth of proactive government. The Warren Court had taken the lead on social justice in the 1950s, striking down racial segregation in the *Brown* decision. But during the 1960s, after the addition of Johnson appointees Thurgood Marshall and Abe Fortas, the Court became the judicial analogue of Great Society liberalism. In a series of controversial decisions, the Court mandated interventionist policies to include the disfranchised in the full blessings of American life and to safeguard the rights of previously dispossessed groups, including criminal defendants, the poor, and racial minorities.

## LBJ AND CIVIL RIGHTS

The upshot of LBJ's legislative, legal, and administrative actions was a profound shift in national social policy. Johnson helped smash the system of Jim Crow, tugging his native South into the national mainstream. Johnson also began efforts to relieve the insidious, informal racial discrimination in northern cities. "When all of the returns are in," African American novelist Ralph Ellison concluded, "perhaps President Johnson will have to settle for being recognized as the greatest American President for the poor and for the Negroes, but that, as I see it, is a very great honor indeed."[40]

Johnson's civil rights policy proved more far-reaching than even Ellison suspected. Bolstered by the Supreme Court, the Johnson administration unleashed a rights revolution, as government seeped into every nook and cranny of American life and federal regulations affected the everyday lives of American citizens in countless, previously unimagined ways. Throughout the late 1960s and into the 1970s, federal agencies adopted the EEOC's strategy of protecting broad-based rights—moving proactively to ensure not only freedom from racial discrimination, but also health and safety, fair business practices, and environmental protection. On the model of the EEOC, the nation created numerous new agencies that promulgated wide-ranging rules for the entire nation and responded to the concerns of various interest groups. The "new social regulation," as economists and public administration experts have termed the explosion of administrative government in the 1960s and 1970s, arose along with the civil rights revolution.

Johnson's civil rights policies also permanently altered the nation's political landscape. The Republican party won over the white South; only once in the three decades after 1964 did a Democratic presidential candidate win a majority of the votes in the South and never did one claim a majority of the white votes. Moreover, while most northern white

Democrats supported the end of southern Jim Crow, the later stages of the civil rights movement hit too close to home. When Martin Luther King, Jr., moved to Chicago in 1966 and began "freedom marches" for jobs and housing into blue-collar white neighborhoods, he met resistance, rocks, and racist jeers.

The Watts riots and the urban explosions that followed them stunned many white Americans, many of whom had supported the civil rights acts and considered themselves liberal Democrats. After 1965, heroic images of nonviolent black protesters against the Ku Klux Klan and Sheriff Clark dissolved into fear-inspiring visions of militants and rioters, arousing alarm about law and order that turned many northern whites from liberalism. Affirmative action drove away still more; eventually, it provoked protests against "reverse discrimination," vindicating Evans and Novak's warning that white Americans would reject "preferential treatment." Johnson lost the New Deal coalition, as many voters who supported FDR, Truman, and Kennedy defected over civil rights.

Nor could LBJ find any solace on the political left. Many civil rights leaders scorned his achievements as half-measures, which painted over the walls of racism but never demolished them. At the same time, many young Americans, black and white, decided that racism and poverty betrayed deep, essential failings in American society. They were not some small aberration, stains on an otherwise noble system that required only presidential leadership and legislative reform to erase. The black revolution, as Martin Luther King, Jr., put it, was "exposing evils that are rooted deeply in the whole structure of our society," evils that manifested themselves in the disfranchisement of black citizens in Mississippi, the repression of student protesters in Berkeley, the bombing of villages in Vietnam.[41]

Especially Vietnam. Over the course of his presidency, leftist critics noted that Johnson allocated twice as much federal funding to missile research as to the war on poverty, that the conflict in Asia was swallowing up the Great Society. "We are fighting an immoral war," Martin Luther King, Jr., declared (see Document 9). "Yet we remain helpless to end the war, to feed the hungry, to make brotherhood a reality."

King's endorsement of the antiwar movement signaled the burgeoning influence of the New Left, the loosely organized coterie of college students, disenchanted youths, intellectuals, and cultural innovators that took shape during the 1960s. New Left radicals distrusted not only President Johnson but also the entire liberal establishment he represented. Seeking a more ethical and participatory form of politics, the student movement viewed liberal reformers as ineffective, hypocritical, and morally bankrupt.

While liberals like LBJ sought reform through electoral politics, executive orders, and legislative mandates, the New Left embraced direct action— marches, community organization, people changing their own lives. Student radicals mocked liberals' faith in established institutions, in their ability to effect change and give voice to the aspirations of ordinary citizens. Liberal reforms, the radicals insisted, never challenged the oppressiveness and cruelty of American life; indeed, by gentling their aspect and beautifying their appearances, the reforms only perpetuated injustices. "For the crisis of our time," one radical professor insisted, "the slow workings of American reform, the limitations on protest and disobedience set by liberals . . . are simply not adequate."[42]

Johnson heard these protests. He knew that the war was dividing the nation, dominating his schedule, compromising his great plans, and killing his presidency. Johnson understood the war's costs, but he could not, would not resist them. His hopes for a liberal reconstruction of America, for a Great Society, for a record of achievement exceeding all other presidents, were rotting in the jungles of Southeast Asia.

## NOTES

[1] *Report of the National Advisory Commission on Civil Disorders* (New York: Bantam, 1968), 1.

[2] *Public Papers of the Presidents of the United States: Lyndon B. Johnson, 1963–1969*, 11 vols. (Washington, D.C.: Government Printing Office, 1964–1969), 1966, 572.

[3] Godfrey Hodgson, *America in Our Time* (New York: Vintage, 1976), 158–59.

[4] *Papers*, 1966, 573.

[5] Joseph A. Califano, Jr., *The Triumph and Tragedy of Lyndon Johnson* (New York: Simon and Schuster, 1991), 11.

[6] Chana K. Lee, "A Passionate Pursuit of Justice," (Ph.D. diss., UCLA, 1993), 296–97, 324–25.

[7] Robert A. Caro, *The Years of Lyndon Johnson: The Path to Power* (New York: Alfred A. Knopf, 1982), xvi–xvii. Eric F. Goldman, *The Tragedy of Lyndon Johnson* (New York: Dell, 1969), 369.

[8] Ibid., xv.

[9] Rowland Evans and Robert Novak, *Lyndon B. Johnson: The Exercise of Power* (New York: Signet Books, 1966), 519.

[10] Goldman, *Tragedy*, 373.

[11] See Document 6.

[12] Ibid. Califano, *Triumph and Tragedy*, 56.

[13] *Papers*, 1966, 840–43.

[14] Joseph A. Califano, interview with Doris Kearns, quoted in Doris Kearns, *Lyndon Johnson and the American Dream* (New York: Harper and Row, 1976), 319.

[15] Ibid. Califano, *Triumph and Tragedy*, 59–62.

[16] *Papers*, 1965, 881–82.

[17] Allen J. Matusow, *The Unraveling of America* (New York: Harper and Row, 1984), 361–62.

[18] Hodgson, *America in Our Time,* 266.

[19] Laura Kalman, *Abe Fortas: A Biography* (New Haven: Yale University Press, 1990), 307.

[20] Bayard Rustin, "From Protest to Politics," in Francis Broderick and August Meier, eds., *Negro Protest Thought in the Twentieth Century* (Indianapolis: Bobbs-Merrill, 1965), 411.

[21] Martin Luther King, Jr., "A Testament of Hope," in Clayborne Carson et al., eds., *Eyes on the Prize: A Reader and Guide* (New York: Penguin, 1987), 234.

[22] Lyndon B. Johnson, *The Vantage Point* (New York: Popular Library, 1971), 167.

[23] Matusow, *Unraveling of America,* 362.

[24] Johnson, *Vantage Point,* 167.

[25] See Document 8.

[26] Ibid.

[27] The term "culture of poverty" derived from the work of a number of urban sociologists. Prominent among them was Oscar Lewis, author of *La Vida* (New York: Vintage, 1965).

[28] Hugh Davis Graham, *Civil Rights and the Presidency* (New York: Oxford University Press, 1992), 105.

[29] Hodgson, *America in Our Time,* 263.

[30] Ibid., 267.

[31] Elinor Graham, "The Politics of Poverty," in Marvin Gettleman and David Mermelstein, eds., *Great Society Reader* (New York: Vintage Books, 1967), 224.

[32] See Document 6.

[33] *Papers,* 1966, 1340–41.

[34] *Papers,* 1967, 721.

[35] Ibid., 722.

[36] Johnson, *Vantage Point,* 177–78.

[37] Ibid., 175–76.

[38] Hodgson, *America in Our Time,* 361.

[39] Graham, *Civil Rights and the Presidency,* 102–03, 118–20.

[40] Jack Valenti, *A Very Human President* (New York: Pocket Books, 1977), 312.

[41] King, "A Testimony of Hope," 235.

[42] Kalman, *Abe Fortas,* 292.

# 6

## "That Bitch of a War": LBJ and Vietnam

"Hey, hey, LBJ, how many boys did you kill today?" taunted antiwar protesters outside the White House throughout 1967 and 1968.[1] The chants followed Johnson wherever he traveled; by the end of 1967, the embattled president rarely left the sanctuary of the Oval Office. Lyndon Johnson's presidency, his plans for a Great Society, and his quest for national unity and universal adulation all sank and rotted in the rain forests and rice paddies of Southeast Asia.

"If not for Vietnam," Ambassador Averell Harriman reflected in 1972, Lyndon Johnson would "have been the greatest President ever." Harriman's regret-tinged words pervade nearly all memoirs of Johnson's career. Few disagree that Vietnam formed, in the words of one team of journalists, "the malignant cancer of the Great Society, somber and oppressive. It infected all else in 1966—a bloody, insoluble dilemma that did not lend itself to the brilliant weapons of power developed by Lyndon Johnson during thirty-five years in politics."[2]

For his part, Lyndon Johnson had never dreamed of becoming preoccupied with a foreign war. Early in his presidency, opponents teased that LBJ was not going to bother with foreign policy and even Lady Bird believed her husband ill-fitted to international affairs. "I just hope that foreign problems do not keep mounting," Lady Bird implored in 1965. "They do not represent Lyndon's kind of Presidency."[3]

Nearly every Johnson-watcher, from the president's wife to his arch enemies, believed him to be out of his element in foreign relations. One newspaperman described LBJ as a Mississippi gambler lost on the high seas—"the riverboat man . . . a swashbuckling master of the political midstream—but only in the crowded, well-traveled familiar inland waterways of domestic politics. He had no taste and scant preparation for the deep waters of foreign policy. . . . He was king of the river and a stranger to the open sea."[4] In making war and negotiating peace, Johnson lacked the detailed command of policy and, especially, the intimate and incisive personal knowledge of his adversaries that made him such a legislative miracle worker in domestic affairs.

Outside the nation's borders the political master seemingly lost his touch. He had to rely on the advice of experts, to navigate by abstract principles rather than by the sure instincts about what really worked that guided him so well in the Congress. Often he misapplied tried-and-true techniques of domestic political combat to international problems, where they were hopelessly out of place. He proposed a giant dam-building project for the Mekong River in Southeast Asia. He envisioned the North Vietnamese leader Ho Chi Minh as an Asian version of Senator Richard Russell or labor union chief George Meany, a political rival he could bring to reason if only they could meet face-to-face. The war, Johnson insisted, would play out "like a filibuster—enormous resistance at first, then a steady whittling away, then Ho hurrying to get it over with."[5] But Johnson's genius for consensus—his ability to persuade—did not translate into foreign tongues; peoples engaged in revolutionary war, a long death struggle for self-rule, would not cut deals like George Meany, would not bow to the Johnson "Treatment" like Richard Russell.

Still, it is easy to exaggerate Johnson's weaknesses as warrior and diplomat. He was not entirely unprepared for world leadership; he had served as majority leader of the Senate, cooperating with President Eisenhower on cold war foreign policy, and he had chaired a congressional committee overseeing the Korean War. Johnson's personality, his peculiar talents and failings, certainly shaped his tragic course in Vietnam, but his assumptions and his decisions reflected a broad-based, widely accepted set of ideas about the United States's role in the world. After all, Johnson's predecessors had all expanded U.S. intervention in Vietnam; his advisers nearly unanimously recommended escalation of the conflict; and until 1968, most Americans supported the war. An instinct that allowed him to transcend the conventional wisdom—*that* was Johnson's gift in domestic politics. In international politics, he was not inept but utterly conventional, a creature of the cold war, an uncritical adherent of liberal anticommunism.

Johnson and his fellow liberals had opposed Senator Joseph McCarthy in the 1950s but had never questioned the monolithic evil of international communism and the United States's duty to defend free peoples everywhere from communist encroachment. Cold war liberals depicted themselves as a "vital center," steering a course between irrational McCarthyites, who sought to roll back reform at home and found communists under every rock, and weak-kneed appeasers, who sought accommodation with the Soviet Union. Liberals believed that an aggressive, bullying

Soviet Union posed the gravest threat to peace and freedom—that the United States had to contain Soviet and Chinese expansion, to apply counterforce wherever the communists sought to extend their power.

Johnson and his principal advisers viewed the world through this ideological prism, this restricted set of lenses. They saw the war in Vietnam as just one battle in a larger struggle against the blood-red tide of communism. "The choice is not simply whether to continue our efforts to keep South Vietnam free and independent," Secretary of Defense Robert McNamara insisted in 1965, "but rather whether to continue our struggle to halt Communist expansion in Asia."[6] Dean Rusk, LBJ's secretary of state, shared this mindset; he viewed the enemy in Vietnam as proxies for the Soviet Union and, especially, "Red China."

So entrenched were these beliefs that contrary evidence would not shake them. Policymakers continued to decry a uniform, unitary international communism even after they learned of the split between China and the Soviet Union. They believed defeat in Vietnam would unleash a communist rampage across East Asia, even when CIA reports suggested otherwise.

Johnson's own anticommunism was not particularly rigid or virulent. On the contrary, he truly hoped for some form of rapprochement with the Soviet Union, some peaceful settlement of the cold war. In his memoirs, he listed the treaty on nonproliferation of nuclear weapons, signed with the Soviets on July 1, 1968, as among his most important accomplishments. Johnson concluded seven other agreements with the Soviets, on issues ranging from cutbacks in production of fissionable nuclear materials to establishing commercial air service between the two nations.

But Johnson's experience with World War II and the cold war taught him that aggression must be repulsed and communism contained, and his memories of McCarthyism made him fear charges of softness in foreign affairs. The communist victory in China had crippled Harry Truman's presidency; LBJ could not risk the loss of Vietnam. "I knew from the start," Johnson told Doris Kearns in 1970, "that I was bound to be crucified either way I moved. If I left the woman I really loved—the Great Society—in order to get involved with that bitch of a war on the other side of the world, then I would lose everything at home. All my programs. . . . But if I left that war and let the Communists take over South Vietnam, then I would be seen as a coward and my nation would be seen as an appeaser and we would both find it impossible to accomplish anything for anybody anywhere on the entire globe."[7] Johnson could not shake his own and the nation's cold war mindset, could not cut America's ties to the losing struggle in Vietnam.

**"There's Money Enough To Support Both Of You —
Now, Doesn't That Make You Feel Better?"**

In 1967, editorial cartoonist Herblock captures the tension between the Vietnam War and the Great Society, as the war diverted the president's attention and the nation's resources away from Johnson's domestic agenda.

## "A FAT, JUICY WORM": THE UNITED STATES AND VIETNAM, 1945–1963

Six American presidents expanded U.S. intervention in Vietnam, each of them reluctantly and inexorably sinking the nation deeper into a political and military morass. The first—Franklin D. Roosevelt—sensed from the start that the United States might be aligning itself on the wrong side of history. During World War II, the Japanese army had occupied the French colony of Indochina, the pendulous peninsula jutting off the Chinese mainland that makes up present-day Vietnam, Laos, and Cambodia. After defeating the Japanese, FDR hoped to lead Indochina toward independence. He disdained colonialism and particularly detested French behavior in Indochina, condemning the French as "poor colonizers" who had "badly mismanaged" Vietnam and its neighbors.[8] The French, however, determined to retake their colonies, and America's British allies, jealous of their own overseas empire, forced FDR to retreat from his program for decolonization in Asia.

A few months after FDR's death, the Vietnamese rebel leader Ho Chi Minh declared independence from France. Ho quoted Thomas Jefferson at the ceremony, the Vietnamese band played "The Star Spangled Banner," and the rebel leader sent a series of letters to President Harry Truman, begging U.S. assistance in his struggle against the French. Truman ignored Ho's appeals, instead approving the return of French troops to Vietnam and financing French efforts to suppress Ho's rebellion. The emerging cold war in Europe, especially the Soviet takeover of Eastern Europe, had reordered American priorities in foreign affairs. The defeat of Germany and Japan had left Communist Russia as the United States's most formidable rival. Fearing that economic hardship and political instability in France might provide fertile ground for communist subversion in Western Europe, the Truman administration decided against stripping France of its Asian empire. Maintaining in Paris "a friendly government to assist in the furtherance of our aims in Europe," the State Department decided, must "take precedence over steps looking toward the realization of our objectives in Indochina."[9]

At the same time, Truman's passionate anticommunism led him to distrust Ho Chi Minh. Although an avowed Marxist, Ho had appealed for U.S. support and proposed opening Vietnam to American trade and leasing the U.S. Navy a base at Cam Ranh Bay. American officials in Vietnam could find no evidence of direct Soviet ties with Ho's movement and reported that the rebel leader had become "the symbol of nationalism and the struggle for freedom to the overwhelming majority of the population." But Truman and his top aides remained unflinching; in the superheated atmosphere of the early cold war they could not, in the words of one State Department document, "afford to assume that Ho is anything but Moscow-directed."[10]

Even with Truman's support, however, the French fared badly. Ho's rebels hid in the countryside, avoiding open battles with the better-equipped colonial army while harassing French outposts with frequent guerrilla raids. "If ever the tiger pauses," Ho explained, likening his guerrillas to the great cat, "the elephant will impale him on his mighty tusks. But the tiger will not pause, and the elephant will die of exhaustion and loss of blood."[11] Just as Ho predicted, the elephantine French army bled slowly, and Truman was forced to step up support for the colonial regime.

Dwight Eisenhower continued and enlarged Truman's policies in Southeast Asia. The Eisenhower administration regarded Ho Chi Minh as an agent of international communism and labeled Indochina a vital interest of the United States—a linchpin in the global defense of freedom. In April 1954, Ike vividly illustrated the significance of Vietnam by comparing the nations of Asia to a row of dominos: "You have a row of dominos set up, you knock over the first one, and what will happen to the last one is the certainty that it will go over very quickly." If the levee broke in Indochina, the communist tide would roll over Thailand, Burma, Malaysia, even the resource-rich islands of Indonesia. Determined to avoid direct U.S. intervention, Ike bankrolled the French in Vietnam, taking over more than three-quarters of the cost of their war effort. He called this "the cheapest way" to protect American interests in Asia.[12]

The cheap, makeshift patch would not hold. In 1954, Ho Chi Minh dealt the French a stunning defeat at Dien Bien Phu. With a French collapse imminent, Eisenhower planned American military operations and warned congressional leaders that he might send in U.S. forces to relieve the French. But Ike held off, especially after the British refused to join in the operation and Senate leaders, including Lyndon Johnson, warned against another war in Asia. Meanwhile, the fall of Dien Bien Phu shifted international attention to the peace conference at Geneva, where Ho Chi Minh reluctantly accepted a temporary partition of Vietnam. Ho's forces would control the urbanized northern part of the country and the French puppet governor would rule the rich agricultural region of South Vietnam until internationally supervised national elections in 1956 reunified the country.

The United States refused to endorse the Geneva agreements and immediately moved to build a strong, anticommunist regime in South Vietnam. The Eisenhower administration eased out the French, sent military advisers to train the South Vietnamese army, and generously supported the tyrannical regime of President Ngo Dinh Diem. A Catholic by belief, Diem persecuted the nation's Buddhist majority and won little sympathy among the peasantry. Ruling with an iron hand, Diem and his family—he filled three of his six cabinet appointments with his own brothers—brought a measure of economic prosperity and political stability to South Vietnam. Not enough, however, according to U.S. intelligence estimates, to prevent Ho Chi Minh from winning the scheduled elections. With strong support from American leaders, Diem refused to hold the elections. In response, Ho's partisans in the South reopened their armed struggle. Calling themselves the National Liberation Front (NLF) and pejoratively christened the Vietcong (for Vietnamese communists) by Diem, the insurgents (with the support of Ho's communist regime in North Vietnam) turned on Diem the same hit-and-run tactics that had frustrated the French.

President Kennedy and Vice President Johnson inherited this unstable situation when they took office in 1961. Kennedy had already committed himself to the defense of South Vietnam. As a senator, JFK had called Vietnam "the cornerstone of the Free World in Southeast Asia, the keystone in the arch, the finger in the dike." Vietnam is "our offspring," Kennedy had admitted in 1956, "we cannot abandon it, we cannot ignore its needs."[13] President Kennedy's early setbacks in Cuba, Laos, and Berlin made defense of Vietnam all the more urgent; he could not afford another defeat. Vietnam became a test of will for JFK, a demonstration to enemies and allies that the United States would stand and fight against communism. Although a few of his Asia experts recommended disengagement from Vietnam, Kennedy rejected any negotiated settlement with the communists.

He also refused to dispatch ground troops, opting instead to send equipment, economic assistance, and several thousand military advisers. Undersecretary of State George Ball warned Kennedy against the adventure. "Within five years," Ball prophesied, "we'll have three hundred thousand men in the paddies and jungles and never find them again. That was the French experience. Vietnam is the worst possible terrain both from a physical and a political point of view." But Kennedy and all of his major advisers believed that the "military advisers," led by the elite forces newly formed into the Green Berets, could hold the fort in Vietnam, at least until the United States could reform Diem and stabilize the South Vietnamese government. "George, I always thought you were one of the brightest guys in town," JFK replied to Ball's ominous prediction, "but this time you're just crazier than hell."[14]

Kennedy gradually increased the number of American soldiers in Vietnam from 948 in November 1961 to over sixteen thousand at the time of his death two years later. In the words of one adviser,

> President Kennedy took the decision to raise the ante through a system of advisers, pilots and supplementary military personnel. . . . In effect, it was decided that the United States would take those additional actions that appeared clearly required to meet the situation, not knowing for sure whether these actions would in fact prove to be adequate, trying . . . not to cross the bridge of still further action, and hoping strongly that what was being taken would prove sufficient.[15]

Kennedy resisted military requests for large numbers of troops. He distrusted the generals' ceaseless demands for ever more men and ammunition. But most of all, Kennedy hesitated because of President Diem's increasingly corrupt and authoritarian behavior. In May 1963, soldiers fired into a group of Buddhists demonstrating against Diem's restrictions on their religious practices. Eight Buddhists died in the massacre, which set off scores of protests around the country. In June, a protesting Buddhist monk immolated himself in downtown Saigon, the capital city of South Vietnam. Pictures of the monk evoked widespread sympathy for the Buddhist cause. The United States could not creditably defend freedom in South Vietnam by supporting so repressive a government. Secretary of State Dean Rusk quietly informed U.S. officials in Saigon that the president would support a military ouster of Diem as long as the coup "has a good chance of succeeding but plans no direct involvement of U.S. armed forces."[16] As Kennedy maintained this see-no-evil pose, his men in Saigon cooperated in the removal and brutal murder of Diem and his associates. Three weeks later, Kennedy himself was assassinated.

In later years, many Americans speculated about Kennedy's ultimate course in Vietnam, suggesting that JFK would not have escalated the war. The hard evidence on this point is distressingly scanty. We know for certain that JFK mistrusted the military—that he questioned the Pentagon's demands for more and more troops and believed that a modest commitment of U.S. personnel could save South Vietnam from communism. We also know that JFK was deeply embarrassed by the depredations of South Vietnam's tyrannical President Ngo Dinh Diem. Kennedy could not fight for the freedom of South Vietnam while it remained in the hands of a cruel, corrupt dictator. But if Kennedy hoped to disengage from Vietnam, he kept those plans to himself (indeed, no one ever suggested that Kennedy would have opposed escalation until years later, after the war became unpopular), and all of JFK's aides, including his brother Bobby, supported military intervention in 1964 and 1965. By the time of his death, Kennedy had come to recognize the intractable problems Vietnam posed for U.S. policy, but he still found it impossible to pull out. In a nationally televised interview, he told Walter Cronkite, "I don't agree with those who say we should withdraw. That would be a great mistake." We had struggled hard to protect Europe, and, Kennedy continued, "We also have to participate—we may not like it—in the defense of Asia." A week later, JFK told NBC news anchors Chet Huntley and David Brinkley that he believed in the domino theory: "I believe it. I think that the struggle is close enough. China is so large, looms so high just beyond the frontiers, that if South Viet-Nam went, it would not only give them an improved geographic position for a guerrilla assault on Malaya but would also give the impression that the wave of the future in Southeast Asia was China and the Communists."[17] Those were not the words of a president trying to prepare the American people for withdrawal from Vietnam. They were rather the words of a man who had decided he would not—could not—lose Vietnam on his watch, even if he recognized and rued the prospects of a protracted, painful war.

Thus, Lyndon Johnson received an ambiguous legacy from JFK—both a determination to keep the war small and an even stronger commitment not to lose South Vietnam to the communists. Johnson even inherited all of JFK's advisers—the very men who masterminded the escalation of the war in Vietnam. Worse yet, he faced the aftermath of Diem's bloody death. As vice president, LBJ had opposed Kennedy's efforts to replace Diem, insisting nine years of supporting him left us no viable alternative. He regarded Diem's assassination as a horrible blunder; having removed Diem, the United States became responsible for his successors however unsavory or incompetent. Complicity in Diem's death tied America not to a particular government, or to a democratizing regime, but to South Vietnam itself, whoever led it.

The day after he took office, President Johnson received Henry Cabot Lodge, the U.S. ambassador to South Vietnam. Hearing Lodge's bleak report on the situation in Saigon, LBJ remembered feeling like a fish that had just "grabbed a big juicy worm with a right sharp hook in the middle of it."[18] But Johnson determined to defend South Vietnam from communism and to continue the policies of his predecessors. He ordered Lodge to "go back and tell those generals in Saigon that Lyndon Johnson intends to stand by our word. . . . "[19] He would not be the one to lose Vietnam.

## AMERICANIZING THE WAR, 1963–1965

Like a crafty trout, LBJ played the line during his first year in office, neither swallowing the bait nor shaking the Vietnam hook. During 1964, he concentrated on domestic affairs and, especially, on defeating Barry Goldwater in the November elections. He left day-to-day management of the war to Secretary of Defense Robert McNamara, whom Johnson called "the ablest man I ever met," National Security Adviser McGeorge Bundy, a Kennedy intimate, and Secretary of State Dean Rusk, a veteran cold warrior whose unswerving loyalty Johnson particularly prized.[20] On the infrequent occasions when Johnson publicly discussed Vietnam, he usually contrasted his own restrained approach with Goldwater's calls for expanding the fighting. "Some others are eager to enlarge the conflict," he told a

New York crowd in an oblique attack on his hawkish opponent. "They ask us to take reckless action. . . . Such action would offer no solution at all to the real problem of Vietnam."[21]

In fact, the major foreign crises of Johnson's first year-and-a-half in office emerged not in Southeast Asia but in Latin America. First, angry Panamanians took to the streets demanding control over the Panama Canal. Johnson rebuffed the protesters for months; he finally agreed to negotiate but offered no concessions. In the spring of 1965, Johnson sent U.S. Marines into the Dominican Republic in order to evacuate American citizens and prevent the triumph of revolutionaries whom Johnson believed harbored communist sympathies. In both cases, Johnson was determined to maintain American dominance over Latin America and to quiet criticism from hawks in the United States that he was too soft on communism. "If we can't clean up the Dominican Republic," Johnson asked, "what can we do in Vietnam?"[22]

Only once during the 1964 campaign did LBJ give Vietnam concerted attention. On August 2, 1964, the U.S. destroyer *Maddox* was patrolling in the Gulf of Tonkin, off the coast of North Vietnam. Returning from a reconnaissance mission, the *Maddox* was fired upon by North Vietnamese torpedo boats. Rather than pulling out of the danger zone, Johnson ordered a second destroyer to accompany the *Maddox* on its next mission. Two nights later, operating in stormy seas, the destroyers reported that they were under attack. To this day, no one knows for certain whether the second attack actually took place. A few days after the incident, Johnson himself questioned the authenticity of the report. "Hell," he told George Ball, "those dumb, stupid sailors were just shooting at flying fish."[23]

In any case, a few hours after the report from the Gulf of Tonkin, LBJ dispatched sixty-four American bombers on a reprisal raid over North Vietnam. Johnson also used the incident to request a congressional resolution authorizing him as commander-in-chief to "take all necessary measures to protect American troops and prevent further aggression in Vietnam."[24] The House of Representatives unanimously endorsed the resolution; in the Senate, a few members questioned the wisdom of granting the president such broad, unspecified authority, but only two senators actually voted against the resolution. Johnson's prompt, decisive response to the alleged attack in the Gulf of Tonkin proved a smashing success at home. Overnight, LBJ's approval rating in the Harris Poll soared from 42 to 72 percent.

With the Tonkin resolution in hand, LBJ stalled further action in Vietnam while he concentrated on defeating Goldwater. In the meantime, the military in Saigon and top civilian officials in the Pentagon became increasingly preoccupied with North Vietnam. This new focus reflected frustration with the losing struggle against the guerrillas in the South. Making war against a regular army—fighting the troops of an invading hostile state—posed a familiar challenge for the armed services; it was what they had done in Korea and World War II. The brass preferred such conventional war to an amorphous political struggle for the hearts and minds of villagers, waged against invisible enemies who stole out of the jungle and refused to stand and fight. For their part, McNamara and his aides assumed that the insurgents in the South operated entirely on the orders of the Hanoi government. A show of strength against North Vietnam would convince Hanoi to call off its minions in the South.

Accordingly, the Pentagon developed a plan for gradually intensified bombing of the North—an "Ouch Strategy" designed to inflict pain on Hanoi and demonstrate American determination to defend South Vietnam. Johnson harbored doubts about the bombing plan; "Generals know only two words—spend and bomb," he often complained. He questioned the efficacy of large-scale bombing and feared that taking the war to the North might provoke the Chinese to join the struggle. In December 1964, he told his ambassador in Vietnam, "I have never felt that this war will be won from the air. . . . "[25] But LBJ was soon convinced, especially because an air war would keep American casualties to a minimum. The administration merely awaited the right opportunity to begin the operation, code-named Rolling Thunder.

The moment arrived on February 6, 1965. Enemy mortars shelled the U.S. Air Force barracks at Pleiku. Eight American service men died in the attack, and more than one hundred were wounded. Johnson ordered immediate retaliatory raids against North Vietnam, personally selecting the targets as he pored over blow-up maps in the White House situation room. It was the beginning of an obsession for him (years later, accusations of indiscriminate bombing angered him because Johnson carefully selected military targets, hoping to minimize civilian casualties). It also launched the pattern of deception that would ultimately undermine his leadership. What was portrayed as retaliation, tit-for-tat raids, was quietly expanded into Rolling Thunder, even though the administration did not publicize its shift from reprisals to sustained attacks. A month later, Johnson landed two battalions of U.S. Marines, fifteen hundred men, to protect the U.S. air base in Da Nang. Soon the number of troops reached fifty thousand, engaging in active combat even though the administration maintained they were only defending U.S. military facilities. Johnson had explicitly approved the change of mission on April 1 and simultaneously ordered that the new policy be kept quiet.

Johnson still hoped to avoid full-scale Americanization of the war. On April 7, 1965, he delivered a major address at Johns Hopkins University, offering to negotiate a settlement with North Vietnam (see Document 10). Invoking the experience of Korea and World War II, Johnson painted the struggle in the familiar hues of liberal anticommunism, as the encroachment by an external invader on a free, sovereign nation. "North Viet-Nam has attacked the independent nation of South Viet-Nam. Its object is total conquest." Beyond that aggression lay another, darker reality—"the deepening shadow of Communist China." In contrast to the conquest-driven madness of Ho and Mao, Johnson declared, "We want nothing for ourselves, only that the people of South Viet-Nam be allowed to guide their own country in their own way. We will do everything necessary to reach that objective." And signaling his desire to minimize American involvement, he added, "We will do only what is absolutely necessary."[26]

If North Vietnam would cease and desist, would end its aggression against the South, Johnson would negotiate a just and lasting peace. He would even provide Indochina with a multibillion-dollar Mekong River project, a dam-building, power, and development scheme that would dwarf anything seen before in the United States. "Peace without conquest" translated Great Society liberalism into a diplomatic charter, the Pedernales into the Mekong, the Hill Country of central Texas into the highlands of central Vietnam. Johnson reiterated his faith in the effectiveness and benevolence of the U.S. government. Liberal activism had delivered the Hill Country from rapacious railroads and greedy utility companies, bringing opportunity and security to poor dirt farmers. It could do the same in Asia—stifling communist tyranny and promoting prosperity along the Mekong. "The ordinary men and women of North Viet-Nam and South Viet-Nam—of China and India—of Russia and America—are brave people," Johnson told the audience at Johns Hopkins. "They are filled with the same proportions of hate and fear, of love and hope. Most of them want the same things for themselves and their families."[27] Like a munificent uncle distributing polka dot ties and unsightly knickknacks to all his poor relations, LBJ promised all those things and more to the Vietnamese. This expansive vision had long animated LBJ's politics and had produced his greatest achievements. He never thought anyone might scorn his gifts, might resent his charity, might even doubt his good intentions. North Vietnam summarily dismissed Johnson's Mekong River project as a "bribe."[28] For Johnson, Hanoi's rejection of his plan proved that negotiating with communists was pointless.

Stepped-up military operations continued but to no avail. A June 1965 intelligence report concluded that U.S. air strikes against North Vietnam "have had no significantly harmful effects on popular morale."[29] In fact, the bombing improved morale—resentment against the raids won for the Communist government the loyalty and resolve of people previously indifferent to the regime and unenthusiastic about the war. Nor did Rolling Thunder cripple the enemy's military capacity; North Vietnam possessed few industrial facilities and bridges were quickly rebuilt. Under thick jungle cover, supply routes—often navigated on foot and by bicycle—remained open. The bombing even backfired in the United States, as Rolling Thunder became the lightning rod for intensified criticism of the war. Senate Majority Leader Mike Mansfield encouraged LBJ to stop the bombing and negotiate a peaceful solution to the conflict.

The time for decision had arrived. In a memo to the president, McGeorge Bundy confessed that "the prospect in Vietnam is grim. The energy and persistence of the Vietcong is astonishing. They can appear anywhere—at almost any time. They have accepted extraordinary losses and they come back for more." Defeat was inevitable without new U.S. action. Bundy admitted that the struggle would be long and arduous, but he offered Johnson no alternative. "There is no way of unloading the burden on the Vietnamese themselves, and there is no way of negotiating ourselves out of Vietnam which offers any serious promise."[30] The awful news pained LBJ; one night he turned to Lady Bird and complained, "I can't get out. I can't finish it with what I have got. So what the hell do I do?"[31]

By June 1965, Johnson could hold off a decision no longer. General William Childs Westmoreland, commander of U.S. forces in Vietnam, informed the White House that South Vietnam would collapse unless the United States immediately committed forty-four battalions of ground troops. Johnson felt trapped. He absolutely refused to lose South Vietnam, convinced it would spell disaster for his presidency, undercut all his other efforts, and ruin his political career (he was vexed, however unreasonably, by the nightmare of Bobby Kennedy blaming him for abandoning JFK's promise to protect the South Vietnamese). Yet he was astute enough to mistrust the military's request for a massive injection of troops.

Johnson convened his advisers for renewed discussion of the issue. Although the president had already made up his mind against losing South Vietnam, LBJ wanted to forge a consensus on the decision to escalate the ground war. He also wanted to delay decisions on Vietnam while the voting rights and Medicare bills struggled through the Congress. A series of crucial meetings ratified the decision to escalate (see Document 11). Secretary McNamara laid out the case for intensifying the war. At the end of his presentation, Johnson looked around the table; everyone except

George Ball seconded McNamara's recommendation. The meeting adjourned for lunch, then devoted the afternoon to Ball's lonely dissent. Ball's argument resonated deeply with Johnson—he too doubted that more men would carry the day, he too worried about fighting a white man's war in Asia and defending corrupt regimes in Saigon, but he could not accept Ball's argument that he could pull out without damaging America's standing in the world.

At the end of July, Johnson issued the orders that would determine the future course of the war and of his career. He approved the immediate deployment of fifty thousand additional troops to South Vietnam and privately committed to send fifty thousand more before the end of the year. He also instructed General Westmoreland to Americanize the war—he allowed U.S. forces to operate independent of South Vietnamese units. In so doing, Johnson made an open-ended promise to assume the burden of defending South Vietnam at whatever cost necessary. Convinced that all-out bombing against the North would bring the Chinese into the war, he vetoed the Joint Chiefs' request to bomb near Vietnam's border with China; but Johnson approved Westmoreland's requests for saturation bombing of the South and gradually intensified air raids against the North.

Even though Johnson took these fateful steps, he decided not to place the country on a war footing. He refused to declare a national emergency, to awaken the patriotic instincts for all-out war, to call up the military reserves, or to ask for a tax increase to pay for the war. With the Medicare and voting rights bills before Congress, with the Great Society still unfinished, LBJ would not convert to a war footing, would not sacrifice his domestic agenda. Franklin Roosevelt and Woodrow Wilson had both become war presidents; they had abandoned the New Deal and the New Freedom to achieve military victories. Johnson would not make that sacrifice. He took the crucial decisions for war but misled both the Congress and the American people about the gravity of the steps he was taking; he instructed his aides, in fact, to escalate the war in "a low-keyed manner" so as to "avoid undue concern and excitement in the Congress and in domestic public opinion."[32]

## "LYNDON JOHNSON'S WAR"

During the fateful July meetings, Johnson had questioned the military's battle plan for the war in Vietnam. But General Earle Wheeler, chairman of the Joint Chiefs of Staff, arrogantly brushed aside the doubts of his commander-in-chief (see Document 11). Johnson's fears proved far more accurate than Wheeler's confident swagger. By 1967, the United States had deployed more than half-a-million combat troops in Vietnam, nearly half of its combat-ready battalions. U.S. aircraft had dropped more bombs in Indochina than in all the theaters of World War II combined. In that year, the war cost $25 billion and more than nine thousand American lives. No longer engaged in a controlled conflict, the nation, in the words of one Defense Department official, was "waging full-throated war on the Southeast Asian peninsula."[33]

For the most part, U.S. troops fought well. But they pursued determined and deadly foes who mastered the countryside, employed unorthodox tactics, and accepted frightening casualties in their all-consuming struggle against the better-equipped U.S. forces. On the rare occasions where they engaged Vietcong units in open combat, American troops usually prevailed. But most of the time, GIs could see neither battlefield nor enemy; they navigated a nightmare landscape of jungles and swamps, villages and rice paddies. A crying infant might be bobby-trapped, ripping off the legs of a soldier who bent down to comfort it, or a GI could unload his rifle into that threatening shadow on the horizon only to find the corpse of an old woman who had been toting water from the stream. Despite repeated claims of progress, the war dragged on without either a diminution in the enemy's will to fight or the stabilization of South Vietnam.

General Wheeler's misplaced confidence about U.S. superiority in men and materiel embodied the essential features of U.S. military strategy in Vietnam. General William Westmoreland, the field commander, pursued a strategy of attrition. In a bewildering guerrilla conflict with no clear frontlines to assail, no territory to capture, no way of knowing for certain who or where the enemy might be, "Westy" decided to wear down the Vietcong and North Vietnamese, to overwhelm them with air power and firepower, gradually sapping their reserves of men, ammunition, and fighting spirit. Westmoreland's campaign relied on so-called search-and-destroy missions: first, B-52 bombers smashed the battlefields in predawn raids; then, detachments of soldiers would fly out in helicopters, pursue the Vietcong throughout the day, count the dead, and return to their bases at night. With attrition as the objective, U.S. forces measured success not in territory captured but in the number of enemy killed, the "body count" of dead Vietcong and North Vietnamese troops. This system encouraged fraud (experts estimate the military padded the body count by as much as 30 percent) and occasionally encouraged horrible abuses—a tendency to shoot first and ask questions later. One marine remembered a patrol when "about fifty people shot this old guy. Everybody claimed they shot him. He got shot cause he started running. . . . Any Vietnamese out at night was the enemy."[34]

Personnel policy compounded military difficulties. Unlike previous wars, when soldiers served "for the duration," GIs in Vietnam served a year-long tour of duty, typically a thirteen-month period with one month off for rest and relaxation. Serving for the duration kept units together; it gave them the common goal of finishing the military task. But during the Vietnam War, the pool of available soldiers far exceeded the immediate need. Keeping the same five hundred thousand men in the jungle, while millions of others never faced battle, would provoke outrage back home. General Westmoreland believed the twelve-month tour expedient politically and good for morale in Vietnam. A certain date of return, Westy believed, "gave a man a goal." Unfortunately, as a soldier's tour approached conclusion, that goal often became self-preservation. Men with a few weeks to go became reluctant to fight; tensions developed as soldiers rotated in and out, some with months left to serve, others counting the days to their discharge. One military expert called the tour "the worst personnel policy in history." (As a result, the armed forces explicitly rejected the Vietnam-era personnel policy during the 1991 Persian Gulf War and announced that all troops would serve for the duration.)[35]

Other military analysts thought that "ticket punching," the policy of rotating commanders every six months so that officers would experience a variety of commands, was even more disruptive. "We fought the same war every six months," one army analyst complained. Frequent rotation not only denied platoon lieutenants a body of combat experience, it also prevented them from developing rapport with their troops. Disrespect for officers was widespread. "What are you going to show me?" one infantryman responded to a pep talk from his platoon leader. "What is it in the scheme of things that's going to give me any insight on this whole situation? You ain't showing me shit."[36]

The soldiers' disrespect for their leaders extended to the highest levels; GIs could not help but mock the clear disjunction between Westmoreland's official reports and the troops' actual experience on the ground. Because U.S. forces inflicted horrendous casualties on the enemy—even with inflated body counts, more than two hundred thousand enemy soldiers had been killed by late 1967—Westmoreland and other military officials claimed to be winning the war. "We are grinding down the Communist enemy in South Vietnam, and there is evidence that manpower problems are emerging in North Vietnam," Westmoreland reported in November 1967. "In two years or less," the general predicted, the United States should "begin phasing down its level of commitment," offering the American people "some light at the end of the tunnel."[37]

But Westy's repeated promises of progress rang particularly hollow with the grunts in the fields; the Vietcong had built thousands of miles of tunnels in the countryside—subterranean channels to sit out American bombing raids, store supplies, launch ambushes, or line with booby traps. No one better understood the enticing but deadly appeal of light at the end of tunnels than Westmoreland's troops. According to a reporter on the scene, one of them, a soldier whose work "kept him 'up to fucking here' in tunnels—flushing out tunnels, lobbing grenades into them, shooting his gun into them, popping CS smoke into them, crawling down into them to bring the bad guys out dead or alive," could only laugh derisively at the general's optimistic predictions and demanded "What does that asshole know about tunnels?"[38]

Search-and-destroy raids failed to overpower the NLF. Preliminary bombing missions softened up the battlefields but also alerted the enemy, allowing them to retreat into tunnels or disappear into villages. Not only did Ho Chi Minh match LBJ step for step, finding a steady supply of soldiers to inject into the war, but the Vietcong initiated most of the combat, fighting only when and where they chose and controlling their losses. Most important, while helicopters whizzed overhead and bombs fell, the NLF concentrated on political organization in the countryside, winning ever more South Vietnamese to their standard as the destruction mounted. The loss of fields and farm stock to bombing, the poisoning of forests and croplands by airplane-dropped chemical defoliants designed to destroy jungle cover and snuff out the enemy, the "zippo raids" (named for the cigarette lighters) where U.S. forces would deny sanctuary to the Vietcong by burning villages—all of these only turned more Vietnamese against the United States and the corrupt regime it supported in Saigon. General Westmoreland expressed little respect for his opposite number, North Vietnamese commander Nguyen Vo Giap. I'm going to kick General Giap's teeth in one-by-one, Westy had promised. But as the U.S. Army chased the elusive NLF into the jungles, abandoning the efforts to win the hearts of Vietnamese peasants in the more populated areas, General Giap smiled broadly, every one of his teeth still shining.

Finally, in late 1967, Secretary of Defense McNamara recognized the futility of the attrition strategy. A former corporate executive who had brought a passion for systems analysis and precise calculations to the Pentagon, McNamara had weighed the costs and benefits of war throughout the conflict and masterminded the controlled escalation from 1961 forward. Now, he recalculated his figures and concluded that "it didn't add up. . . . What I was trying to find out was how the hell the war went on year after year when we stopped the infiltration [from North Vietnam] or

Johnson greets U.S. soldiers at Cam Ranh Bay in South Vietnam (1966). The grim onlooker with hands on his hips is General William C. Westmoreland, commander of U.S. troops in Vietnam.

shrunk it and when we had a very high body count and so on. It just didn't make sense."[39] No longer able to support the president's policy—his own policy—McNamara submitted his resignation.

The defection of his once most trusted Vietnam adviser added insult to injury, for the mounting disaster in Southeast Asia exhausted and pained LBJ. "We couldn't break him of the habit," an aide remembered, "even for health reasons, of getting up at 4:30 or 5:00 every morning to go down to the operations room and check on the casualties from Vietnam, each one of which took a little piece out of him."[40] In January 1966, Joe Califano noticed that LBJ had stopped drinking. Johnson did not mention the fact, but the numbing burden of sending boys to their death, the daily decisions on their fate, convinced him to forego the Cutty Sark whiskey he had long enjoyed. Even when Lady Bird begged him to have just one scotch to relax, Johnson almost invariably demurred.

As the military stalemate became manifest, Johnson hunkered down in the White House, deriding the "nervous nellies who break ranks under the strain." "This is not Johnson's war. This is America's war," LBJ furiously scolded a journalist in October 1967. "If I drop dead tomorrow, this war will still be with you."[41] And, of course, in large measure, Johnson spoke accurately. He had inherited the war—and the assumptions that underlay it—from Truman, Eisenhower, and Kennedy. After he retired, Richard Nixon would pursue it with renewed and expanded fury. But LBJ plunged the nation into the quagmire. In his efforts to cloak the conflict, to keep its costs from the American people, to prevent it from obscuring his other purposes, Johnson had repeatedly deceived the Congress, the press, and the public. A quick victory might have vindicated his underhanded strategy—in Congress, Johnson's compromises and shady dealings nearly always registered a success on the Senate floor. Vietnam destroyed his credibility. It *had* become "Lyndon Johnson's War."

# THE CREDIBILITY GAP
# AND THE HOME FRONT

The chants outside his doors erased any doubt that Americans held Lyndon Johnson responsible for the war in Vietnam. "Hey, Hey, LBJ" dogged the president at every public appearance. Sometimes, the hecklers even voiced their support for the enemy: "Ho, Ho, Ho Chi Minh/Ho Chi Minh is going to win!" *New York Post* reporter Pete Hamill interviewed hundreds of protesters and concluded that " . . . much of the virulence of the anti–Vietnam War movement can be traced to the character of Lyndon B. Johnson. Not a single student I've talked to in the past several weeks—left, right, and indifferent—respects the President. They think of him as vain, cornball, intellectually muddled, power-mad. . . . "[42]

The war intensified New Left disdain for Johnson in particular and liberalism in general. Before 1965, university-based radicals had directed their protests at a variety of targets—restrictive regulations on campus, civil rights, urban decay. There had been many movements but little organized movement. The war focused the efforts of student radicals and galvanized thousands of apolitical students into protest. Antiwar students denounced what they saw as the nation's amoral intervention in the affairs of another people, an unjust war hideously and hypocritically defended as a battle for freedom. They bridled at the direct connections between their universities and the nation's war machine—ROTC-trained officers, academic research financed by the Defense Department and the CIA, weapons companies recruiting new employees on campus. For young Americans, the bombing in Vietnam exposed the hollowness of liberal rhetoric; it epitomized all that was wrong with America. It rallied them into concerted, mass protest.

At an antiwar demonstration in Washington, Paul Potter, president of Students for a Democratic Society (SDS), offered the New Left analysis of Lyndon Johnson's war, linking the carnage in Southeast Asia to the fundamental injustice of American society (see Document 13). Promising to create a "massive social movement" built around the issue of Vietnam, Potter declared, "We must name that system. We must name it, describe it, analyze it, understand it, and change it." Seven months later, Potter's successor as SDS president stood up at another antiwar rally and completed the task. The evil system was liberalism, New Left protesters had concluded. Johnson and his top advisers "are not moral monsters," a student leader admitted. "They are all honorable men. They are all liberals." But this liberalism was "not so human at all."[43] With their emphasis on effectiveness, their willingness to compromise, liberals were blind to the moral and human costs of their policies. For the New Left, Vietnam was preeminently a liberal's war.

Student protest baffled LBJ, who felt some sympathy for the young rebels. "I just don't understand those young people," he told Doris Kearns near the end of his life. "Don't they realize I'm really one of them? I always hated cops when I was a kid, and just like them I dropped out of school and took off for California. I'm not some conformist middle-class personality." He believed the student movement misguided, misinformed, manipulated. They had not lived through World War II and Korea, they had never tangled with Hitler and Stalin, they "wouldn't know a communist if they tripped over one." Leftist professors thought their pronouncements about the "death of the domino theory . . . could make the Communist threat vanish overnight."[44]

If Johnson was puzzled and hurt by young people's hatred, he reserved special scorn for the opponents he best knew and understood, the growing congressional opposition to his policies in Vietnam. As majority leader, Johnson had prided himself on his cooperation with Eisenhower in foreign affairs; Senator Johnson had muted all open debate with the president on international matters. He expected similar support from his Congress. When Senator Clifford Case of New Jersey defected, criticizing the war on the Senate floor, Johnson saw only crass, self-serving ambition. "You all know," he remarked, "that whenever most Senators look in a mirror, they see a President. Well, they tell me Clifford Case has been looking in the mirror an awful lot lately."[45]

No opponent of the war frustrated Johnson so much as Senator J. William Fulbright of Arkansas, the chairman of the Senate Foreign Relations Committee. A Rhodes Scholar and the driving force behind an international academic exchange program, Fulbright criticized Johnson and the war, gradually becoming a darling of the antiwar movement for his eloquent warnings against the arrogance of American power. Fulbright's criticism aroused desperate fury from the president. When the senator scheduled televised hearings about Johnson's conduct of the war in February 1966, LBJ immediately set off for Honolulu, his first presidential trip outside the North American continent, and took with him all the officials supposed to testify before Fulbright's committee. On one occasion, LBJ vividly encapsulated his opinion of his rival: "You know, when you're milking a cow and you have all that foamy white milk in the bucket and you're just about through when all of a sudden the cow switches her tail through a pile of manure and slaps it into that foamy white milk. That's Bill Fulbright."[46]

Johnson particularly resented the respect afforded the urbane, cultivated Arkansan in academic circles and by the liberal eastern press, the same people that regarded LBJ as a vulgar, uncultured hick. Fulbright had opposed many reform measures dear to the eastern establishment, he had signed the southern manifesto against school integration, and he had opposed the civil rights movement. Johnson believed him a racist — willing to sacrifice the Vietnamese to the communists because they were brown.

Desperate and defeated, Johnson grasped at straws, blaming his loss of support on Fulbright's motives or on communist agents within the peace movement. He longed to reestablish some kind of consensus, to rebuild the national unity so essential to his brand of liberal leadership. "Put away all the childish divisive things," he begged, "if you want the maturity and the unity that is the mortar of a nation's greatness."[47] Assailed by hawks and doves, by radicals and antiwar liberals who blamed him for the carnage in Vietnam, and by conservatives who claimed he was not pursuing the battle vigorously enough, Johnson felt caught in tightening pincers (see Document 12). "I stuck to the middle ground," Johnson wrote in his memoirs. "That course was not comfortable. It would have been easier in the short run to break out the flag for an all-out military effort, and perhaps easier still to abandon our commitment in Asia and concentrate on domestic tasks." So Johnson held his course, what he sometimes called his "dawk policy."[48] But Johnson could not build a consensus on Vietnam, could not stake out a middle ground because there was none. By the end of 1967, both hawks and doves overwhelmingly disapproved of him. The pincers were closing.

As his popularity plummeted, Johnson moved toward the right. At the beginning of his presidency, Johnson had feared the hawks far more than the doves. He plunged into Vietnam because withdrawal would have aroused the conservatives in Congress, revived McCarthyism, and killed the Great Society. But as the protests mounted, Johnson increasingly blamed the student left for rising public sentiment against the war and his own low ratings in the polls. He cozied up to hawks and conservatives, preferring to shield himself from criticism of the war, and he tried to destroy the antiwar movement. In violation of the CIA's charter, which prohibited it from operating within the United States, LBJ ordered the agency to begin surveillance of antiwar leaders—to prove that they were communist agents of foreign governments. When Operation Chaos, as the illegal plan was called, failed to uncover any such links, Johnson turned from spying to active harassment. Undercover FBI agents infiltrated peace organizations and attempted to disrupt their activities.

Criticized on both sides, Johnson needed to win over the press and the people; and this, above all, LBJ was ill-prepared to achieve. Television had become the nation's primary news medium and LBJ, never a brilliant public speaker, looked terrible on the tube—his wordy, folksy style looked forced, phony. Special assistant Jack Valenti, who as president of the Motion Picture Association of America understood mass media, tried to coach LBJ for his TV appearances, but the president would not be bothered by Valenti's advice on television demeanor. Johnson's dealings with the press proved equally clumsy. Flattery and favoritism, Johnson's old tactics in the Senate, could not win favorable coverage from the White House press corps—a professional crew anxious to maintain their independence from the man they covered. Reporters resented Johnson's crude attempts to manipulate them, his occasional refusals to talk, his last-minute press conferences, his unnecessary Sunday announcements which pulled them away from their families. Never thick-skinned, Johnson believed that so much criticism of the president was bad for the country, especially when *he* was president; and he increasingly blamed unfair press coverage for the nation's waning support of the war in Vietnam. About his relationship with the press, LBJ said, "I feel like a hound bitch in heat in the country. If you run, they chew your tail off; if you stand still, they slip it to you."[49]

Particularly damaging were doubts about Johnson's truthfulness—what became known in 1965 as "the credibility gap." In Joseph Califano's words, LBJ's "fixation with keeping options open on any new policy venture until he had every political stone turned and set in place was, in good part, why he was such an effective legislator. But the misleading body language played badly with the press corps and the public, who like to bear witness to the struggles and machinations of their presidents."[50] Johnson's subterfuges, his dealmaking, exaggerations, and tactical reversals infuriated the reporters he often led astray. "How do you know when Lyndon Johnson is telling the truth?" began an oft-repeated joke in the White House press room. "Well, when he goes like this"—finger beside nose—"he's telling the truth. When he goes like this"—pulling an ear lobe—"he's telling the truth. When he goes like this"—rubbing the chin—"he's telling the truth. But when he starts moving his lips, that's when he's lying."[51]

Charges about his honesty had vexed Johnson throughout his career, but the credibility gap only became damaging, only lost Johnson the support of middle America, when the emerging truth of the debacle in Vietnam belied Johnson's bold promises and confident reports. For deception lay at the heart of LBJ's Vietnam strategy. He consistently downplayed the true costs and extent of the war so that he ended up with egg on his face when the real story emerged. Rolling Thunder involved steady bombing, not reprisals; "advisers" fought combat missions; more troops were needed than Johnson admitted, and so on. Worst of all, reporters on the scene could see for themselves that the war was going badly. The Johnson administration's repeated claims of victory aroused scorn from the reporters "in country" and their viewers and readers at home. Johnson and his aides mooned on about the light at the end of the tunnel, while TV screens revealed chaos, defeat, and death.

The credibility gap exploded into an uncrossable chasm during the Tet offensive. In the wee hours of January 30, 1968, during Tet, the celebration of the Vietnamese New Year, commandos blasted a hole in the protective wall surrounding the U.S. Embassy in Saigon. For six hours, nineteen guerrillas fired mortars into the building, the most visible symbol of the American presence in South Vietnam. The audacious embassy raid, captured by television cameras, formed only a tiny part of a simultaneous assault on every major urban area in South Vietnam. Marching under the general order "move forward to achieve final victory," North Vietnamese and NLF forces took the Americans by surprise (U.S. intelligence reports indicated that the enemy did not have the resources to mount such an attack), seized the city of Hue, and struck at more than one hundred targets up and down the entire length of Vietnam. Eventually, U.S. troops beat back the offensive, recapturing the cities and hamlets, inflicting horrific casualties on the Vietcong, and maintaining the South Vietnamese government's precarious hold on its embattled country. Elated by the communists' breakout into open battle, General Westmoreland claimed a major victory: "The enemy exposed himself by virtue of his strategy and he suffered heavy casualties."[52]

Tet turned out to be the decisive engagement of Lyndon Johnson's war, not on the battlefields of Vietnam as General Westmoreland hoped, but in the living rooms of America. Westy's claim of success provoked disbelief from the assembled reporters who recorded it, and a chorus of discontent and derisive laughter followed President Johnson when he echoed his commander's assessment. For years, the administration had promised that victory lay around the corner. Tet showed there was fight left in the enemy, that it could attack at will—even the U.S. headquarters in Saigon was at risk. Americans only love a winner; support for the war drained away instantly, as Tet vividly demonstrated that U.S. strategy had failed. Immediately before the offensive, despite years of antiwar protest, only 28 percent of Americans called themselves doves. Twice as many, 56 percent, told Gallup pollsters they were hawks. One month later, each side tallied 40 percent. Tet had changed millions of minds. Major mainstream opinion leaders—*Life, Time, Newsweek,* NBC—all voiced serious criticism of the war; and CBS anchorman Walter Cronkite, the nation's most revered and trusted television figure, stuck the last fork into Johnson's Vietnam policy. "We have been too often disappointed by the optimism of the American leaders, both in Vietnam and Washington, to have faith any longer in the silver linings they find in the darkest clouds," Cronkite intoned. "To say we are mired in stalemate seems the only realistic, yet unsatisfactory conclusion."[53] Johnson's attempt to fight a war in Vietnam and maintain the Great Society at home was done.

In the aftermath of Tet, military leaders asked immediately for two hundred and six thousand additional troops and pressed Johnson to call up the reserves and expand the war. Johnson directed his new secretary of defense, Clark Clifford, to determine how to meet the military's requests for more men and materiel. Confident that Clifford, a sturdy supporter of his policy, would develop a workable proposal, LBJ instructed him to "give me the lesser of two evils." But after studying the situation, Clifford could only tell the president what he did not want to hear. No progress had been made during four painful years of fighting. "As we build up our forces, they build up theirs. . . . We seem to have a sinkhole. We put in more—they match it. I see more and more fighting with more and more casualties on the U.S. side and no end in sight to the action."[54]

Clifford knew his man. He realized Johnson would reject the dire news so he summoned the "Wise Men" to Washington, a group of distinguished former high officials, including Dean Acheson, secretary of state under Truman; Korean War commander Matthew Ridgeway; and John J. McCloy, the allied high commissioner in Germany after World War II. The administration had first assembled these pillars of the American establishment in November 1967. Then, they had unanimously approved the conduct of the war and dismissed withdrawal as unthinkable. Their support had considerably buoyed LBJ. Now, receiving the latest political and military briefings in March 1968, even the Wise Men changed their minds. The inventors of cold war strategy, including the very architects of the limited conflict in Vietnam, told Johnson the war was unwinnable, wasteful, doomed. As he listened, a dejected LBJ scribbled on his notepad, "Can no longer do the job we set out to do . . . Adjust our course . . . move to disengage." After the meeting adjourned, resignation gave way to rage. "The establishment bastards have bailed out," Johnson fumed.[55]

Meanwhile, popular discontent with Johnson swelled. On March 12, 1968, President Johnson won the Democratic presidential primary in New Hampshire with 49 percent of the vote. But his little-known opponent, antiwar Senator Eugene McCarthy of Minnesota, shocked the nation by polling 42 percent of the vote in the conservative New England state. The close call, widely interpreted as a defeat for LBJ, prompted Robert Kennedy to announce his own candidacy for the presidency. The Vietnam War would drag on for another seven years, but for Lyndon Johnson it ended on March 31, 1968. That day he appeared on national television, listing steps to wind down the war and open negotiations with the North Vietnamese. He ended the speech with a shocking announcement of his retirement from national politics. "I will not seek and will not accept the nomination of my party for another term as your president."[56]

## "NO MORE VIETNAMS"

Johnson's failure, America's failure in Vietnam, has continued to vex historians, policymakers, and the entire nation. Americans of every political persuasion swear by the slogan "No more Vietnams," even though the words carry very different meanings for conservatives and liberals, hawks and doves. For some, including President Ronald Reagan, Vietnam represented a failure of will; Johnson and his minions refused to pull out all the military stops, to support the boys in the trenches with everything they had. Never again, Reagan promised, would Americans send men into battle without overwhelming force and unquestioned popular support.

Critics of the war drew other lessons from the nation's failure in Indochina—lessons about the limits of American power, the hubris, folly, and injustice of involvement in the affairs of other nations. For Americans of this persuasion, "No more Vietnams" pointed away from brash, arrogant interventionism abroad and toward a more restrained foreign policy.

It expressed a feeling that in other places, even America's best intentions could backfire. During the Tet offensive, U.S. artillery had destroyed most of the village of Ben Tre in the Mekong Delta region of South Vietnam. "We had to destroy it in order to save it," one officer told an AP reporter.[57] For many observers, that comment epitomized the folly of American involvement in Vietnam and the danger of adventurism abroad. Vietnam critics also sought restraints on presidential power, on the ability of the chief executive to plunge the nation into battle without a congressional declaration of war. In 1975, Congress created such restrictions with the War Powers Act.

The ghost of Vietnam has haunted every subsequent American military operation. Even those who derided the "Vietnam syndrome" and supported a more interventionist foreign policy labored under the shadow of Johnson's failures. After a brief 1983 foray into Lebanon, President Reagan withdrew the U.S. Marines because the action did not meet his administration's conditions for American military actions. According to Reagan's secretary of defense, Caspar Weinberger, the United States would only commit troops to missions with clearly defined and easily achieved objectives, of limited duration, and possessing clear popular support. And President Reagan himself enunciated the "Reagan doctrine," support for indigenous anticommunist guerrillas in places such as Angola and Nicaragua in lieu of direct U.S. military action.

In the wake of the 1991 Persian Gulf War, President George Bush announced the demise of the "Vietnam syndrome," but Bush's pronouncement turned out to be premature. The Gulf War itself met Weinberger's definition of a limited conflict; and after a quick victory in Kuwait, Bush would not stomach an extended battle against Iraq and its dictator, Saddam Hussein. The exit of U.S. soldiers from Somalia in 1993 and the reluctance of Bush and his successor, Bill Clinton, to intervene in Bosnia revealed the continuing influence of the Vietnam legacy.

Analysis of the war remains so impassioned and contentious because Americans cannot even agree on what they are discussing, for not one but many wars were waged in Vietnam. First, Southeast Asia formed the battleground in the global geopolitical struggle against international communism. Vietnam appeared only as the latest test in the long cold war that had turned hot in Korea, Berlin, Greece, Iran, and Cuba. This was the war Lyndon Johnson fought; its requirements forced the president's hand and foreclosed his military options. In geopolitical terms, withdrawal seemed impossible; it would have meant a major defeat for the free world, disgracing Johnson's presidency and exposing all of East Asia to further communist expansion. But all-out war, so desired by hawks, remained equally unpalatable. Johnson and his top aides believed that the use of tactical nuclear weapons, the invasion of North Vietnam, even massive escalation of conventional bombing and ground action would bring the Chinese into the war and risk conflagrations around the globe. All-out war also would undermine U.S. moral leadership—the country's position as a defender of freedom rather than an agent of conquest.

General Westmoreland fought a second, separate conflict—the conventional war of attrition against North Vietnam and organized units of the NLF. By traditional military standards, U.S. armed forces fought well, winning most of the battles, inflicting heavy casualties. Westmoreland frequently asserted that General Giap could not have lasted two weeks in an American uniform, that any U.S. commander who accepted such losses would have been sacked immediately and probably court-martialed. Of course, neither Giap nor any of his soldiers wore American uniforms, and all of Westmoreland's assumptions proved wrong-headed—that North Vietnam could not absorb high casualties, that bombing would cripple its military capacity, that U.S. military superiority would sap their will to resist. The conventional war also deflected attention from the counterinsurgency campaign against South Vietnam-based guerrillas.

That insurgency was the third Vietnam war, the one waged by the National Liberation Front (NLF). In the early 1960s, American officials had recognized that pacification of the countryside was South Vietnam's top priority, but as the war escalated, South Vietnam gradually abandoned the effort. By 1967, "the American-guided pacification program had become," in the words of a high Defense Department official, a "transparent monstrosity, an example of American optimism and messianic zeal gone off the deep end." Winning the hearts and minds of the Vietnamese peasantry, fighting a "political counter-revolution in the interests of democracy," this official concluded, would have been difficult for any group of outsiders, "particularly white men."[58] But the United States lost any chance at all of defeating the insurgency as long as the conventional war destroyed the country. Search-and-destroy missions leveled villages, chemical defoliants poisoned crops, and combat forced millions of rural Vietnamese off the land. At one time or another, a quarter of the Vietnamese population were refugees, crowding in squalid camps or flooding cities corrupted by the massive military presence. The United States abandoned the field to the NLF; without pacification of the countryside, the guerrillas could fight on indefinitely.

Finally, and most importantly, the Vietnam War centered on political struggle in the South. The entire American strategy—the whole point of intervention from Eisenhower onward—had been the maintenance of a secure, independent South Vietnam as a bulwark against communist expansion in Southeast Asia. But the South Vietnamese government's very dependence on American intervention and the U.S. support for a series of corrupt, tyrannical regimes played into the hands of the Vietcong. The huge American presence turned South Vietnam, in Senator Fulbright's words, into a "gigantic whorehouse."[59] It allowed the NLF to transform the conflict; it became not a war of democracy against communism, or even South Vietnam versus North Vietnam, but Asians against Americans.

Over and over again, military, diplomatic, and political tactics miscarried in Vietnam as LBJ tried more and more of the same—more troops, more air raids, more offers of bombing pauses, more support for the troubled government in Saigon. President Johnson bore the brunt of responsibility for these repeated failures. But, perhaps, as State Department official Leslie H. Gelb tellingly noted in 1971, the war stands not as a failure of the system at all but as the logical outcome, even "success," of a bureaucratic system and a political strategy tragically unequal to the challenges of Vietnam. Our leaders, Gelb recognized, knew what was happening and what they were doing in Vietnam; "U.S. involvement did not stem from a failure to foresee consequences" but from an inability and unwillingness to break free of inherited assumptions, "to seek new answers and new policies."[60] The tragedy of Vietnam, Gelb concluded, was that the system worked.

Johnson's liberal anticommunist worldview forced him to hold on in Southeast Asia although he understood the dangers of "that bitch of a war." His personal and political experience precluded any serious rethinking of the relation of Vietnam to American security and world leadership. His liberal faith in the potency of government action, in the capacity of the federal government to foster freedom and opportunity at home, misled him about the efficacy of U.S. intervention in distant lands. In Southeast Asia, LBJ's political philosophy was tested and found wanting.

## NOTES

[1] George Reedy, *The Twilight of the Presidency* (New York: New American Library, 1970), 72.

[2] Rowland Evans and Robert Novak, *Lyndon B. Johnson: The Exercise of Power* (New York: Signet Books, 1966), 599. Doris Kearns, *Lyndon Johnson and the American Dream* (New York: Signet Books, 1976), 263.

[3] Eric F. Goldman, *The Tragedy of Lyndon Johnson* (New York: Dell, 1969), 447–48.

[4] Philip Geyelin, quoted in Townsend Hoopes, *The Limits of Intervention*, rev. ed. (New York: W. W. Norton, 1987), 8.

[5] Kearns, *Johnson and the American Dream,* 278.

[6] Tom Wicker, *JFK and LBJ* (New York: Pelican Books, 1969), 273.

[7] Kearns, *Johnson and the American Dream,* 263.

[8] George Herring, *America's Longest War,* 2nd ed. (New York: Alfred A. Knopf, 1986), 7.

[9] Ibid., 9.

[10] Ibid., 10.

[11] Ibid., 11.

[12] Larry Berman, *Planning A Tragedy* (New York: W. W. Norton, 1982), 9. Loren Baritz, *Backfire* (New York: Ballantine, 1985), 63.

[13] Herring, *America's Longest War,* 43.

[14] George Ball, *The Past Has Another Pattern* (New York: W. W. Norton, 1982), 365–66.

[15] Berman, *Planning A Tragedy,* 29–30.

[16] Ibid., 26–27.

[17] Kennedy, television interviews of September 2 and 9, 1963, in William Appleman Williams et al., eds., *America in Vietnam: A Documentary History* (New York: W. W. Norton, 1989), 198–201.

[18] Herring, *America's Longest War,* 110.

[19] Ibid.

[20] Wicker, *JFK and LBJ,* 198.

[21] Lyndon B. Johnson, *Quotations from Chairman LBJ* (New York: Simon and Schuster, 1968), 64.

[22] Laura Kalman, *Abe Fortas: A Biography* (New Haven: Yale University Press, 1990), 232–33.

[23] Baritz, *Backfire,* 129. Larry Berman quotes the remark as "For all I know, our Navy was shooting at whales out there." See Berman, *Planning A Tragedy,* 32–33.

[24] U.S. Congress, "Gulf of Tonkin Resolution," in Williams et al., eds., *America in Vietnam,* 237.

[25] Berman, *Planning A Tragedy,* 34–35. Evans and Novak, *Exercise of Power,* 564.

[26] See Document 10.

[27] Ibid.

[28] Baritz, *Backfire,* 156.

[29] Berman, *Planning A Tragedy,* 51.

[30] Ibid., 43–44.

[31] Lady Bird Johnson, *A White House Diary* (New York: Holt, Rinehart, and Winston, 1970), 248.

[32] Herring, *America's Longest War,* 140.

[33] Hoopes, *Limits of Intervention,* 57.

[34] Michael Schaller et al., *Present Tense* (Boston: Houghton Mifflin, 1992), 297.

[35] Ibid., 304–05.

[36] Ibid., 305. Robert Jay Lifton, *Home From the War* (New York: Simon and Schuster, 1973).

[37] Larry Berman, *Lyndon Johnson's War* (New York: W. W. Norton, 1989), 120.

[38] Baritz, *Backfire,* 168.

[39] Berman, *Lyndon Johnson's War,* 37.

[40] Ibid., 142.

[41] Ibid., xi. Johnson, address at Chicago, Illinois, May 17, 1966, in *Quotations from Chairman LBJ,* 11–12.

[42] Robert Sherrill, *The Accidental President* (New York: Pyramid Books, 1967), 13.

[43] Carl Oglesby, quoted in Robert J. McMahon, *Major Problems in the History of the Vietnam War* (Lexington: D.C. Heath and Co., 1990), 477–78.

[44] Kearns, *Johnson and the American Dream,* 345–49. Herring, *America's Longest War,* 181.

[45] Joseph A. Califano, Jr., *The Triumph and Tragedy of Lyndon Johnson* (New York: Simon and Schuster, 1991), 248.

[46] Johnson, quoted in *Newsweek,* Sept. 4, 1967.

[47] Johnson, address at Chicago, Illinois, May 17, 1966, quoted in *New York Times,* May 18, 1966, 8.

[48] Goldman, *Tragedy,* 491. Berman, *Lyndon Johnson's War,* 27.

[49] Berman, *Lyndon Johnson's War,* 183.

[50] Califano, *Triumph and Tragedy,* 173.

[51] Goldman, *Tragedy,* 484–85.

[52] Berman, *Lyndon Johnson's War,* 145. Herring, *America's Longest War,* 186.

[53] Herring, *America's Longest War,* 200–01.

[54] Berman, *Lyndon Johnson's War,* 176–80.

[55] Ibid., 195, 199–200, 206.

[56] *Public Papers of the Presidents of the United States: Lyndon B. Johnson, 1963–1969,* 11 vols. (Washington, D.C.: Government Printing Office, 1963–1969), 1968, 475.

[57] Herring, *America's Longest War,* 192.

[58] Hoopes, *Limits of Intervention,* 66, 69.

[59] Schaller et al., *Present Tense,* 300.

[60] Leslie H. Gelb, "Vietnam: The System Worked," *Foreign Policy,* Summer 1971, 140–55, 159–67.

# 7

## Dumping Johnson:
## The Decline and Fall
## of American Liberalism

In 1964, Lyndon Johnson celebrated a dazzling electoral victory over antigovernment conservative Barry Goldwater. Carrying more than 60 percent of the popular vote, LBJ's coattails swept in a liberal majority in both houses of the Congress and left the opposition Republican party defeated and discredited. Yet only four years later, Johnson's successor as Democratic presidential candidate, Vice President Hubert H. Humphrey, eked out a paltry 42.7 percent of the vote. Humphrey finished a close second to Republican nominee Richard M. Nixon, but together Nixon and third-party candidate George Wallace tallied almost as many votes as Johnson had won. The same overwhelming majority that produced a liberal landslide in 1964 chose conservative candidates in 1968, ushering in two decades of Republican preeminence in American national politics. The nation thoroughly repudiated Johnson's can-do, activist liberalism—his promise of aggressive government action on behalf of all Americans. The Democratic party dumped Johnson, and the nation discarded his brand of politics.

The 1972 election further confirmed the nation's rejection of Johnson and liberalism. Democratic party leaders warned LBJ to stay away from the national convention in Miami, and the weeklong festivities barely took note of the party's one-time champion. "President Johnson," former LBJ aide Jack Valenti complained, had become "a non-person, expunged from the Democratic Party with the same kind of scouring effectiveness that Marxist revisionists use to rewrite Communist history. As a final petty insult, the managers of the convention made sure LBJ's picture was absent among the portraits of FDR, Truman, Stevenson, and JFK."[1] On election day, the Republican president Richard Nixon was reelected by a thundering margin, matching the proportions of Johnson's own landslide victory in

1964. Nixon began his second term by warning his fellow Americans not to expect too much from Washington. "In trusting too much in government," Nixon cautioned, "we have asked more of it than we can deliver."[2]

By the end of the 1970s, few Americans even honored Johnson's dream of a Great Society. Ronald Reagan of California, a prominent supporter of Barry Goldwater in 1964, won the presidency in 1980 and launched a conservative counterrevolution against the achievements of Lyndon Johnson and his war on poverty. Government is not the solution to the nation's troubles, Reagan declared, "government is the problem." One month after his inauguration, Reagan laid out his program for economic recovery. Calling for "a new beginning," Reagan recommended tax cuts, spending controls, strengthening defense, and drastically cutting antipoverty programs to eliminate "fraud" and "unintended" benefits. Reagan promised to reduce the role of the federal government in all its dimensions.

The American public seemed to endorse Reagan's interpretation of recent history; opinion polls placed Lyndon Johnson at the very bottom of ratings of post-World War II presidents, and the title *liberal* became a badge of dishonor, saucily dismissed as "the L word." Why did Johnson and his ambitious agenda fall so far so fast? Why did the nation reject Lyndon Johnson and cast out activist government along with him? The depth and passion of the nation's scorn certainly pained LBJ. "How is it possible," the retired president demanded from his bed at the LBJ ranch, "that all these people could be so ungrateful to me after I had given them so much?"[3]

## GUNS, BUTTER, AND STAGFLATION

Historians can offer no simple answers to Johnson's plaintive cry; the rejection of liberalism encompassed discontent with racial militance, crime, the war in Vietnam, economic stagnation, welfare programs, and Johnson's own vulgarity and deceitfulness. No decision, however, so compromised Johnson's presidency as his determination to secure both guns and butter—to fight simultaneous wars against communism and poverty and to finance both through a dangerous fiscal sleight of hand.

As he escalated the Vietnam War in 1965, LBJ rejected the counsel of his economic advisers that he call on the nation to sacrifice—raising taxes to finance the war effort and control inflation. Theoretically, liberal Keynesian economics demanded tax increases just as often as tax cuts; federal action had to cool an economy overheating with wartime demand as well as stoke a sluggish economy. The New Economics, however,

was far less appealing in 1965, when Johnson's Council of Economic
Advisers explained the need for higher taxes than in 1963 when it had
recommended a cut. As LBJ put it in his memoirs, "It is not too difficult to
convince someone that he will be better off with more take-home pay. But
try to convince him that he will be better off tomorrow by losing part of his
income today."[4]

For Johnson, the political dangers of new taxes were doubly magnified
by his own legislative success. He would have difficulty winning congressional approval for a tax hike so soon after brilliantly persuading
Congress to cut taxes. More important, LBJ understood that requests for
new revenues would prompt investigations and debate on Capitol Hill;
Congress would raise taxes to support the war but only if Johnson came
clean about its true costs and put aside his plans for urban renewal,
highway beautification, medical care, and education. Johnson decided,
fatefully, that he could protect the Great Society only by downplaying the
costs of his two-front war and by delaying a tax increase as long as
possible.

Initially, LBJ's gambit proved successful. He raised revenues by selling
federal property and assets, economized on expenditures, and resisted
inflationary pressures by intervening in and negotiating settlements to
several major industrial disputes. "Six months after his decision to pursue
the Great Society and the war without a tax increase," Joseph Califano
recalled, "it almost seemed as if LBJ could hold down wages and prices by
the force and presence of his personality."[5] He scavenged government
stockpiles for salable commodities and unloaded tons of reserved copper,
zinc, aluminum, and rubber. He brought labor and management leaders to
the White House and bullied them into accepting contracts that met his
wage and price targets.

Still, wartime demand intensified inflationary pressures, which in turn
drove up interest rates and eroded the value of most Americans' savings.
Johnson would not budge. In his January 1966 State of the Union Address,
Johnson insisted that "this Nation is mighty enough, its society healthy
enough, its people are strong enough, to pursue our goals in the rest of the
world while still building a Great Society here at home" (see Document
14). He rejected a general tax increase for 1966, but he conceded that
"because of Vietnam, we cannot do all that we should or all that we would
like to do." So although Johnson pressed ahead with a scaled-back version
of the Great Society, he allowed his dear child only a niggardly allowance.

Not even these painful economies solved the government's budget
problems or slowed the spiral of inflation. Johnson's policies had exacerbated a host of economic woes—stimulating inflation, slowing

growth, weakening the dollar in international currency markets, intensifying an unfavorable balance of payments in foreign trade, even undercutting the Great Society. Reluctantly, in August 1967, Johnson threw in his hand and asked the Congress for more taxes, specifically for a 10 percent surcharge on individual and corporate income taxes. To protect the needy, Johnson's plan exempted low-income taxpayers from the surcharge and increased Social Security payments to the aged and disabled. "If we don't act soon," LBJ told congressional leaders in a private meeting, "we'll wreck the republic."[6]

These alarms could not alone convince restless committee chairmen on Capitol Hill to approve his plan. Led by Arkansas congressman Wilbur Mills, chairman of the tax-writing House Ways and Means Committee, the Congress insisted on savage cuts in Great Society spending as a condition for passing the tax bill. No friend of the war on poverty, Mills maintained that the poor did not deserve federal aid and that government programs could not remedy their fundamentally moral personal failings. Racial bias informed Mills's position; his antiwelfare homilies always described black families and black illegitimate children. Mills's attitudes represented the white backlash against civil rights and the war on poverty that spread throughout the United States after 1966 and became the dominant political force of the 1970s. "You have got to go on TV," the Arkansan instructed the president in 1967, and tell the country that "because of Vietnam we must cut domestic spending and pass a tax increase. . . . "[7]

Johnson balked. Budget director Charles Schulze reported that Mills's cuts would be "very heavy in health, housing, pollution, and poverty . . . reducing some programs to a shambles." Schulze thought Mills and his allies were "playing 'chicken' in an eyeball-to-eyeball confrontation. . . . " He predicted that "if we are willing to take a strong and unyielding stand, they will blink first."[8] If Johnson had asked for a tax increase in 1965, at the height of his power and popularity, he might have stared down Wilbur Mills as he had other conservative southern congressmen on civil rights and urban renewal. But in late 1967, Mills held most of the cards and he knew it. The House Ways and Means Committee voted to set aside the tax bill until Johnson came around on spending cuts. The stalemate held until after Johnson withdrew from the presidential campaign, when the President signed a revenue act containing both the surcharge and the six billion dollars in cuts Mills had demanded.

The 1968 tax bill offered too little too late to relieve the economic crisis that Johnson's guns-and-butter strategy had aggravated. By delaying the tax increase, Johnson allowed inflation to take root. Consumer prices shot up, commercial interest rates doubled, the dollar lost value, and the national debt escalated. For the next twenty-five years, from 1969 to 1984, federal economic policy concentrated on the problems of stagflation—the combination of economic stagnation with high rates of inflation. Slow growth and lagging productivity depressed real income, while the Arab oil embargoes of the 1970s, farm price subsidies, and a kind of economic arteriosclerosis kept pushing prices upward. Presidents Nixon, Ford, and Carter seesawed between contractionary policies—tax surcharges, reduced spending, high interest rates—designed to curb inflation—and fiscal stimuli aimed at relieving unemployment and repeated recessions.

Already by the late 1960s, a growing number of economists had questioned the liberal Keynesian faith in government fiscal policy as the "ultimate stabilizer" of an uncertain marketplace and the guarantor of economic security and prosperity. Led by Nobel Prize-winner Milton Friedman, these "monetarist" economists portrayed interventionist economic policies as "counterproductive agitations." Reversing the Keynesian perspective of the Kennedy and Johnson administrations, monetarists characterized government action as the destabilizing factor in an otherwise shock-absorbing, self-adjusting system. They argued for a hands-off approach, challenging the faith of every chief executive from FDR to LBJ that the president could and should oversee the national economy.

## THE END OF THE JOHNSON ERA

The economic turmoil of the late 1960s did not merely discredit the New Economics and its liberal adherents in the White House. It brought real uncertainty and hardship to many Americans; wages could not keep up with gains in prices, inflation ate away the value of savings and fixed incomes. At the same time, long-term economic trends, most of them out of the control of the White House, signaled an end to the long period of unprecedented prosperity that had blessed the United States for a generation. World War II had left the United States at the summit of the world, its industrial muscles flexed as never before while the nation's rivals for international economic supremacy, Europe and Japan, lay in ruins. By 1969, the rest of the world was beginning to catch up. The United States, to be sure, remained the world's largest, most productive, richest economy, but its lead had dwindled, its unchallenged dominance eroded. Japan passed the United States as the world's fastest-growing national economy, the European Economic Community became the world's largest economic entity, and America's share of world trade declined.

All these changes threatened the ever-rising standards of living that had elevated so many working Americans into comfortable middle-class status during the 1950s and 1960s and had financed the liberal programs that eased their upward passage — student loans for college education, federal mortgages, Social Security, worker safety laws, and minimum wage regulations. Preserving and spreading the benefits of prosperity, these government programs sustained the liberal electoral coalition first fashioned by Franklin D. Roosevelt. But economic decline, especially higher taxes and ruinous inflation, threatened to cut working people off from the very programs and benefits that had brought them into the liberal coalition in the first place.

This coalition included minorities and the poor, labor and selected segments of the business community, academics and artists; but at its heart, what made the coalition a majority were white urban ethnics — Boston's Irish, Buffalo's Poles, New York's Jews, Milwaukee's Germans — and their children in suburban communities around the nation. Liberal Democrats had won their loyalty during the Great Depression, and sustained it after World War II, by providing them with unions and job security, college educations and home ownership, Social Security for their retirement, and highways for their cars. But gradually over the course of the 1960s, these people found their lives and their neighborhoods changing; they came to view liberalism in general and the Democratic party in particular as enemies rather than allies.

The white backlash against civil rights coiled at the heart of this political realignment, expressing, according to Martin Luther King, Jr., "the congenital deformity of racism that has crippled the nation from its conception."[9] Certainly, racism played a large part in white resistance to civil rights, north and south; many white Americans, themselves steadfast liberals on economic and political issues, simply refused to live side-by-side with blacks, to hire them, to send their children to the same schools.

But racism alone could not explain the disintegration of the liberal coalition. Racial tension, declining economic prospects, and decaying cities became tied up with a series of explosive political issues in the 1960s. First among them in the late 1960s was concern about law and order. The term *law and order* became a sort of code word for opposition to protest movements on the campuses and in the ghettos, but it also expressed frustration with deteriorating conditions in the nation's cities and fear of urban riots. People living on the thresholds of dangerous, depressed slums felt the federal government ignored their needs, that Great Society programs rewarded rioters while their own neighborhoods became more dangerous.

Bitter opposition to welfare accompanied the rising concern about law and order. Middle-class and lower-middle-class white Americans resented government programs they viewed as unresponsive to their needs—programs they felt lavished their hard-earned tax dollars on the undeserving poor, rewarding rioters and freeloaders. Although these perceptions rested on gross distortions—even at the height of the war on poverty, federal programs never devoted to the poor more than a fraction of the benefits apportioned to more affluent Americans—they powerfully gripped the imaginations of struggling Americans unnerved by the civil rights revolution and the economic squeeze. Increasingly, loyal Democratic voters viewed welfare as wasteful, unnecessary, damaging—an unwarranted boon for noisy protesters, for irresponsible parents, for parasites living on the public trough as they sat behind the wheels of "welfare Cadillacs." White ethnic voters, the stalwarts of the New Deal coalition, resented paying higher taxes for "them."

Racial desegregation in the North, including mandatory busing and affirmative action, accelerated the flight from liberalism. Busing departed from the tradition of neighborhood schools and sometimes required long rides into unknown, uncertain areas. Hiring and admissions practices aimed at recruiting more minority workers and students struck some Americans as unfair "reverse discrimination." Both policies aggravated a sense of grievance, a feeling that working-class whites were paying for something that was not their fault. This discontent expressed itself in protests against busing, in violence against black schoolchildren bused into white neighborhoods, in lawsuits against affirmative action, in white flight to the suburbs. It also fostered resentment against elite upper-class liberals, comfortably insulated from these tensions in their suburban homes, and toward Democratic politicians who backed these policies. One study revealed a dramatic shift in the party loyalties of low-income workers during the 1960s. In 1960, nearly 60 percent of low-income workers had cast their votes for the Democratic ticket; in 1968 and again in 1972, only 35 percent of this group remained loyal to the party of FDR and LBJ.

These social issues carried a symbolic resonance beyond their substantive economic and political foundations. The perception of an intrusive, bureaucratic government—concerned with the rights of outsiders, criminals, and protesters but neglectful of the needs and fears of ordinary working people—exerted a powerful hold of its own, quite separate from the actual rhetoric and reality of liberal policies (see Document 15). Conservative Republicans wasted no opportunity to reinforce and sharpen this unflattering portrait of liberalism.

For many disillusioned liberal Democrats, government had outgrown its britches, had become too big, too pushy. Federal agencies told employers who to hire, students which schools to attend, airlines which flights to schedule, and doctors which procedures to prescribe. Johnsonian liberalism had vastly expanded the regulatory state, moving it into nearly every facet of American life. Discontent festered about the explosion of new regulations and, in a stagnant economy, about the burdens of taxation and inflation. Democratic voters became easy targets for Republicans like Richard Nixon and conservative populists like George Wallace—candidates who exploited resentments against a more intrusive government and assailed the "pointy-headed intellectuals" and "briefcase-toting bureaucrats" who staffed it. At the close of LBJ's presidency, *Time* magazine reported on the state of the nation and uncovered the end of an era: "The notion—often myth—of individualism has stood for many different things in American life," *Time* reported. "New Deal liberalism through Lyndon Johnson's day saw individualism as requiring the paternal protection of the Federal Government. Lately a longing for individualism has reappeared in reaction against the welfare state. . . . "[10] Americans stopped turning toward the government to solve their problems; they had had enough.

By 1970, a majority of Americans had become skeptical of government activism; they were more concerned about the taxes they paid than about the benefits they received. They no longer looked to Washington as their friend and benefactor. And when Americans rejected liberal government and dethroned King Politics, they banished his most devoted and influential courtier—Lyndon B. Johnson—with him.

For when conservatives lambasted liberalism for "throwing money at problems," for granting government benefits to anyone and everyone like some doting parent, they had Lyndon Johnson's number. Johnson, according to one member of his cabinet, was a compulsive giver. From his youth, he constantly made extravagant gifts, and as president he handed out photos, pens, pictures, and cuff links to every visitor. This all-consuming, even selfish generosity, a desire to help people and win their gratitude and affection, animated Johnson's personal life and his politics. Politics and political struggles mattered so much to Lyndon Johnson because he never doubted that government could, should, and would change Americans' lives, improve them, bestow gifts upon them.

So expansive and generous a presidency, Lyndon Johnson believed, required a foundation of national unity. No one understood the need to preserve the liberal coalition so well as LBJ. In 1964 he had gathered nearly all Americans into his tent, promising to renew and outdo Roosevelt's New Deal, to unite the nation happily around Lyndon Johnson's campfire. But he could not keep the embers burning, could not satisfy everyone. "In 1968," one commentator wrote during that tumultuous year, "1964 seems decades in the past. A mere four years ago, we were more nearly a united people than we had ever been in this century; today we seem in an advanced state of disintegration."[11]

"A viable political consensus rests upon an expectation of benefits by all members of the coalition," one writer noted in his journalistic autopsy of the Great Society.[12] When LBJ could not deliver these benefits, when conflict over race relations and the Vietnam war polarized the nation, Johnson's magic powers over the Congress and country vanished. He appeared a charlatan, a wheeler-dealer whose bluster and backroom maneuvers no longer worked. "This country's ultimate strength lies in the unity of our people," a weary LBJ told a national television audience in March 1968. "There is division in the American house. There is divisiveness among us all tonight."[13] He recognized that his power had dissipated, that his days of accomplishment had ended.

Still, many of the people closest to LBJ thought he would fight for another term, even after the Tet offensive and McCarthy's stunning performance in the New Hampshire primary. If nothing else, Johnson's friends reasoned, pride and spite would force him to battle on. Richard Nixon was sure to be the Republican standard-bearer, and Johnson relished the opportunity to defeat him. "I was never more sure of anything in my political career than of the fact that I could beat Richard Nixon," he told Joseph Califano, and for years Johnson "just knew in my heart that it was not right for Dick Nixon to ever be President of this country." Moreover, Bobby Kennedy's entry in the race seemed certain to keep LBJ in the hunt. "If I ever had any doubts about Johnson's running," one old LBJ confidante maintained, "I would have lost them the day Kennedy announced because he is not about to turn the country over to Bobby."[14] Hardly anyone could believe that this man who lived and breathed politics would willingly give up his life's passion without a fight. But Johnson, his health deteriorating and his power undermined by divisions in the body politic, decided to retire.

The withdrawal gave LBJ new vitality, a final second wind. By renouncing personal ambition for the first time in his long political career, Johnson won new credibility with and sympathy from the American people. He used the death of Martin Luther King, Jr., to secure passage of the Open Housing Act and the assassination of Robert Kennedy to push for gun control. He opened peace talks with North Vietnam and set aside thousands of acres of wilderness. Finally, the last day of his term arrived and Johnson returned to Texas. On his first night as a private citizen in over thirty years, Lyndon and Lady Bird surveyed their vast cattle ranch and noticed the quiet, the absence of the large retinue that had always followed them. Lady Bird turned to her husband and smiled. "The coach has turned back into a pumpkin," she sighed, "and the mice have all run away."[15]

In retirement, Johnson composed his memoirs, established the Johnson Presidential Library and the Johnson School of Public Affairs at the University of Texas, and supervised his sprawling ranch on the Pedernales. He hectored the managers of his library to keep the doors open from early morning to late evening so that his museum would receive more visitors than any other presidential library. He threw himself into ranch management with the same intensity that he had devoted to politics. He visited with his grandchildren. Occasionally, he commiserated with old friends like Abe Fortas and Thurgood Marshall. On January 22, 1973, while taking an afternoon nap at the ranch, Johnson suffered a heart attack. He phoned for help but died alone in his room before assistance could reach him. Four years after Johnson's death, Marshall remembered the conversations he had had with a disconsolate LBJ and surmised that Johnson would "still be alive today if he had been reelected. He died," Marshall said, "of a broken heart."[16]

Johnson's political vision, then, followed its champion gently into the night. His faith in government action, his universalism, and his belief in national unity largely passed into oblivion behind him. At the beginning of his presidency, in a speech in Austin, he had rallied his audience to the liberal standard by insisting that all Americans shared a common destiny and that only federal action could ensure it. The alternative, he warned, was conflict, polarization, stagnation, inequality. "Will you leave the future a society where lawns are clipped and the countryside cluttered, where store buildings are new and school buildings are old; a society of private satisfaction for some in the midst of public squalor for all? Or will you join to build the Great Society?"[17] The answer to that final question, in the twenty years after Johnson's retirement, tolled a resounding no.

Johnson's record remains. Medicare, Head Start, voting rights, and environmental regulation are permanent features of the American political landscape. Bill Clinton, another extroverted southerner in the White House, wrestles daily with the Johnson legacy, simultaneously reaffirming the need for generous government programs and billing himself as a "New Democrat," free from the excesses of the Great Society. Contemporary liberals pose as both heirs and critics of LBJ, mindful of the middle class as well as the dispossessed, willing to use military force overseas but recognizing the limits of American power.

For nearly half a century, Lyndon Johnson bestrode the world of American politics like a colossus, embodying in his ambition and compassion, his opportunism and vision, his anticommunism and his devotion to the wretched of the earth, all the events and controversies that dominated his era. He left a record of achievement unmatched by any other president and a legacy of failure, deceit, and bitterness that eroded Americans' faith in the presidency, mired the nation in a brutal, unpopular war, and ultimately undermined his party, his politics, and his own career. With liberalism in eclipse, LBJ's reputation has never recovered. His martyred predecessor John F. Kennedy and even his disgraced successor Richard Nixon consistently place ahead of LBJ in public ratings of the presidents, even though they never came close to matching Johnson's accomplishments. Johnson is the one modern president most Americans refuse to look in the eye, to consider in all his vulgarity, passion, weakness, and greatness. Perhaps the French leader Charles de Gaulle best understood our national reluctance to come to terms with Lyndon Johnson—who tells us too much about ourselves, not, like John F. Kennedy, about who we long to become. "This man Kennedy is America's mask," de Gaulle understood. "But this man Johnson, he is the country's real face."[18]

# NOTES

[1] Jack Valenti, *A Very Human President* (New York: Pocket Books, 1977), 301–03.

[2] Richard Nixon, Second Inaugural Address, Jan. 20, 1972. Text reprinted in the *New York Times*, Jan. 21, 1972.

[3] Doris Kearns, *Lyndon Johnson and the American Dream* (New York: Signet Books, 1976), 356.

[4] Lyndon B. Johnson, *The Vantage Point* (New York: Popular Library, 1971), 440.

[5] Joseph A. Califano, Jr., *The Triumph and Tragedy of Lyndon Johnson* (New York: Simon and Schuster, 1991), 105.

[6] Larry Berman, *Lyndon Johnson's War* (New York: W. W. Norton, 1989), xii.

[7] Kearns, *Johnson and the American Dream*, 315.

[8] Allen J. Matusow, *The Unraveling of America* (New York: Harper and Row, 1984), 171.

[9] Martin Luther King, Jr., *Where Do We Go From Here?* (New York: Bantam, 1968), 80–81.

[10] *Time*, Jan. 24, 1969, 35.

[11] Richard Rovere, *Waist Deep in the Big Muddy* (Boston: Little, Brown, 1968), 31.

[12] Robert Lekachman, "Death of a Slogan—The Great Society 1967," *Commentary*, January 1967, 56.

[13] *Public Papers of the Presidents: Lyndon B. Johnson 1963–1969*, 11 vols. (Washington, D.C.: Government Printing Office, 1964–1969), 1968, 475.

[14] Califano, *Triumph and Tragedy,* 291. Lyndon B. Johnson, *Quotations from Chairman LBJ* (New York: Simon and Schuster, 1968). Kearns, *Johnson and the American Dream,* 354.

[15] Johnson, *Vantage Point,* 568.

[16] Thurgood Marshall, quoted in the *Washington Post,* Jan. 31, 1993, A10.

[17] Johnson, *Quotations from Chairman LBJ,* 35.

[18] Charles de Gaulle, quoted in Robert Dallek, *Lone Star Rising: Lyndon Johnson and His Times* (New York: Oxford University Press, 1991), 7.

# PART TWO

# The Documents

# 8

## Perspectives on the Great Society

### DOCUMENT 1. "LET US CONTINUE": LBJ'S FIRST SPEECH AS PRESIDENT

In his first speech as president, Lyndon Johnson attempted to soothe a nation shocked by John F. Kennedy's violent death. Mourning his slain predecessor, LBJ promised to complete Kennedy's program. Significantly, he translated Kennedy's tragic death into a mandate for legislative action, particularly to engineer breakthroughs on the stalled civil rights and tax cut bills.

### LYNDON B. JOHNSON
## Address before a Joint Session of the Congress
#### November 27, 1963

*Mr. Speaker, Mr. President, Members of the House, Members of the Senate, my fellow Americans:*

All I have I would have given gladly not to be standing here today.

The greatest leader of our time has been struck down by the foulest deed of our time. Today John Fitzgerald Kennedy lives on in the immortal words and works that he left behind. He lives on in the mind and memories of mankind. He lives on in the hearts of his countrymen.

No words are sad enough to express our sense of loss. No words are strong enough to express our determination to continue the forward thrust of America that he began.

Address before a Joint Session of the Congress, November 27, 1963, *Public Papers of the Presidents of the United States: Lyndon B. Johnson, 1963–64,* vol. 1 (Washington, D.C.: Government Printing Office, 1964), 8–10.

The dream of conquering the vastness of space—the dream of partnership across the Atlantic—and across the Pacific as well—the dream of a Peace Corps in less developed nations—the dream of education for all of our children—the dream of jobs for all who seek them and need them—the dream of care for our elderly—the dream of an all-out attack on mental illness—and above all, the dream of equal rights for all Americans, whatever their race or color—these and other American dreams have been vitalized by his drive and by his dedication.

And now the ideas and the ideals which he so nobly represented must and will be translated into effective action.

Under John Kennedy's leadership, this Nation has demonstrated that it has the courage to seek peace, and it has the fortitude to risk war. We have proved that we are a good and reliable friend to those who seek peace and freedom. We have shown that we can also be a formidable foe to those who reject the path of peace and those who seek to impose upon us or our allies the yoke of tyranny.

This Nation will keep its commitments from South Viet-Nam to West Berlin. We will be unceasing in the search for peace; resourceful in our pursuit of areas of agreement even with those with whom we differ; and generous and loyal to those who join with us in common cause.

In this age when there can be no losers in peace and no victors in war, we must recognize the obligation to match national strength with national restraint. We must be prepared at one and the same time for both the confrontation of power and the limitation of power. We must be ready to defend the national interest and to negotiate the common interest. This is the path that we shall continue to pursue. Those who test our courage will find it strong, and those who seek our friendship will find it honorable. We will demonstrate anew that the strong can be just in the use of strength; and the just can be strong in the defense of justice.

And let all know we will extend no special privilege and impose no persecution. We will carry on the fight against poverty and misery, and disease and ignorance, in other lands and in our own.

We will serve all the Nation, not one section or one sector, or one group, but all Americans. These are the United States—a united people with a united purpose.

Our American unity does not depend upon unanimity. We have differences; but now, as in the past, we can derive from those differences strength, not weakness, wisdom, not despair. Both as a people and a government, we can unite upon a program, a program which is wise and just, enlightened and constructive.

For 32 years Capitol Hill has been my home. I have shared many moments of pride with you, pride in the ability of the Congress of the

United States to act, to meet any crisis, to distill from our differences strong programs of national action.

An assassin's bullet has thrust upon me the awesome burden of the Presidency. I am here today to say I need your help; I cannot bear this burden alone. I need the help of all Americans, and all America. This Nation has experienced a profound shock, and in this critical moment, it is our duty, yours and mine, as the Government of the United States, to do away with uncertainty and doubt and delay, and to show that we are capable of decisive action; that from the brutal loss of our leader we will derive not weakness, but strength; that we can and will act and act now.

From this chamber of representative government, let all the world know and none misunderstand that I rededicate this Government to the unswerving support of the United Nations, to the honorable and determined execution of our commitments to our allies, to the maintenance of military strength second to none, to the defense of the strength and the stability of the dollar, to the expansion of our foreign trade, to the reinforcement of our programs of mutual assistance and cooperation in Asia and Africa, and to our Alliance for Progress in this hemisphere.

On the 20th day of January, in 1961, John F. Kennedy told his countrymen that our national work would not be finished "in the first thousand days, nor in the life of this administration, nor even perhaps in our lifetime on this planet. But," he said, "let us begin."

Today, in this moment of new resolve, I would say to all my fellow Americans, let us continue.

This is our challenge—not to hesitate, not to pause, not to turn about and linger over this evil moment, but to continue on our course so that we may fulfill the destiny that history has set for us. Our most immediate tasks are here on this Hill.

First, no memorial oration or eulogy could more eloquently honor President Kennedy's memory than the earliest possible passage of the civil rights bill for which he fought so long. We have talked long enough in this country about equal rights. We have talked for one hundred years or more. It is time now to write the next chapter, and to write it in the books of law.

I urge you again, as I did in 1957 and again in 1960, to enact a civil rights law so that we can move forward to eliminate from this Nation every trace of discrimination and oppression that is based upon race or color. There could be no greater source of strength to this Nation both at home and abroad.

And second, no act of ours could more fittingly continue the work of President Kennedy than the early passage of the tax bill for which he fought all this long year. This is a bill designed to increase our national income and Federal revenues, and to provide insurance against recession. That bill, if passed without delay, means more security for those now working, more jobs for those now without them, and more incentive for our economy.

In short, this is no time for delay. It is a time for action—strong, forward-looking action on the pending education bills to help bring the light of learning to every home and hamlet of America—strong, forward-looking action on youth employment opportunities; strong, forward-looking action on the pending foreign aid bill, making clear that we are not forfeiting our responsibilities to this hemisphere or to the world, nor erasing Executive flexibility in the conduct of our foreign affairs—and strong, prompt, and forward-looking action on the remaining appropriation bills.

In this new spirit of action, the Congress can expect the full cooperation and support of the executive branch. And in particular, I pledge that the expenditures of your Government will be administered with the utmost thrift and frugality. I will insist that the Government get a dollar's value for a dollar spent. The Government will set an example of prudence and economy. This does not mean that we will not meet our unfilled needs or that we will not honor our commitments. We will do both.

As one who has long served in both Houses of the Congress, I firmly believe in the independence and the integrity of the legislative branch. And I promise you that I shall always respect this. It is deep in the marrow of my bones. With equal firmness, I believe in the capacity and I believe in the ability of the Congress, despite the divisions of opinions which characterize our Nation, to act—to act wisely, to act vigorously, to act speedily when the need arises.

The need is here. The need is now. I ask your help.

We meet in grief, but let us also meet in renewed dedication and renewed vigor. Let us meet in action, in tolerance, and in mutual understanding. John Kennedy's death commands what his life conveyed—that America must move forward. The time has come for Americans of all races and creeds and political beliefs to understand and to respect one another. So let us put an end to the teaching and the preaching of hate and evil and violence. Let us turn away from the fanatics of the far left and the far right, from the apostles of bitterness and bigotry, from those defiant of law, and those who pour venom into our Nation's bloodstream.

I profoundly hope that the tragedy and the torment of these terrible days will bind us together in new fellowship, making us one people in our hour of sorrow. So let us here highly resolve that John Fitzgerald Kennedy did not live—or die—in vain. And on this Thanksgiving eve, as we gather together to ask the Lord's blessing, and give Him our thanks, let us unite in those familiar and cherished words:

> America, America,
> God shed His grace on thee,
> And crown thy good
> With brotherhood
> From sea to shining sea.

# DOCUMENT 2. LAUNCHING THE GREAT SOCIETY

During the early months of his administration, Johnson walked a political tightrope, carefully honoring the memory of John F. Kennedy while slowly placing his own marks on the presidency. Johnson mapped out an ambitious legislative agenda and simultaneously groped for a slogan to encapsulate his version of American liberalism, one that would rival FDR's "New Deal," Truman's "Fair Deal," and JFK's "New Frontier." Johnson's aides canvassed many of the nation's leading writers and thinkers for ideas, including novelist John Steinbeck, whose lines about the Great Society as a constant challenge—an objective never fully realized, always in the process of becoming—captured the president's imagination and made their way into his official statements.

In the selection that follows, excerpted from a commencement address at the University of Michigan in 1964, Johnson brought together the major themes of his previous presidential speeches and embraced the term *Great Society* as the name for his program. Johnson promised to complete the unfinished business of his predecessors, but he suggested that unbridled economic growth, the central objective of American liberals in the 1950s and early 1960s, was no longer sufficient. He laid out a new, broader program for American liberalism, encompassing not only economic prosperity but also quality of life.

# LYNDON B. JOHNSON

# *Remarks at the University of Michigan*

## *May 22, 1964*

I have come today from the turmoil of your Capital to the tranquility of your campus to speak about the future of your country.

The purpose of protecting the life of our Nation and preserving the liberty of our citizens is to pursue the happiness of our people. Our success in that pursuit is the test of our success as a Nation.

For a century we labored to settle and to subdue a continent. For half a century we called upon unbounded invention and untiring industry to create an order of plenty for all of our people.

The challenge of the next half century is whether we have the wisdom to use that wealth to enrich and elevate our national life, and to advance the quality of our American civilization.

Your imagination, your initiative, and your indignation will determine whether we build a society where progress is the servent of our needs, or a society where old values and new visions are buried under unbridled growth. For in your time we have the opportunity to move not only toward the rich society and the powerful society, but upward to the Great Society.

The Great Society rests on abundance and liberty for all. It demands an end to poverty and racial injustice, to which we are totally committed in our time. But that is just the beginning.

The Great Society is a place where every child can find knowledge to enrich his mind and to enlarge his talents. It is a place where leisure is a welcome chance to build and reflect, not a feared cause of boredom and restlessness. It is a place where the city of man serves not only the needs of the body and the demands of commerce but the desire for beauty and the hunger for community.

It is a place where man can renew contact with nature. It is a place which honors creation for its own sake and for what it adds to the understanding of the race. It is a place where men are more concerned with the quality of their goals than the quantity of their goods.

But most of all, the Great Society is not a safe harbor, a resting place, a final objective, a finished work. It is a challenge constantly renewed,

Remarks at the University of Michigan, May 22, 1964 (as excerpted), *Public Papers of the Presidents of the United States: Lyndon B. Johnson, 1963–64,* Vol. 1 (Washington, D.C.: Government Printing Office, 1964), 704–07.

beckoning us toward a destiny where the meaning of our lives matches the marvelous products of our labor.

So I want to talk to you today about three places where we begin to build the Great Society—in our cities, in our countryside, and in our classrooms. . . .

Many of you will live to see the day, perhaps 50 years from now, when there will be 400 million Americans—four-fifths of them in urban areas. In the remainder of this century urban population will double, city land will double, and we will have to build homes, highways, and facilities equal to all those built since this country was first settled. So in the next 40 years we must rebuild the entire urban United States.

Aristotle said: "Men come together in cities in order to live, but they remain together in order to live the good life." It is harder and harder to live the good life in American cities today.

The catalog of ills is long: there is the decay of the centers and the despoiling of the suburbs. There is not enough housing for our people or transportation for our traffic. Open land is vanishing and old landmarks are violated.

Worst of all expansion is eroding the precious and time honored values of community with neighbors and communion with nature. The loss of these values breeds loneliness and boredom and indifference.

Our society will never be great until our cities are great. Today the frontier of imagination and innovation is inside those cities and not beyond their borders.

New experiments are already going on. It will be the task of your generation to make the American city a place where future generations will come, not only to live but to live the good life. . . .

A second place where we begin to build the Great Society is in our countryside. We have always prided ourselves on being not only America the strong and America the free, but America the beautiful. Today that beauty is in danger. The water we drink, the food we eat, the very air that we breathe are threatened with pollution. Our parks are over-crowded, our seashores overburdened. Green fields and dense forests are disappearing.

A few years ago we were greatly concerned about the "Ugly American."[1] Today we must act to prevent an ugly America.

For once the battle is lost, once our natural splendor is destroyed, it

---

[1] A term derived from the title of the best-selling 1958 novel *The Ugly American* by Eugene Burdick and William J. Lederer (New York: Norton, 1958) that has come to refer to boorish American travelers in foreign countries. It signifies Americans who are insensitive to the culture, history, and concerns of the lands they visit.

can never be recaptured. And once man can no longer walk with beauty or wonder at nature his spirit will wither and his sustenance be wasted.

A third place to build the Great Society is in the classrooms of America. There your children's lives will be shaped. Our society will not be great until every young mind is set free to scan the farthest reaches of thought and imagination. We are still far from that goal.

Today, 8 million adult Americans, more than the entire population of Michigan, have not finished 5 years of school. Nearly 20 million have not finished 8 years of school. Nearly 54 million—more than one-quarter of all America—have not even finished high school.

Each year more than 100,000 high school graduates, with proved ability, do not enter college because they cannot afford it. And if we cannot educate today's youth, what will we do in 1970 when elementary school enrollment will be 5 million greater than 1960? And high school enrollment will rise by 5 million. College enrollment will increase by more than 3 million.

In many places, classrooms are overcrowded and curricula are outdated. Most of our qualified teachers are underpaid, and many of our paid teachers are unqualified. So we must give every child a place to sit and a teacher to learn from. Poverty must not be a bar to learning, and learning must offer an escape from poverty.

But more classrooms and more teachers are not enough. We must seek an educational system which grows in excellence as it grows in size. This means better training for our teachers. It means preparing youth to enjoy their hours of leisure as well as their hours of labor. It means exploring new techniques of teaching, to find new ways to stimulate the love of learning and the capacity for creation.

These are three of the central issues of the Great Society. While our Government has many programs directed at those issues, I do not pretend that we have the full answer to those problems. . . .

Within your lifetime powerful forces, already loosed, will take us toward a way of life beyond the realm of our experience, almost beyond the bounds of our imagination.

For better or for worse, your generation has been appointed by history to deal with those problems and to lead America toward a new age. You have the chance never before afforded to any people in any age. You can help build a society where the demands of morality, and the needs of the spirit, can be realized in the life of the Nation.

So, will you join in the battle to give every citizen the full equality which God enjoins and the law requires, whatever his belief, or race, or the color of his skin?

Will you join in the battle to give every citizen an escape from the crushing weight of poverty?

Will you join in the battle to make it possible for all nations to live in enduring peace — as neighbors and not as mortal enemies?

Will you join in the battle to build the Great Society, to prove that our material progress is only the foundation on which we will build a richer life of mind and spirit?

There are those timid souls who say this battle cannot be won; that we are condemned to a soulless wealth. I do not agree. We have the power to shape the civilization that we want. But we need your will, your labor, your hearts, if we are to build that kind of society.

Those who came to this land sought to build more than just a new country. They sought a new world. So I have come here today to your campus to say that you can make their vision our reality. So let us from this moment begin our work so that in the future men will look back and say: It was then, after a long and weary way, that man turned the exploits of his genius to the full enrichment of his life.

## DOCUMENT 3.  A POVERTY WARRIOR
## DEFENDS THE GREAT SOCIETY

For the past twenty-five years, liberals, conservatives, and radicals have debated the merits of the Great Society, disagreeing about both the worthiness of its objectives and the extent of its success. In 1984, the LBJ School of Public Affairs at the University of Texas marked the twentieth anniversary of the Great Society by convening a group of scholars and public officials to assess the legacy of Johnson's program. In the following selection, Joseph A. Califano, Jr., one of the participants in the symposium and also LBJ's principal adviser on domestic affairs from 1965 to 1969, describes the achievements and mistakes of the Great Society.

# JOSEPH A. CALIFANO, JR.
## *How Great Was the Great Society?*

Historians should make no mistake in judging the Johnson administration. What Lyndon Johnson and the Great Society were about twenty years ago was revolution.

President Johnson came to office in an America where the economy had been stagnant for several years; an America where movie theaters and restaurants within a short walk of our nation's Capitol were still segregated, for whites only; an America of unparalleled abundance and prosperity in which more than 20 percent of the people lived in poverty.

It was also an America feeling the birth pains of urbanization and the world's first postindustrial society, a nation becoming a lonely crowd, troubled by the organization men in gray flannel suits, the beat generation, and everything getting bigger than life.

The modern age that had brought America unprecedented material riches had also brought an assault on the individuality of the human spirit. The loneliness of the large city was replacing the friendliness of the rural hamlet. Chain stores with anonymous clerks and thousands of products were turning the neighborhood grocer, haberdasher, and druggist into Norman Rockwell antiques. Computers were replacing people as bill collectors. The mass production of automobiles exceeded our ability to construct and repair roads. Real estate was owned and being traded by people who never saw it. Products were sold and money lent by distant corporations, far away from buyers and borrowers across America. Television was nationalizing culture and taste, reshaping politics and entertainment, and bringing bad news into living rooms every night.

The task of preserving personal identity and human dignity was difficult enough for the affluent middle class of America; it was impossible for the poor who struggled in a supersociety that threatened to engulf the individual with its supermarketplace, superuniversities, overcrowded urban schools and courts, big unions, big corporations, big governments.

Against this backdrop, it's not surprising that Lyndon Johnson's historic University of Michigan commencement speech described the Great Society which he aspired to create as "a place where men are more concerned

Joseph A. Califano, Jr., "How Great Was the Great Society?" in Barbara C. Jordan and Elspeth D. Rostow, eds., *The Great Society: A Twenty-Year Critique* (Austin: Lyndon B. Johnson Library, 1986), 123–31.

with the quality of their goals than the quantity of their goods . . . a challenge constantly renewed, beckoning us toward a destiny where the meaning of our lives matches the marvelous products of our labor." President Johnson voiced the hope that in the future men would look back and say: "It was then, after a long and weary way, that man turned the exploits of his genius to the full enrichment of his life."

How much of Johnson's hope did the Great Society realize? Was it good or bad for America?

The cornerstone of the Great Society was a robust economy. With that, the overwhelming majority of the people could get their fair share of America's prosperity. A growing economic pie also allowed the affluent to take bigger pieces, even as we committed a larger portion to the public sector.

Despite a growing economy, some citizens needed special help. There were those who needed the sort of support most of us got from our mothers and fathers: a decent place to live, clothing, health care, an education to develop their talents. Great Society programs like elementary and secondary education, financial aid for college, job training, and much of the health care effort were designed to put them on their own feet, not on the taxpayer's back.

There were also Americans who, largely through no fault of their own, were unable to take care of themselves. For them, the Great Society sought to provide either money or the services that money could buy, so they could live at a minimum level of human dignity. Among these were the poor children, the permanently disabled, and the elderly.

Did the Great Society programs fail? Many who come at them with the political hindsight of the contemporary right think so. But —

Ask the 11 million students who have received loans for their college education whether the Higher Education Act failed.

Ask the 4 million blacks who registered to vote in eleven Southern states and the 6,000 blacks who held elective public office in 1984 whether the Voting Rights Act failed.

Ask the 8 million children who have been through Head Start whether the Poverty Program failed.

Ask the millions of Americans who have enjoyed the 14,000 miles of scenic trails, 7,200 miles of scenic rivers, 45 new national parks, 83 million acres of wilderness areas, and 833 endangered species of plants, animals, and birds that have been preserved—ask them whether the 278 conservation and beautification laws, including the Wilderness Act of 1964, the Endangered Species Preservation Act of 1966, and the Scenic Trails System and Wild and Scenic Rivers Acts of 1968 failed.

Ask the 2 million senior citizens who were raised above the poverty level by the minimum payment requirements of the Social Security Act amendments of 1966 whether that legislation failed.

Ask the millions of visitors whether the laws establishing the Kennedy Center and Hirschorn Museum failed.

Ask the 400 professional theater companies, the 200 dance companies, and the 100 opera companies that have sprung up since 1965 whether the National Endowments for the Arts and Humanities failed.

Ask San Franciscans that use BART, Washingtonians that use Metro, Atlantans that use MARTA, and cities and counties that use the 56,000 buses purchased since 1966 — the equivalent of our entire national fleet — whether the Urban Mass Transit Act failed.

Ask the millions of workers who gained new skills through the Manpower Development and Training Act, the Job Corps, and the National Alliance for Businessmen, whether those programs failed.

Ask the 10 million Americans living in the 3 million housing units funded by the federal aid whether the Great Society Housing Acts of 1964 and 1968 failed.

What would America be like if there had been no Great Society programs?

Perhaps no better examples exist than the changes brought about by health laws, civil rights statutes, and consumer legislation.

*Health.* Without Medicare and Medicaid; the heart, cancer and stroke legislation; and forty other health bills, life expectancy would be several years shorter, and deaths from heart disease, stroke, diabetes, pneumonia, and influenza would be much higher. Since 1962, life expectancy has jumped five years, from seventy to seventy-five. Life expectancy for blacks has risen even more, with a stunning eight-year improvement for black women. This year, for the first time in America, a black baby girl at birth has a life expectancy greater than that of a white baby boy.

*Civil rights.* In 1965, when the Voting Rights Act was passed, there were 79 black elected officials in the South; now there are nearly 3,000. Nationally, the percentage of blacks registered to vote has grown from less than 30 percent to almost 60 percent. Before the Civil Rights Act of 1964, black people in large parts of this country could not sleep in most hotels, eat in most restaurants, try on clothes at department stores, or get a snack at a lunch counter. Today, this seems a foreign and distant memory. Black enrollment in higher education has tripled, and the proportion of blacks holding professional, technical, and management jobs has more than doubled.

*Consumer protection.* The Great Society's consumer legislation sought to give the individual a fair chance in the world of products sold with the aid of the best designers and marketers, money lent on notes prepared by the shrewdest lawyers and accountants, meat and poultry from chemically fed animals, thousands of products from baby cribs that choked to refrigerator doors that couldn't be pushed open from the inside. So the Great Society gave birth to the Truth in Packaging, Truth in Lending, Wholesome Meat, Wholesome Poultry, and Product Safety Acts. And if you want to know why it's so hard to open a Tylenol bottle, blame the Great Society's child safety legislation. Auto and Highway Safety Acts gave us seat belts, padded dash boards, and a host of automobile design changes.

Has America changed?

— When Lyndon Johnson spoke at the University of Michigan in 1964, he noted that 8 million adult Americans had not finished five years of school, 20 million had not finished eight years, and 54 million had not completed high school. Today, only 3 million have not completed five years, 8 million have not completed 8 years, and 28 million have not completed high school.

— Infant mortality has been cut by more than half, from 26 deaths per 1,000 live births in 1963 to 10.9 in 1983.

— More than 30,000 schools have received funds under the Elementary and Secondary Education Act to teach remedial math and reading to disadvantaged students.

— Thanks to Highway Beautification, 600,000 billboards have been removed from highways and 10,000 junkyards have been cleaned up.

And what of the overall impact of the Great Society on poverty in America? In 1960, 22 percent of the American people lived below the official poverty level. When Lyndon Johnson left office in 1969, that had dropped to 13 percent. Despite the relatively flat economy of the 1970s, the official poverty level did not rise. Indeed, by 1979 it was still about 12 percent. But, and this is a but we must repeat again and again, if we count the income effects of the Great Society service programs, such as those for health care, job training, aid to education, and rehabilitation for the handicapped, by the mid-1970s the poverty rate had been reduced to less than 7 percent. The early 1980s have sadly seen the rate rise up again.

And the Great Society has been invaluable to President Reagan, not just as a political whipping boy, but as the key to his attack on inflation. President Reagan was able to drive down inflation with a sledgehammer because of the cushions Lyndon Johnson's Great Society provided: liberalization of welfare, food stamps and unemployment compensation;

Medicaid and Medicare; community health centers; work training; housing; and a host of other programs. Ronald Reagan taught us that we can rapidly wring inflation out of the economy because the remnants of a compassionate, interventionist government are there not only to keep the mobs off the streets, but to keep most needy families at a minimum living standard and adequately fed.

I've always felt that Lyndon Johnson died convinced that the civil rights programs, notably the Voting Rights Act, marked his administration's finest hours. He certainly spent his political capital generously to enact these programs. To me, the Great Society's achievements with older Americans have also been remarkable. The combination of Medicare, Medicaid's support of nursing homes (forty-three cents of each Medicaid dollar goes to them), minimum Social Security benefits, senior citizen centers and food programs, and improved Veterans Administration benefits, along with private-sector retirement plans, virtually eliminated poverty among the elderly in America. As LBJ used to say, much remains to be done; I believe a great deal of our energies and resources in the future must be devoted to poor children and single-parent families.

I've given many examples of the successes of the Great Society. What of its shortcomings?

Did we legislate too much? Perhaps. We seemed to have a law for everything. Fire safety. Water safety. Pesticide control for the farm. Rat control for the ghetto. Bail reform. Immigration reform. Medical libraries. Presidential disability. Juvenile delinquency. Safe streets. Tire safety. Age discrimination. Fair housing. Corporate takeovers. International monetary reform. Sea grant colleges.[2] When we discovered that poor students needed a good lunch, we devised legislation for a school lunch program. When we later found out that breakfast helped them learn better, we whipped up a law for a school breakfast program. When a pipeline exploded, we proposed the Gas Pipeline Safety Act. When my son Joe swallowed a bottle of aspirin, President Johnson sent Congress a Child Safety Act. When it was too hard for citizens to get information out of the government, we drafted a Freedom of Information Act. When we needed more doctors, or nurses, or teachers, we legislated programs to train them.

Did we stub our toes? Of course.

---

[2] The Johnson administration established a program to support university research in marine science and oceanography, eventually administered by the National Oceanic and Atmospheric Administration. Participating institutions were called sea grant colleges, a variation on the land grant colleges established during the nineteenth century to teach agricultural science.

We made our mistakes, plenty of them. In health, our Great Society quest to provide access to health care for the elderly and the poor led us to accede to the demands of hospitals and physicians for open-ended cost-plus and fee-for-service payments. As a result, with Medicare and Medicaid, we adopted inherently wasteful and inefficient reimbursement systems. Incidentally, we recognized the danger of exploding health care costs in 1968, but Congress denied President Johnson's request to change Medicare's payment system.

There were too many narrow categorical grant programs created in health, education, and social services. It's one thing to embark upon a program to help states educate millions of poor children, or to provide scholarships so that any American with the brains and talent can go to college. It's quite another to set curriculum priorities from Washington with funds that must be spent on specific subjects of education, such as environmental or ethnic studies or metric education.

The struggle for civil rights left us deeply and often unjustifiably suspicious of the motives and intentions of institutional and middle America. It influenced our attitudes about consumer safety, occupational health, environmental protection, and transportation. It undermined our trust in the states.

As a result, many federal laws were written in far too much detail. And regulation writers cast aside the great American common-law principle that every citizen is presumed to obey the law. Quite the contrary, we wrote laws and regulations on the theory that each citizen would seek to circumvent them. We became victims of the self-defeating and self-fulfilling premise that, unless we were protected by a law or regulation, we were vulnerable. As regulations got into too many nooks and crannies of American life, they created testy resistance and needlessly invited ridicule. But we should remember that the massive influx of regulations that so irritated Americans came not during the Johnson years, but the decade that followed. It was the seventies, not the sixties, that brought us 6,000 schedule codes under Medicare, pages and pages of regulations under the Occupational Health and Safety legislation, hundreds of pages of education regulations.

At times we may have lost sight of the fact that these laws—hundreds of them—were not an end in themselves. Often we did not recognize that government could not do it all. And, of course, there were overpromises. But they were based on high hopes and great expectations and fueled by the frustration of seeing so much poverty and ignorance and illness amidst such wealth. We simply could not accept poverty, ignorance, and hunger as intractable, permanent features of American society. There was no child we could not feed; no adult we could not put to work; no disease we could not cure; no toy, food, or appliance we could not make safer; no air or water we could not clean. But it was all part of asking "not how much, but how good; not only how to create wealth, but how to use it; not only how fast we [were] going, but where we [were] headed."

This twentieth anniversary of the Great Society is not a time for giving up on those precious goals to which so many of us devoted so much of our energy and our lives. It is not even a time for hunkering down. The Great Society is alive and well—in Medicare and Medicaid; in the air we breathe and the water we drink, in the rivers and lakes we swim in; in the schools and colleges our students attend; in the medical miracles from the National Institutes of Health; in housing and transportation and equal opportunity. We can build on the best of it, and recognize our mistakes and correct them.

We must once again join our talents and experience to make our government a responsive servant of the people. For a democratic government to respond means to lead, to forge the claims of narrow groups on the anvil of government to serve the needs of all of our people, to know the special importance of protecting the individual in the modern bureaucracy, to recognize the fundamental right of each person to live in human dignity.

That was what the Great Society at its best did. It converted the hopes and aspirations of all kinds of Americans into a political force that brought out much of the good in each of us. The result was a social revolution in race relations that even a bloody civil war could not achieve; a revolution in education that opened college to any American with the ability and ambition to go; a revolution in health that provided care for all the elderly and many of the poor; a sea change in the relationship of consumers to big corporate sellers and lenders; a born-again respect for our land and air and water that is still gaining momentum.

The achievements of the Great Society did not come easily. As everyone in this room knows, that kind of work in government is hard, often frustrating, sometimes exasperating. But the rewards are far greater for those in a democracy who work persistently to build and shape government to serve the people, than for those who tear it apart or lash out in despair and frustration because the task is too much for them. I deeply believe that the Great Society teaches that we can succeed in that work of building and shaping. Like G. K. Chesterton,[3] "I do not believe in a fate that befalls people however they act. But I do believe in fate that befalls them unless they act."

[3] British journalist, novelist, and philosopher (1874–1936).

Too many of us, including many of our young Americans and some in government, don't try because the tasks seem too difficult, sometimes impossible. Of course those who govern will make mistakes, plenty of them. But we must not fear failure. What we should fear above all is the judgment of God and history if we, the most affluent people on God's earth, free to act as we wish, choose not to govern justly, not to distribute our riches fairly, and not to help the most vulnerable among us—or worse, if we choose not even to try. Whatever historians of the Great Society say twenty years later, they must admit that we tried, and I believe they will conclude that America is a better place because we did.

## DOCUMENT 4. A HISTORIAN CRITIQUES THE GREAT SOCIETY

In this selection, historian Allen J. Matusow of Rice University, another participant in the symposium on the twentieth anniversary of the Great Society, analyzes what he sees as the fundamental defects of Johnson's programs. Matusow, the author of a critical study of American liberalism in the 1960s, concludes that the war on poverty failed and that its failure stemmed from the inherent weaknesses of and contradictions within liberalism itself.

## ALLEN J. MATUSOW
# From *The Great Society: A Twenty-Year Critique*

I think that the panelists yesterday who praised the civil rights legislation were right on the money—that those laws were the great achievement of twentieth-century liberalism and that Lyndon Johnson has earned a place of honor in American history for his role in passing those laws. On the other hand, I am much more skeptical of claims that the War on Poverty was successful. In fact, I argue in my book and I am going to argue here that while there were some successes, on balance that war failed.

Allen J. Matusow, Statement in Barbara C. Jordan and Elspeth D. Rostow, eds., *The Great Society: A Twenty-Year Critique* (Austin: Lyndon B. Johnson Library, 1986), 143–47.

I don't think that the failure was the result of a lack of compassion or failure of ideals; the administration had ideals and compassion in spades. I think that the root problem of the War on Poverty was a political problem. President Johnson was a politician of consensus in a middle-class country, and that meant that whatever he did for the poor, he had to do with the permission of the affluent classes. And that, I think, was the root of the difficulties that followed. The truth of it is, if you want to fight a real war on poverty, you are going to have to recognize that the interests of the poor will at some crucial point be in conflict with the interests of the middle classes.

Political constraints on the president determined, for instance, the definition of poverty, and this is crucial. The administration defined poverty as a fixed condition: if a family of four had an income of $3,000 or less, it was poor. That is a politically useful definition, but it's not an intellectually defensible one. In modern industrial societies, poverty is a relative deprivation; that is, it is an aspect of inequality. The poor are poor if they continue to lag as far behind everybody else as before, despite rising living standards.

If that definition is the correct one, then the only way to combat poverty is to undertake a redistribution of income. And no national politician in a middle-class country can propose to do that, and that included President Johnson. As a result, there has been no income redistribution since the War on Poverty or, for that matter, before.

At the beginning of the century, the bottom 20 percent who were regarded as poor received 5 percent of the national income. That was true in the twenties. In 1964, when the president declared war on poverty, the 20 percent of the population he said was poor received 5 percent of the money income. And today, the bottom 20 percent receives 5 percent of the national income. By that measurement, despite the figures you have heard in this symposium, there has been no reduction in the incidence of poverty.

It seems to me that the same political constraints that compelled an inadequate definition of the poverty problem also were responsible for serious flaws on individual measures; that is, in order to get bills passed, middle-class constituencies had to be satisfied, with the result that there were crippling flaws in the major antipoverty measures. I would like briefly to refer to two of these measures. I am going to talk about education and medicine because these programs of the Great Society were the most defensible and most popular and they were the ones addressed by yesterday's panelists.

Let me start with education. Title I of the Elementary and Secondary

Education Act of 1965 provided grants to local school districts for compensatory education programs to benefit low-income students with a hope that those grants would equalize educational achievement among social classes. That was a worthy objective. In order to achieve it, however, the administration had to appease middle-class school boards and middle-class school bureaucracies at the local level who would never permit any program to pass unless they controlled it, which in that legislation they were permitted to do.

Now, the problem with that is that middle-class school boards and middle-class administrators are not famous for their sympathy for poor students. They are on the whole—at least on the average—more sympathetic to their middle-class constituencies. In 1966 a poll of school superintendents showed that 70 percent of them did not think that Title I benefits should service poor students. As a result, over the years of administering the program, the local school districts were able to exploit anomalies in it and make sure that the benefits were not exclusively directed to the poor.

President Johnson always believed that Title I was an antipoverty program. The local school districts made sure that it was not. In 1977, a study conducted by the federal government showed that almost two-thirds of the beneficiaries of Title I programs were not poor, that more than half were not low achievers, and that 40 percent were neither poor nor low-achieving.

It should be said that when this law was passed, no one knew whether compensatory education would work; or, if it would work, how. Unfortunately, a study done for Congress in the late 1970s showed that Title I had no long-term impact on the educational achievement of low-income students.

Let me just quickly talk about Medicaid. Medicaid is another program that was shaped to accommodate an existing vested middle-class interest, and that's the interest of doctors and hospital administrators; that is, to pass the bill, the administration had to promise doctors and hospitals that it would not interfere with the conduct of the medical profession.

It's quite often implied by people who talk about Medicaid that in the old days if you didn't have money, you didn't have access to medical services. That is not true. There was an extensive system of charity medicine before Medicaid was passed. For example, in 1964, if you were in a family with an income of less than $3,000, your hospital admission rate was 107 per 1,000; whereas if you were in a family of over $10,000, it was 89 per 1,000. And poor people saw doctors on an average of 4.3 times a year compared to 5.1 times for more affluent classes.

That doesn't mean that access was not a problem. There were pockets of poor people in America that did not have access to medical treatment. But if you were the average poor person, you had access to a fairly well-developed charity medical system.

Now, if the point of Medicaid was to increase access to medical care, Medicaid was somewhat successful, because the hospital admission rate for poor people jumped from 107 per 1,000 to 122 per 1,000, and poor people actually began to see the doctor slightly more than nonpoor people after Medicaid was passed.

But the point is that most of the medical services received by poor people after Medicaid would have been received anyway under the charity medical system.

Here are the points that can be raised by someone skeptical of Medicaid: First, the primary beneficiaries were the doctors and hospitals who received payment for services they once rendered free of charge or at reduced payment.

Second, the program very quickly exceeded all cost estimates, so that within ten years six dollars out of every ten dollars spent on public assistance in the United States was spent for Medicaid. Almost certainly, most poor people would have rather had the cash.

Third, the charity medical system was always a two-tiered system— that is, if you were in the charity medical system, you received second-class treatment—and the charity medical system was not changed by Medicaid. It was simply subsidized. For example, in the state of New York only 8 percent of the 12,000 doctors in that city will take Medicaid patients and they, by report, are mostly the marginal practitioners.

Finally, there is a question of whether the additional medical services provided under Medicaid really lead to improved health. This is a very complicated subject, and I don't pretend to have the final answer, but I am highly skeptical of the claims that beyond a certain point more consumption of medical services results in better health.

The most popular claim of those who think that more medical care under Medicaid promotes more health is that there has been a radical reduction of black infant mortality rates since Medicaid. In fact, the black infant mortality rate in the first decade went down about 26 percent, which is significant but not historically unusual: it went down *40* percent in the 1940s. There was extensive treatment of the average pregnant poor black woman before Medicaid; that is, the average poor pregnant woman saw a doctor about 6.5 times before Medicaid, compared to 9.5 times later. The question is, did these additional visitations pay off?

Well, the single thing that a doctor can do for a pregnant woman that will enhance the chances of the survival of her child in the first year is to make sure that the body weight of the infant will be in a normal range, because low-weight births are the most significant corollary to infant mortality. As it turns out, there has been no reduction in the incidence of low-weight births since 1965.

The other day it occurred to me there existed a possible test to measure what the effect of Medicaid is on black infant mortality rates. Not all the states implemented Medicaid at the same time. A few began to implement Medicaid in January of 1966, and about a dozen didn't implement Medicaid until January of 1970; that is four years of this ten-year period in which it's possible to examine black infant mortality in states with and without Medicaid.

So I took the two largest industrial states that initiated Medicaid in January of 1966, that is, Pennsylvania and Illinois, and I compared them with two states, also industrial, that did not introduce Medicaid until four years later, that is, Indiana and New Jersey. I found that the infant mortality rate was significantly lower in the states that did not have Medicaid. There was only one Southern state, Louisiana, that initiated Medicaid in 1966; I compared it with Mississippi and Alabama, and concerning infant mortality there is virtually no difference. I am not going to conclude from that that there is a correlation betwen Medicaid and infant mortality, but I think these figures should induce a certain skepticism about the nature of the claims made for these programs.

# DOCUMENT 5. POVERTY: THE STATISTICAL RECORD, 1960–1990

Central to the ongoing debate about the efficacy of Johnson's antipoverty program are rival—and irreconcilable—interpretations of the official statistics. Johnson's defenders note that the proportion of the American population living in poverty dropped precipitously during the 1960s, while critics of the Great Society attribute that decline to the economic boom stimulated by the Vietnam War and note the persistence of high rates of poverty among African Americans. Even today, more than 30 percent of African Americans live below the official poverty line, distressing testimony to the intractability of hard-core poverty in the nation's inner cities.

The Census Bureau table that follows allows readers to draw their own conclusions.

**Persons Below Poverty Level and Below 125 Percent of Poverty Level: 1959 to 1990 [Persons as of March of the following year.]**

| YEAR | PERCENT BELOW POVERTY LEVEL | | | | BELOW 125 PERCENT OF POVERTY LEVEL | |
|---|---|---|---|---|---|---|
| | ALL RACES[1] | WHITE | BLACK | HISPANIC[2] | NUMBER (MIL.) | PERCENT OF TOTAL POPULATION |
| 1959 | 22.4 | 18.1 | 55.1 | (NA) | 54.9 | 31.1 |
| 1960 | 22.2 | 17.8 | (NA) | (NA) | 54.6 | 30.4 |
| 1966 | 14.7 | 12.2 | 41.8 | (NA) | 41.3 | 21.3 |
| 1969 | 12.1 | 9.5 | 32.2 | (NA) | 34.7 | 17.4 |
| 1970 | 12.6 | 9.9 | 33.5 | (NA) | 35.6 | 17.6 |
| 1975 | 12.3 | 9.7 | 31.3 | 26.9 | 37.2 | 17.6 |
| 1976 | 11.8 | 9.1 | 31.1 | 24.7 | 35.5 | 16.7 |
| 1977 | 11.6 | 8.9 | 31.3 | 22.4 | 35.7 | 16.7 |
| 1978 | 11.4 | 8.7 | 30.6 | 21.6 | 34.2 | 15.8 |
| 1979[4] | 11.7 | 9.0 | 31.0 | 21.8 | 36.6 | 16.4 |
| 1980 | 13.0 | 10.2 | 32.5 | 25.7 | 40.7 | 18.1 |
| 1981 | 14.0 | 11.1 | 34.2 | 26.5 | 43.7 | 19.3 |
| 1982 | 15.0 | 12.0 | 35.6 | 29.9 | 46.5 | 20.3 |
| 1983[5] | 15.2 | 12.1 | 35.7 | 28.0 | 47.2 | 20.3 |
| 1984 | 14.4 | 11.5 | 33.8 | 28.4 | 45.3 | 19.4 |
| 1985 | 14.0 | 11.4 | 31.3 | 29.0 | 44.2 | 18.7 |
| 1986 | 13.6 | 11.0 | 31.1 | 27.3 | 43.5 | 18.2 |
| 1987[6] | 13.4 | 10.4 | 32.4 | 28.0 | 43.0 | 17.9 |
| 1988 | 13.0 | 10.1 | 31.3 | 26.7 | 42.6 | 17.5 |
| 1989 | 12.8 | 10.0 | 30.7 | 26.2 | 42.7 | 17.3 |
| 1990 | 13.5 | 10.7 | 31.9 | 28.1 | 44.8 | 18.0 |

NA Not available. [1] Includes other races not shown separately. [2] Hispanic persons may be of any race. [3] Beginning 1981, income cutoffs for nonfarm families are applied to all families, both farm and nonfarm. [4] Population controls based on 1980 census; see text, sections 1 and 14. [5] Beginning 1983, based on revised Hispanic population controls; data not directly comparable with prior years. [6] Beginning 1987, based on revised processing procedures; data not directly comparable with prior years.

| YEAR | NUMBER BELOW POVERTY LEVEL (MIL.) | | | | AVERAGE INCOME CUTOFFS FOR NON-FARM FAMILY OF 4[3] | |
| | ALL RACES[1] | WHITE | BLACK | HISPANIC[2] | AT POVERTY LEVEL | AT 125 PERCENT OF POVERTY LEVEL |
| --- | --- | --- | --- | --- | --- | --- |
| 1959 | 39.5 | 28.5 | 9.9 | (NA) | $2,973 | $3,716 |
| 1960 | 39.9 | 28.3 | (NA) | (NA) | 3,022 | 3,778 |
| 1966 | 28.5 | 20.8 | 8.9 | (NA) | 3,317 | 4,146 |
| 1969 | 24.1 | 16.7 | 7.1 | (NA) | 3,743 | 4,679 |
| 1970 | 25.4 | 17.5 | 7.5 | (NA) | 3,968 | 4,960 |
| 1975 | 25.9 | 17.8 | 7.5 | 3.0 | 5,500 | 6,875 |
| 1976 | 25.0 | 16.7 | 7.6 | 2.8 | 5,815 | 7,269 |
| 1977 | 24.7 | 16.4 | 7.7 | 2.7 | 6,191 | 7,739 |
| 1978 | 24.5 | 16.3 | 7.6 | 2.6 | 6,662 | 8,328 |
| 1979[4] | 26.1 | 17.2 | 8.1 | 2.9 | 7,412 | 9,265 |
| 1980 | 29.3 | 19.7 | 8.6 | 3.5 | 8,414 | 10,518 |
| 1981 | 31.8 | 21.6 | 9.2 | 3.7 | 9,287 | 11,609 |
| 1982 | 34.4 | 23.5 | 9.7 | 4.3 | 9,862 | 12,328 |
| 1983[5] | 35.3 | 24.0 | 9.9 | 4.6 | 10,178 | 12,723 |
| 1984 | 33.7 | 23.0 | 9.5 | 4.8 | 10,609 | 13,261 |
| 1985 | 33.1 | 22.9 | 8.9 | 5.2 | 10,989 | 13,736 |
| 1986 | 32.4 | 22.2 | 9.0 | 5.1 | 11,203 | 14,004 |
| 1987[6] | 32.2 | 21.2 | 9.5 | 5.4 | 11,611 | 14,514 |
| 1988 | 31.7 | 20.7 | 9.4 | 5.4 | 12,092 | 15,115 |
| 1989 | 31.5 | 20.8 | 9.3 | 5.4 | 12,674 | 15,843 |
| 1990 | 33.6 | 22.3 | 9.8 | 6.0 | 13,359 | 16,699 |

*Source:* U.S. Bureau of the Census, *Current Population Reports,* series P-60, No. 175, and earlier reports.
U. S. Bureau of the Census, *Statistical Abstract of the United States: 1992,* prepared by the Geography Division in cooperation with the Housing Division, Bureau of the Census. (Washington, D.C.: Government Printing Office, 1992), 456.

# 9

# Racial Conflict
# and the Civil Rights Revolution

## DOCUMENT 6. "WE SHALL OVERCOME": THE VOTING RIGHTS SPEECH

On March 15, 1965, in the wake of the dramatic civil rights protests in Selma, Alabama, Johnson summoned both houses of Congress to a special evening joint session and addressed the nation on television from the rostrum of the House of Representatives. Johnson announced his support for a tough voting rights bill that would wipe out, once and for all, the restrictions that denied black citizens the ballot in southern states. But Johnson moved beyond his normal strategy of advocating specific legislation by identifying himself clearly and openly with the civil rights movement, embracing the goals of the Selma protesters as "our cause too," and adopting as his own the civil rights movement's anthem, "We Shall Overcome."

In many ways, the speech signaled a turning point in the civil rights struggle, marking the beginning of the end of the largely southern struggle for political rights and desegregation and ushering in the national debates over economic opportunity, political empowerment, and affirmative action. Johnson's warning that the privileges of citizenship required more than legal rights foreshadowed the coming, more controversial stage in civil rights politics.

# LYNDON B. JOHNSON
## The American Promise:
## Special Message to the Congress
### March 15, 1965

*Mr. Speaker, Mr. President, Members of the Congress:*

I speak tonight for the dignity of man and the destiny of democracy.

I urge every member of both parties, Americans of all religions and of all colors, from every section of this country, to join me in that cause.

At times history and fate meet at a single time in a single place to shape a turning point in man's unending search for freedom. So it was at Lexington and Concord. So it was a century ago at Appomattox. So it was last week in Selma, Alabama.

There, long-suffering men and women peacefully protested the denial of their rights as Americans. Many were brutally assaulted. One good man, a man of God, was killed.[1]

There is no cause for pride in what has happened in Selma. There is no cause for self-satisfaction in the long denial of equal rights of millions of Americans. But there is cause for hope and for faith in our democracy in what is happening here tonight.

For the cries of pain and the hymns and protests of oppressed people have summoned into convocation all the majesty of this great Government—the Government of the greatest Nation on earth.

Our mission is at once the oldest and the most basic of this country: to right wrong, to do justice, to serve man.

In our time we have come to live with moments of great crisis. Our lives have been marked with debate about great issues; issues of war and peace, issues of prosperity and depression. But rarely in any time does an issue lay bare the secret heart of America itself. Rarely are we met with a challenge, not to our growth or abundance, our welfare or our security, but rather to the values and the purposes and the meaning of our beloved Nation.

The issue of equal rights for American Negroes is such an issue. And should we defeat every enemy, should we double our wealth and conquer

---

[1]Johnson refers here to the Rev. James Reeb, the northern clergyman murdered in Selma, Alabama, during civil rights demonstrations in 1965. See pages 108–111.

Special Message to the Congress: The American Promise, March 15, 1965 (as excerpted), *Public Papers of the Presidents of the United States: Lyndon B. Johnson, 1965*, Vol. 1 (Washington, D.C.: Government Printing Office, 1965), 281–87.

the stars, and still be unequal to this issue, then we will have failed as a people and as a nation.

For with a country as with a person, "What is a man profited, if he shall gain the whole world, and lose his own soul?"

There is no Negro problem. There is no Southern problem. There is no Northern problem. There is only an American problem. And we are met here tonight as Americans—not as Democrats or Republicans—we are met here as Americans to solve that problem.

This was the first nation in the history of the world to be founded with a purpose. The great phrases of that purpose still sound in every American heart, North and South: "All men are created equal"—"government by consent of the governed"—"give me liberty or give me death." Well, those are not just clever words, or those are not just empty theories. In their name Americans have fought and died for two centuries, and tonight around the world they stand there as guardians of our liberty, risking their lives.

Those words are a promise to every citizen that he shall share in the dignity of man. This dignity cannot be found in a man's possessions; it cannot be found in his power, or in his position. It really rests on his right to be treated as a man equal in opportunity to all others. It says that he shall share in freedom, he shall choose his leaders, educate his children, and provide for his family according to his ability and his merits as a human being.

To apply any other test—to deny a man his hopes because of his color or race, his religion or the place of his birth—is not only to do injustice, it is to deny America and to dishonor the dead who gave their lives for American freedom.

## The Right to Vote

Our fathers believed that if this noble view of the rights of man was to flourish, it must be rooted in democracy. The most basic right of all was the right to choose your own leaders. The history of this country, in large measure, is the history of the expansion of that right to all of our people.

Many of the issues of civil rights are very complex and most difficult. But about this there can and should be no argument. Every American citizen must have an equal right to vote. There is no reason which can excuse the denial of that right. There is no duty which weighs more heavily on us than the duty we have to ensure that right.

Yet the harsh fact is that in many places in this country men and women are kept from voting simply because they are Negroes.

Every device of which human ingenuity is capable has been used to deny this right. The Negro citizen may go to register only to be told that the day is wrong, or the hour is late, or the official in charge is absent. And if he persists, and if he manages to present himself to the registrar, he may be disqualified because he did not spell out his middle name or because he abbreviated a word on the application.

And if he manages to fill out an application he is given a test. The registrar is the sole judge of whether he passes this test. He may be asked to recite the entire Constitution, or explain the most complex provisions of State law. And even a college degree cannot be used to prove that he can read and write.

For the fact is that the only way to pass these barriers is to show a white skin.

Experience has clearly shown that the existing process of law cannot overcome systematic and ingenious discrimination. No law that we now have on the books—and I have helped to put three of them there —can ensure the right to vote when local officials are determined to deny it.

In such a case our duty must be clear to all of us. The Constitution says that no person shall be kept from voting because of his race or his color. We have all sworn an oath before God to support and to defend that Constitution. We must now act in obedience to that oath.

## Guaranteeing the Right to Vote

Wednesday I will send to Congress a law designed to eliminate illegal barriers to the right to vote.

The broad principles of that bill will be in the hands of the Democratic and Republican leaders tomorrow. After they have reviewed it, it will come here formally as a bill. I am grateful for this opportunity to come here tonight at the invitation of the leadership to reason with my friends, to give them my views, and to visit with my former colleagues.

I have had prepared a more comprehensive analysis of the legislation which I had intended to transmit to the clerk tomorrow but which I will submit to the clerks tonight. But I want to really discuss with you now briefly the main proposals of this legislation.

This bill will strike down restrictions to voting in all elections— Federal, State, and local—which have been used to deny Negroes the right to vote.

This bill will establish a simple, uniform standard which cannot be used, however ingenious the effort, to flout our Constitution.

It will provide for citizens to be registered by officials of the United States Government if the State officials refuse to register them.

It will eliminate tedious, unnecessary lawsuits which delay the right to vote.

Finally, this legislation will ensure that properly registered individuals are not prohibited from voting. . . .

## The Need for Action

There is no constitutional issue here. The command of the Constitution is plain. There is no moral issue. It is wrong—deadly wrong—to deny any of your fellow Americans the right to vote in this country.

There is no issue of States rights or national rights. There is only the struggle for human rights.

I have not the slightest doubt what will be your answer.

The last time a President sent a civil rights bill to the Congress it contained a provision to protect voting rights in Federal elections. That civil rights bill was passed after 8 long months of debate. And when that bill came to my desk from the Congress for my signature, the heart of the voting provision had been eliminated.

This time, on this issue, there must be no delay, no hesitation and no compromise with our purpose.

We cannot, we must not, refuse to protect the right of every American to vote in every election that he may desire to participate in. . . .

## We Shall Overcome

But even if we pass this bill, the battle will not be over. What happened in Selma is part of a far larger movement which reaches into every section and State of America. It is the effort of American Negroes to secure for themselves the full blessings of American life.

Their cause must be our cause too. Because it is not just Negroes, but really it is all of us, who must overcome the crippling legacy of bigotry and injustice.

And we shall overcome.

As a man whose roots go deeply into Southern soil I know how agonizing racial feelings are. I know how difficult it is to reshape the attitudes and the structure of our society.

But a century has passed, more than a hundred years, since the Negro was freed. And he is not fully free tonight.

It was more than a hundred years ago that Abraham Lincoln, a great President of another party, signed the Emancipation Proclamation, but emancipation is a proclamation and not a fact.

A century has passed, more than a hundred years, since equality was promised. And yet the Negro is not equal.

A century has passed since the day of promise. And the promise is unkept.

The time of justice has now come. I tell you that I believe sincerely that no force can hold it back. It is right in the eyes of man and God that it should come. And when it does, I think that day will brighten the lives of every American.

For Negroes are not the only victims. How many white children have gone uneducated, how many white families have lived in stark poverty, how many white lives have been scarred by fear, because we have wasted our energy and our substance to maintain the barriers of hatred and terror?

So I say to all of you here, and to all in the Nation tonight, that those who appeal to you to hold on to the past do so at the cost of denying you your future.

This great, rich, restless country can offer opportunity and education and hope to all: black and white, North and South, sharecropper and city dweller. These are the enemies: poverty, ignorance, disease. They are the enemies and not our fellow man, not our neighbor. And these enemies too, poverty, disease and ignorance, we shall overcome. . . .

## Rights Must Be Opportunities

The bill that I am presenting to you will be known as a civil rights bill. But, in a larger sense, most of the program I am recommending is a civil rights program. Its object is to open the city of hope to all people of all races.

Because all Americans just must have the right to vote. And we are going to give them that right.

All Americans must have the privileges of citizenship regardless of race. And they are going to have those privileges of citizenship regardless of race.

But I would like to caution you and remind you that to exercise these privileges takes much more than just legal right. It requires a trained mind and a healthy body. It requires a decent home, and the chance to find a job, and the opportunity to escape from the clutches of poverty.

Of course, people cannot contribute to the Nation if they are never taught to read or write, if their bodies are stunted from hunger, if their sickness goes untended, if their life is spent in hopeless poverty just drawing a welfare check.

So we want to open the gates to opportunity. But we are also going to give all our people, black and white, the help that they need to walk through those gates.

## DOCUMENT 7. A NEW MILITANCE IN BLACK AMERICA

In July 1965, civil rights leader James Farmer addressed a national convention of his organization, the Congress on Racial Equality (CORE). Farmer's remarks joined a chorus of more militant African-American voices in the mid-1960s, as frustration mounted with the slow pace of reform and continued racial injustice. Stokely Carmichael, newly elected president of the Student Non-Violent Coordinating Committee, toured Mississippi replacing the old slogan of "Freedom Now" by leading chants of "Black Power!" Malcolm X advocated black nationalism in northern cities, repudiating Martin Luther King, Jr.'s insistence on nonviolence and promising active self-defense against racism. King himself began protests in Chicago and committed himself to securing "positive and necessary power for black people."

Farmer's CORE address reflects the atmosphere of growing militance and desperation, exacerbated by the violent disturbances in Watts and other cities. He declares that civil rights advocates must no longer rely on the federal government but instead gain power directly for themselves. The new militance fostered a political crisis for the Johnson administration, simultaneously estranging LBJ from the civil rights community and alienating white liberals.

## JAMES FARMER

# "We Must Be in a Position of Power"
# Address before the CORE National Convention

### July 1, 1965

As CORE meets at its 23rd Annual Convention, we have behind us many successes achieved and victories won. But this report will not be a recounting of past successes; to rest on one's laurels is to atrophy and die. Past victories—in public accommodations, in voting rights, in the support of law and public policy—have been in battles preceding the major encounter.

The major war now confronting us is aimed at harnessing the awesome political potential of the black community in order to effect basic social and economic changes for all Americans, to alter meaningfully the lives of the Black Americans (our plight has not been and will not be changed by past victories), and to bring about a real equality of free men.

*This job cannot be done for us by the Government.* In the first place, the establishments—Federal, State, and Local—have too much built-in resistance to fundamental change. Any establishment by definition seeks its own perpetuation and rejects that which threatens it. For example, politicians take over and seek to make the antipoverty programs an adjunct of their political aspirations. They attack community action programs of the antipoverty war as being anti-city hall. School Boards, which have already lost the dropouts and other underprivileged youth, reach out greedily to control community education programs and see that they do not shake up the school systems. Powerful lobbies, such as the financial and the real estate interests, exert tremendous pressure to see that programs to relieve poverty do not threaten their interests.

Further, it is impossible for the Government to mount a decisive war against poverty and bigotry in the United States while it is pouring billions down the drain in a war against people in Viet Nam. The billion dollars available to fight poverty is puny compared with the need and insignificant compared with the resources expended in wars.

Thus, we must be constructive critics of the antipoverty program, using its resources for our fight where we can, insisting that local anti-

James Farmer, "We Must Be in a Position of Power": Address before the CORE National Convention, Durham, N.C., July 1, 1965 (as excerpted), reprinted in Francis L. Broderick and August Meier, eds., *Negro Protest Thought in the Twentieth Century* (Indianapolis: Bobbs-Merrill, 1965), 422–24, 428.

poverty boards be truly representatives of the deprived communities and the minorities which they are supposed to help, and attacking waste and pork-barreling wherever it occurs.

Yet it would be fatal to think that the antipoverty program alone can make the necessary changes in the social and economic life of Black Americans. It can be no more a solution to our problems than the Civil Rights Acts of 1957, 1960, 1964 were, or the Voter Rights Act of 1965 will be. Like those laws, the antipoverty program has to be seen as no more than a tool, useful at times but inadequate at best to do the job.

We can rely upon none but ourselves as a catalyst in the development of the potential power of the black community in its own behalf and in behalf of the nation. CORE alone has the nationwide network of militant chapters required, unshackled by compromising entanglements, political commitments and alliances. CORE alone has the flexibility to move in the new directions demanded by this phase of the war, while it fulfills its commitments to the unfinished tasks of the last phase.

In this new phase of our war to change the life of the Negro in a changed America, there are two aspects: Community organization and Political organization. It must be clearly seen that neither aspect is an end in itself. Community organization, including social services, for its own sake is mere social uplift and has no basic importance in changing the life role of the Negro. Political organization for its own sake is sheer opportunism. While both aspects must be undertaken simultaneously, the first, community organization, may be seen as a step to increase the effectiveness of the second, political organization. Or another way of viewing it is to see community organization as a tool—a tool to build a vehicle. Political organization, then, is the vehicle to take us to the desired objective. That objective is an open society free of race discrimination and forced segregation, shorn of poverty and unemployment, with decent housing and high-quality education for all. The objective, in a word, is a new society, a free and open society.

## DOCUMENT 8. FROM CIVIL RIGHTS TO AFFIRMATIVE ACTION

President Johnson acknowledged the new challenges posed by the success of his civil rights and voting rights bills and by the increasing concern about subtle, informal forms of racial discrimination in the North. In the following document, Johnson announced the opening of a new stage in his civil rights program, a shift from removing legal barriers against racial equality to providing genuine opportunity to victims of racial discrimination—from equality as a right and a theory to equality as a fact and a result. Excerpted from a commencement address at Howard University, a historically black college in Washington, D.C., the speech represented another major crossroads in American race relations. Johnson promised much broader federal action to promote racial equality in employment, education, and social life—a controversial program that provoked racial backlash among many whites who formerly supported him and the Democratic party. He also endorsed the portrait of poverty embodied in the Moynihan Report, a controversial analysis that offended many African Americans.

## LYNDON B. JOHNSON
### *"To Fulfill These Rights": Commencement Address at Howard University*
### *June 4, 1965*

Our earth is the home of revolution. In every corner of every continent men charged with hope contend with ancient ways in the pursuit of justice. They reach for the newest of weapons to realize the oldest of dreams, that each may walk in freedom and pride, stretching his talents, enjoying the fruits of the earth.

Our enemies may occasionally seize the day of change, but it is the banner of our revolution they take. And our own future is linked to this process of swift and turbulent change in many lands in the world. But nothing in any country touches us more profoundly, and nothing is more freighted with meaning for our own destiny than the revolution of the Negro American.

In far too many ways American Negroes have been another nation: deprived of freedom, crippled by hatred, the doors of opportunity closed to hope.

In our time change has come to this Nation, too. The American Negro, acting with impressive restraint, has peacefully protested and marched, entered the courtrooms and the seats of government, demanding a justice

Commencement Address at Howard University: "To Fulfill These Rights" (as excerpted), June 4, 1965, *Public Papers of the Presidents of the United States: Lyndon B. Johnson, 1965,* Vol. 1 (Washington, D.C.: Government Printing Office, 1965), 635–40.

that has long been denied. The voice of the Negro was the call to action. But it is a tribute to America that, once aroused, the courts and the Congress, the President and most of the people, have been the allies of progress. . . .

The voting rights bill will be the latest, and among the most important, in a long series of victories. But this victory—as Winston Churchill said of another triumph for freedom—"is not the end. It is not even the beginning of the end. But it is, perhaps, the end of the beginning."

That beginning is freedom; and the barriers to that freedom are tumbling down. Freedom is the right to share, share fully and equally, in America society—to vote, to hold a job, to enter a public place, to go to school. It is the right to be treated in every part of our national life as a person equal in dignity and promise to all others.

## Freedom Is Not Enough

But freedom is not enough. You do not wipe away the scars of centuries by saying: Now you are free to go where you want, and do as you desire, and choose the leaders you please.

You do not take a person who, for years, has been hobbled by chains and liberate him, bring him up to the starting line of a race and then say, "you are free to compete with all the others," and still justly believe that you have been completely fair.

Thus it is not enough just to open the gates of opportunity. All our citizens must have the ability to walk through those gates.

This is the next and the more profound stage of the battle for civil rights. We seek not just freedom but opportunity. We seek not just legal equity but human ability, not just equality as a right and a theory but equality as a fact and equality as a result.

For the task is to give 20 million Negroes the same chance as every other American to learn and grow, to work and share in society, to develop their abilities—physical, mental and spiritual, and to pursue their individual happiness.

To this end equal opportunity is essential, but not enough, not enough. Men and women of all races are born with the same range of abilities. But ability is not just the product of birth. Ability is stretched or stunted by the family that you live with, and the neighborhood you live in—by the school you go to and the poverty or the richness of your surroundings. It is the product of a hundred unseen forces playing upon the little infant, the child, and finally the man.

## Progress for Some

This graduating class at Howard University is witness to the indomitable determination of the Negro American to win his way in American life.

The number of Negroes in schools of higher learning has almost doubled in 15 years. The number of nonwhite professional workers has more than doubled in 10 years. The median income of Negro college women tonight exceeds that of white college women. And there are also the enormous accomplishments of distinguished individual Negroes—many of them graduates of this institution, and one of them the first lady ambassador in the history of the United States.

These are proud and impressive achievements. But they tell only the story of a growing middle-class minority, steadily narrowing the gap between them and their white counterparts.

## A Widening Gulf

But for the great majority of Negro Americans—the poor, the unemployed, the uprooted, and the dispossessed—there is a much grimmer story. They still, as we meet here tonight, are another nation. Despite the court orders and the laws, despite the legislative victories and the speeches, for them the walls are rising and the gulf is widening.

Here are some of the facts of this American failure.

Thirty-five years ago the rate of unemployment for Negroes and whites was about the same. Tonight the Negro rate is twice as high.

In 1948 the 8 percent unemployment rate for Negro teenage boys was actually less than that of whites. By last year that rate had grown to 23 percent, as against 13 percent for whites unemployed.

Between 1949 and 1959, the income of Negro men relative to white men declined in every section of this country. From 1952 to 1963 the median income of Negro families compared to white actually dropped from 57 percent to 53 percent.

In the years 1955 through 1957, 22 percent of experienced Negro workers were out of work at some time during the year. In 1961 through 1963 that proportion had soared to 29 percent.

Since 1947 the number of white families living in poverty has decreased 27 percent while the number of poorer nonwhite families decreased only 3 percent.

The infant mortality of nonwhites in 1940 was 70 percent greater than whites. Twenty-two years later it was 90 percent greater.

Moreover, the isolation of Negro from white communities is increasing, rather than decreasing as Negroes crowd into the central cities and become a city within a city.

Of course Negro Americans as well as white Americans have shared in our rising national abundance. But the harsh fact of the matter is that in the battle for true equality too many—far too many—are losing ground every day.

## The Causes of Inequality

We are not completely sure why this is. We know the causes are complex and subtle. But we do know the two broad basic reasons. And we do know that we have to act.

First, Negroes are trapped—as many whites are trapped—in inherited, gateless poverty. They lack training and skills. They are shut in, in slums, without decent medical care. Private and public poverty combine to cripple their capacities.

We are trying to attack these evils through our poverty program, through our education program, through our medical care and our other health programs, and a dozen more of the Great Society programs that are aimed at the root causes of this poverty.

We will increase, and we will accelerate, and we will broaden this attack in years to come until this most enduring of foes finally yields to our unyielding will.

But there is a second cause—much more difficult to explain, more deeply grounded, more desperate in its force. It is the devastating heritage of long years of slavery; and a century of oppression, hatred, and injustice.

## Special Nature of Negro Poverty

For Negro poverty is not white poverty. Many of its causes and many of its cures are the same. But there are differences—deep, corrosive, obstinate differences—radiating painful roots into the community, and into the family, and the nature of the individual.

These differences are not racial differences. They are solely and simply the consequence of ancient brutality, past injustice, and present prejudice. They are anguishing to observe. For the Negro they are a constant reminder of oppression. For the white they are a constant reminder of guilt. But they must be faced and they must be dealt with and they must be overcome, if we are ever to reach the time when the only difference between Negroes and whites is the color of their skin.

Nor can we find a complete answer in the experience of other American minorities. They made a valiant and a largely successful effort to emerge from poverty and prejudice.

The Negro, like these others, will have to rely mostly upon his own efforts. But he just can not do it alone. For they did not have the heritage of centuries to overcome, and they did not have a cultural tradition which had been twisted and battered by endless years of hatred and hopelessness, nor were they excluded—these others—because of race or color—a feeling whose dark intensity is matched by no other prejudice in our society.

Nor can these differences be understood as isolated infirmities. They are a seamless web. They cause each other. They result from each other. They reinforce each other.

Much of the Negro community is buried under a blanket of history and circumstance. It is not a lasting solution to lift just one corner of that blanket. We must stand on all sides and we must raise the entire cover if we are to liberate our fellow citizens.

## The Roots of Injustice

One of the differences is the increased concentration of Negroes in our cities. More than 73 percent of all Negroes live in urban areas compared with less than 70 percent of the whites. Most of these Negroes live in slums. Most of these Negroes live together—a separated people.

Men are shaped by their world. When it is a world of decay, ringed by an invisible wall, when escape is arduous and uncertain, and the saving pressures of a more hopeful society are unknown, it can cripple the youth and it can desolate the men.

There is also the burden that a dark skin can add to the search for a productive place in our society. Unemployment strikes most swiftly and broadly at the Negro, and this burden erodes hope. Blighted hope breeds despair. Despair brings indifferences to the learning which offers a way out. And despair, coupled with indifferences, is often the source of destructive rebellion against the fabric of society.

There is also the lacerating hurt of early collision with white hatred or prejudice, distaste or condescension. Other groups have felt similar intolerance. But success and achievement could wipe it away. They do not change the color of a man's skin. I have seen this uncomprehending pain in the eyes of the little, young Mexican-American schoolchildren that I taught many years ago. But it can be overcome. But, for many, the wounds are always open.

## Family Breakdown

Perhaps most important—its influence radiating to every part of life—is the breakdown of the Negro family structure. For this, most of all, white America must accept responsibility. It flows from centuries of oppression and persecution of the Negro man. It flows from the long years of degradation and discrimination, which have attacked his dignity and assaulted his ability to produce for his family.

This, too, is not pleasant to look upon. But it must be faced by those whose serious intent is to improve the life of all Americans.

Only a minority—less than half—of all Negro children reach the age of 18 having lived all their lives with both of their parents. At this moment, tonight, little less than two-thirds are at home with both of their parents. Probably a majority of all Negro children receive federally aided public assistance sometime during their childhood.

The family is the cornerstone of our society. More than any other force it shapes the attitude, the hopes, the ambitions, and the values of the child. And when the family collapses it is the children that are usually damaged. When it happens on a massive scale the community itself is crippled.

So, unless we work to strengthen the family, to create conditions under which most parents will stay together—all the rest: schools, and playgrounds, and public assistance, and private concern, will never be enough to cut completely the circle of despair and deprivation.

## To Fulfill These Rights

There is no single easy answer to all of these problems.

Jobs are part of the answer. They bring the income which permits a man to provide for his family.

Decent homes in decent surroundings and a chance to learn—an equal chance to learn—are part of the answer.

Welfare and social programs better designed to hold families together are part of the answer.

Care for the sick is part of the answer.

An understanding heart by all Americans is another big part of the answer.

And to all of these fronts—and a dozen more—I will dedicate the expanding efforts of the Johnson administration.

But there are other answers that are still to be found. Nor do we fully understand even all of the problems. Therefore, I want to announce tonight that this fall I intend to call a White House conference of scholars, and experts, and outstanding Negro leaders—men of both races—and officials of Government at every level.

This White House conference's theme and title will be "To Fulfill These Rights."

Its object will be to help the American Negro fulfill the rights which, after the long time of injustice, he is finally about to secure.

To move beyond opportunity to achievement.

To shatter forever not only the barriers of law and public practice, but the walls which bound the condition of many by the color of his skin.

To dissolve, as best we can, the antique enmities of the heart which diminish the holder, divide the great democracy, and do wrong—great wrong—to the children of God.

And I pledge you tonight that this will be a chief goal of my administration, and of my program next year, and in the years to come. And I hope, and I pray, and I believe, it will be a part of the program of all America.

## What Is Justice?

For what is justice?

It is to fulfill the fair expectations of man.

Thus, American justice is a very special thing. For, from the first, this has been a land of towering expectations. It was to be a nation where each man could be ruled by the common consent of all—enshrined in law, given life by institutions, guided by men themselves subject to its rule. And all—all of every station and origin—would be touched equally in obligation and in liberty.

Beyond the law lay the land. It was a rich land, glowing with more abundant promise than man had ever seen. Here, unlike any place yet known, all were to share the harvest.

And beyond this was the dignity of man. Each could become whatever his qualities of mind and spirit would permit—to strive, to seek, and, if he could, to find his happiness.

This is American justice. We have pursued it faithfully to the edge of our imperfections, and we have failed to find it for the American Negro.

So, it is the glorious opportunity of this generation to end the one huge wrong of the American Nation and, in so doing, to find America for ourselves, with the same immense thrill of discovery which gripped those who first began to realize that here, at last, was a home for freedom.

All it will take is for all of us to understand what this country is and what this country must become.

The Scripture promises: "I shall light a candle of understanding in thine heart, which shall not be put out."

Together, and with millions more, we can light that candle of understanding in the heart of all America.

And, once lit, it will never again go out.

## DOCUMENT 9. WAR AT HOME AND ABROAD: MARTIN LUTHER KING, JR., OPPOSES THE VIETNAM WAR

Lyndon Johnson often described his civil rights and Vietnam policies in parallel terms—as different parts of his struggle to promote freedom, peace, and justice at home and around the world. As the war in Vietnam escalated, however, civil rights organizations increasingly criticized the president and joined the antiwar movement. Like Johnson, African American leaders drew an equation between race relations in the United States and the struggle in Southeast Asia; but in the charged, militant atmosphere of the late 1960s, black leaders identified the war not with the struggle for freedom but with the forces of oppression, racism, and imperialism.

In the document which follows, a sermon at the Riverside Church in New York City in 1967, Martin Luther King, Jr., links the civil rights and antiwar causes. The speech vividly illustrated the breakup of the liberal coalition that had elected Johnson in 1964 and supported the Great Society in 1965.

## MARTIN LUTHER KING, JR.

### *"Beyond Vietnam": Speech at Riverside Church Meeting*

#### *April 4, 1967*

. . . I come to this platform tonight to make a passionate plea to my beloved nation. This speech is not addressed to Hanoi or to the National Liberation Front. It is not addressed to China or to Russia.

Martin Luther King, Jr., "Beyond Vietnam," Speech at Riverside Church Meeting, New York, N.Y., April 4, 1967, reprinted in Clayborne Carson et al., eds., *Eyes on the Prize: A Reader and Guide* (New York: Penguin, 1987), 201–04.

Since I am a preacher by trade, I suppose it is not surprising that I have several reasons for bringing Vietnam into the field of my moral vision. There is at the outset a very obvious and almost facile connection between the war in Vietnam and the struggle I, and others, have been waging in America. A few years ago there was a shining moment in that struggle. It seemed as if there was a real promise of hope for the poor—both black and white—through the Poverty Program. There were experiments, hopes, new beginnings. Then came the build-up in Vietnam and I watched the program broken and eviscerated as if it were some idle political plaything of a society gone mad on war, and I knew that America would never invest the necessary funds or energies in rehabilitation of its poor so long as adventures like Vietnam continued to draw men and skills and money like some demoniacal destructive suction tube. So I was increasingly compelled to see the war as an enemy of the poor and to attack it as such.

Perhaps the more tragic recognition of reality took place when it became clear to me that the war was doing far more than devastating the hopes of the poor at home. It was sending their sons and their brothers and their husbands to fight and to die in extraordinarily high proportions relative to the rest of the population. We were taking the black young men who had been crippled by our society and sending them 8,000 miles away to guarantee liberties in Southeast Asia which they had not found in Southwest Georgia and East Harlem. So we have been repeatedly faced with the cruel irony of watching Negro and white boys on TV screens as they kill and die together for a nation that has been unable to seat them together in the same schools. . . .

My third reason moves to an even deeper level of awareness, for it grows out of my experience in the ghettos of the North over the last three years—especially the last three summers. As I have walked among the desperate, rejected and angry young men I have told them that Molotov cocktails and rifles would not solve their problems. I have tried to offer them my deepest compassion while maintaining my convictions that social change comes most meaningfully through non-violent action. But they asked—and rightly so—what about Vietnam? They asked if our own nation wasn't using massive doses of violence to solve its problems, to bring about the changes it wanted. Their questions hit home, and I knew that I could never again raise my voice against the violence of the oppressed in the ghettos without having first spoken clearly to the greatest purveyor of violence in the world today—my own government. . . .

For those who ask the question, "Aren't you a Civil Rights leader?" and thereby mean to exclude me from the movement for peace, I have this further answer. In 1957 when a group of us formed the Southern Christian Leadership Conference, we chose as our motto: "To save the soul of America." We were convinced that we could not limit our vision to certain rights for black people, but instead affirmed the conviction that America would never be free or saved from itself unless the descendants of its slaves were loosed completely from the shackles they still wear. . . .

And as I ponder the madness of Vietnam and search within myself for ways to understand and respond in compassion my mind goes constantly to the people of that peninsula. I speak now not of the soldiers of each side, not of the junta in Saigon, but simply of the people who have been living under the curse of war for almost three continuous decades now. I think of them too because it is clear to me that there will be no meaningful solution there until some attempt is made to know them and hear their broken cries.

They watch as we poison their water, as we kill a million acres of their crops. They must weep as the bulldozers roar through their areas preparing to destroy the precious trees. They wander into the hospitals, with at least 20 casualties from American firepower for one Vietcong-inflicted injury. They wander into the towns and see thousands of the children, homeless, without clothes, running in packs on the streets like animals. They see the children degraded by our soldiers as they beg for food. They see the children selling their sisters to our soldiers, soliciting for their mothers. . . .

Perhaps the more difficult but no less necessary task is to speak for those who have been designated as our enemies. What of the National Liberation Front—that strangely anonymous group we call VC or Communists? What must they think of us in America when they realize that we permitted the repression and cruelty of Diem which helped to bring them into being as a resistance group in the South? What do they think of our condoning the violence which led to their own taking up of arms? How can they believe in our integrity when now we speak of "aggression from the North" as if there were nothing more essential to the war? How can they trust us when now we charge them with violence after the murderous reign of Diem, and charge them with violence while we pour every new weapon of death into their land? Surely we must understand their feelings even if we do not condone their actions. Surely we must see that the men we supported pressed them to their violence. Surely we must see that our own computerized plans of destruction simply dwarf their greatest acts.

How do they judge us when our officials know that their membership is less than 25 percent Communist and yet insist on giving them the blanket name? What must they be thinking when they know that we are aware of their control of major sections of Vietnam and yet we appear ready to allow national elections in which this highly organized political parallel government will have no part? They ask how we can speak of free elections when the Saigon press is censored and controlled by the military junta. And they are surely right to wonder what kind of new government we plan to help form without them—the only party in real touch with the peasants. They question our political goals and they deny the reality of a peace settlement from which they will be excluded. Their questions are frighteningly relevant. Is our nation planning to build on political myth again and then shore it up with the power of new violence?

Here is the true meaning of value and compassion and nonviolence when it helps us to see the enemy's point of view, to hear his questions, to know his assessment of ourselves. For from his view we may indeed see the basic weaknesses of our own condition, and if we are mature, we may learn and grow and profit from the wisdom of the brothers who are called the opposition.

So, too, with Hanoi. In the North, where our bombs now pummel the land, and our mines endanger the waterways, we are met by a deep but understandable mistrust. To speak for them is to explain this lack of confidence in western words, and especially their distrust of American intentions now. In Hanoi are the men who led the nation to independence against the Japanese and the French, the men who sought membership in the French commonwealth and were betrayed by the weakness of Paris and the willfulness of the colonial armies. It was they who led a second struggle against French domination at tremendous costs, and then were persuaded to give up the land they controlled between the 13th and 17th parallel as a temporary measure at Geneva. After 1954 they watched us conspire with Diem to prevent elections which would have surely brought Ho Chi Minh to power over a united Vietnam, and they realized they had been betrayed again. . . .

At this point I should make it clear that while I have tried in these last few minutes to give a voice to the voiceless on Vietnam and to understand the arguments of those who are called enemy, I am as deeply concerned about our own troops there as anything else. For it occurs to me that what we are submitting them to in Vietnam is not simply the brutalizing process that goes on in any war where armies face each other and seek to destroy. We are adding cynicism to the process of death, for they must know after a short period there that none of the things we claim to be fighting for are really involved. Before long they must know that their government has sent them into a struggle among Vietnamese, and the more sophisticated surely realize that we are on the side of the wealthy and the secure while we create a hell for the poor.

If we continue there will be no doubt in my mind and in the mind of the world that we have no honorable intentions in Vietnam. It will become clear that our minimal expectation is to occupy it as an American colony and men will not refrain from thinking that our maximum hope is to goad China into a war so that we may bomb her nuclear installations. If we do not stop our war against the people in Vietnam immediately, the world will be left with no other alternative than to see this as some horribly clumsy and deadly game we have decided to play.

In order to atone for our sins and errors in Vietnam, we should take the initiative in bringing a halt to this tragic war. I would like to suggest five concrete things that our Government should do immediately to begin the long and difficult process of extricating ourselves from this nightmarish conflict:

1. End all bombing in North and South Vietnam.
2. Declare a unilateral cease-fire in the hope that such action will create the atmosphere for negotiation.
3. Take immediate steps to prevent other battlegrounds in Southeast Asia by curtailing our military build-up in Thailand and our interference in Laos.
4. Realistically accept the fact that the National Liberation Front has substantial support in South Vietnam and must thereby play a role in any meaningful negotiations and in any future Vietnam government.
5. Set a date that we will remove all foreign troops from Vietnam in accordance with the 1954 Geneva Agreement.

Part of our ongoing commitment might well express itself in an offer to grant asylum to any Vietnamese who fears for his life under a new regime which included the Liberation Front. Then we must make what reparations we can for the damage we have done. We must provide the medical aid that is badly needed, making it available in this country if necessary.

Meanwhile we in the churches and synagogues have a continuing task while we urge our Government to disengage itself from a disgraceful commitment. We must continue to raise our voices if our nation persists in its perverse ways in Vietnam. We must be prepared to match actions with words by seeking out every creative means of protest possible.

# 10
## Vietnam

## DOCUMENT 10. LBJ OUTLINES HIS WAR AIMS

In April 1965, Lyndon Johnson delivered a major statement on his objectives in Vietnam. In a speech at Johns Hopkins University, in Baltimore, Maryland, LBJ explained his reasons for "Why We Are in Vietnam" and pledged to maintain the independence of South Vietnam. Johnson evoked Woodrow Wilson's promise of "peace without victory" in World War I, echoing Wilson's declaration that the United States had no selfish purpose in intervening in a foreign land. In the first of many fruitless attempts to bring the enemy to the negotiating table on his terms, Johnson also offered incentives to communist North Vietnam, promising a massive economic development project for the Mekong River Valley if Ho Chi Minh would end the war.

### LYNDON B. JOHNSON
## *Peace Without Conquest: Address at Johns Hopkins University*
### *April 7, 1965*

I have come here to review once again with my own people the views of the American Government.

Tonight Americans and Asians are dying for a world where each people may choose its own path to change.

Address at Johns Hopkins University: "Peace Without Conquest," April 7, 1965, *Public Papers of the Presidents of the United States: Lyndon B. Johnson, 1965,* Vol. 1 (Washington, D.C.: Government Printing Office, 1965), 394–98.

This is the principle for which our ancestors fought in the valleys of Pennsylvania. It is the principle for which our sons fight tonight in the jungles of Viet-Nam.

Viet-Nam is far away from this quiet campus. We have no territory there, nor do we seek any. The war is dirty and brutal and difficult. And some 400 young men, born into an America that is bursting with opportunity and promise, have ended their lives on Viet-Nam's steaming soil.

Why must we take this painful road?

Why must this Nation hazard its ease, and its interest, and its power for the sake of a people so far away?

We fight because we must fight if we are to live in a world where every country can shape its own destiny. And only in such a world will our own freedom be finally secure.

This kind of world will never be built by bombs or bullets. Yet the infirmities of man are such that force must often precede reason, and the waste of war, the works of peace.

We wish that this were not so. But we must deal with the world as it is, if it is ever to be as we wish.

## The Nature of the Conflict

The world as it is in Asia is not a serene or peaceful place.

The first reality is that North Viet-Nam has attacked the independent nation of South Viet-Nam. Its object is total conquest.

Of course, some of the people of South Viet-Nam are participating in attack on their own government. But trained men and supplies, orders and arms, flow in a constant stream from north to south.

This support is the heartbeat of the war.

And it is a war of unparalleled brutality. Simple farmers are the targets of assassination and kidnapping. Women and children are strangled in the night because their men are loyal to their government. And helpless villages are ravaged by sneak attacks. Large-scale raids are conducted on towns, and terror strikes in the heart of cities.

The confused nature of this conflict cannot mask the fact that it is the new face of an old enemy.

Over this war—and all Asia—is another reality: the deepening shadow of Communist China. The rulers in Hanoi are urged on by Peking. This is a regime which has destroyed freedom in Tibet, which has attacked India, and has been condemned by the United Nations for aggression in Korea. It is a nation which is helping the forces of violence in almost every continent. The contest in Viet-Nam is part of a wider pattern of aggressive purposes.

## Why Are We in Viet-Nam?

Why are these realities our concern? Why are we in South Viet-Nam? *We are there because we have a promise to keep.* Since 1954 every American President has offered support to the people of South Viet-Nam. We have helped to build, and we have helped to defend. Thus, over many years, we have made a national pledge to help South Viet-Nam defend its independence.

And I intend to keep that promise.

To dishonor that pledge, to abandon this small and brave nation to its enemies, and to the terror that must follow, would be an unforgivable wrong.

*We are also there to strengthen world order.* Around the globe, from Berlin to Thailand, are people whose well-being rests, in part, on the belief that they can count on us if they are attacked. To leave Viet-Nam to its fate would shake the confidence of all these people in the value of an American commitment and in the value of America's word. The result would be increased unrest and instability, and even wider war.

*We are also there because there are great stakes in the balance.* Let no one think for a moment that retreat from Viet-Nam would bring an end to conflict. The battle would be renewed in one country and then another. The central lesson of our time is that the appetite of aggression is never satisfied. To withdraw from one battlefield means only to prepare for the next. We must say in southeast Asia—as we did in Europe—in the words of the Bible: "Hitherto shalt thou come, but no further."

There are those who say that all our effort there will be futile—that China's power is such that it is bound to dominate all Southeast Asia. But there is no end to that argument until all of the nations of Asia are swallowed up.

There are those who wonder why we have a responsibility there. Well, we have it there for the same reason that we have a responsibility for the defense of Europe. World War II was fought in both Europe and Asia, and when it ended we found ourselves with continued responsibility for the defense of freedom.

## Our Objective in Viet-Nam

Our objective is the independence of South Viet-Nam, and its freedom from attack. We want nothing for ourselves—only that the people of South Viet-Nam be allowed to guide their own country in their own way.

We will do everything necessary to reach that objective. And we will do only what is absolutely necessary.

In recent months attacks on South Viet-Nam were stepped up. Thus, it became necessary for us to increase our response and to make attacks by air. This is not a change of purpose. It is a change in what we believe that purpose requires.

We do this in order to slow down aggression.

We do this to increase the confidence of the brave people of South Viet-Nam who have bravely borne this brutal battle for so many years with so many casualties.

And we do this to convince the leaders of North Viet-Nam—and all who seek to share their conquest—of a very simple fact:

We will not be defeated.

We will not grow tired.

We will not withdraw, either openly or under the cloak of a meaningless agreement.

We know that air attacks alone will not accomplish all of these purposes. But it is our best and prayerful judgment that they are a necessary part of the surest road to peace.

We hope that peace will come swiftly. But that is in the hands of others besides ourselves. And we must be prepared for a long continued conflict. It will require patience as well as bravery, the will to endure as well as the will to resist.

I wish it were possible to convince others with words of what we now find it necessary to say with guns and planes: Armed hostility is futile. Our resources are equal to any challenge. Because we fight for values and we fight for principles, rather than territory or colonies, our patience and our determination are unending.

Once this is clear, then it should also be clear that the only path for reasonable men is the path of peaceful settlement.

Such peace demands an independent South Viet-Nam—securely guaranteed and able to shape its own relationships to all others—free from outside interference—tied to no alliance—a military base for no other country.

These are the essentials of any final settlement.

We will never be second in the search for such a peaceful settlement in Viet-Nam.

There may be many ways to this kind of peace: in discussion or negotiation with the governments concerned; in large groups or in small ones; in the reaffirmation of old agreements or their strengthening with new ones.

We have stated this position over and over again, fifty times and more, to friend and foe alike. And we remain ready, with this purpose, for unconditional discussions.

And until that bright and necessary day of peace we will try to keep conflict from spreading. We have no desire to see thousands die in battle—Asians or Americans. We have no desire to devastate that which the people of North Viet-Nam have built with toil and sacrifice. We will use our power with restraint and with all the wisdom that we can command.

But we will use it.

This war, like most wars, is filled with terrible irony. For what do the people of North Viet-Nam want? They want what their neighbors also desire: food for their hunger; health for their bodies; a chance to learn; progress for their country; and an end to the bondage of material misery. And they would find all these things far more readily in peaceful association with others than in the endless course of battle.

## A Cooperative Effort for Development

These countries of southeast Asia are homes for millions of impoverished people. Each day these people rise at dawn and struggle through until the night to wrestle existence from the soil. They are often wracked by disease, plagued by hunger, and death comes at the early age of 40.

Stability and peace do not come easily in such a land. Neither independence nor human dignity will ever be won, though, by arms alone. It also requires the work of peace. The American people have helped generously in times past in these works. Now there must be a much more massive effort to improve the life of man in that conflict-torn corner of our world.

The first step is for the countries of southeast Asia to associate themselves in a greatly expanded cooperative effort for development. We would hope that North Viet-Nam would take its place in the common effort just as soon as peaceful cooperation is possible.

The United Nations is already actively engaged in development in this area. As far back as 1961 I conferred with our authorities in Viet-Nam in connection with their work there. And I would hope tonight that the Secretary General of the United Nations could use the prestige of his great office, and his deep knowledge of Asia, to initiate, as soon as possible, with the countries of that area, a plan for cooperation in increased development.

For our part I will ask the Congress to join in a billion dollar American investment in this effort as soon as it is underway.

And I would hope that all other industrialized countries, including the Soviet Union, will join in this effort to replace despair with hope, and terror with progress.

The task is nothing less than to enrich the hopes and the existence of more than a hundred million people. And there is much to be done.

The vast Mekong River can provide food and water and power on a scale to dwarf even our own TVA.[1]

The wonders of modern medicine can be spread through villages where thousands die every year from lack of care.

Schools can be established to train people in the skills that are needed to manage the process of development.

And these objectives, and more, are within the reach of a cooperative and determined effort.

I also intend to expand and speed up a program to make available our farm surpluses to assist in feeding and clothing the needy in Asia. We should not allow people to go hungry and wear rags while our own warehouses overflow with an abundance of wheat and corn, rice and cotton.

So I will very shortly name a special team of outstanding, patriotic, distinguished Americans to inaugurate our participation in these programs. This team will be headed by Mr. Eugene Black, the very able former President of the World Bank.

In areas that are still ripped by conflict, of course development will not be easy. Peace will be necessary for final success. But we cannot and must not wait for peace to begin this job.

## The Dream of World Order

This will be a disorderly planet for a long time. In Asia, as elsewhere, the forces of the modern world are shaking old ways and uprooting ancient civilizations. There will be turbulence and struggle and even violence. Great social change—as we see in our own country now—does not always come without conflict.

We must also expect that nations will on occasion be in dispute with us. It may be because we are rich, or powerful; or because we have made some mistakes; or because they honestly fear our intentions. However, no nation need ever fear that we desire their land, or to impose our will, or to dictate their institutions.

[1] TVA is the acronym for Tennessee Valley Authority, one of the most ambitious programs of Franklin D. Roosevelt's New Deal. Through dam building, production of cheap hydroelectric power, navigation improvements, fertilizer development, and other programs, the TVA sought comprehensive economic development of the depressed Tennessee River Valley region of the southeastern United States. The TVA offered the model for the Lower Colorado River Authority in LBJ's home state and for his proposed Mekong River project in Vietnam. See pages 20–22, 136.

But we will always oppose the effort of one nation to conquer another nation.

We will do this because our own security is at stake.

But there is more to it than that. For our generation has a dream. It is a very old dream. But we have the power and now we have the opportunity to make that dream come true.

For centuries nations have struggled among each other. But we dream of a world where disputes are settled by law and reason. And we will try to make it so.

For most of history men have hated and killed one another in battle. But we dream of an end to war. And we will try to make it so.

For all existence most men have lived in poverty, threatened by hunger. But we dream of a world where all are fed and charged with hope. And we will help to make it so.

The ordinary men and women of North Viet-Nam and South Viet-Nam—of China and India—of Russia and America—are brave people. They are filled with the same proportions of hate and fear, of love and hope. Most of them want the same things for themselves and their families. Most of them do not want their sons to ever die in battle, or to see their homes, or the homes of others, destroyed.

Well, this can be their world yet. Man now has the knowledge—always before denied—to make this planet serve the real needs of the people who live on it.

I know this will not be easy. I know how difficult it is for reason to guide passion, and love to master hate. The complexities of this world do not bow easily to pure and consistent answers.

But the simple truths are there just the same. We must all try to follow them as best we can.

## Conclusion

We often say how impressive power is. But I do not find it impressive at all. The guns and the bombs, the rockets and the warships, are all symbols of human failure. They are necessary symbols. They protect what we cherish. But they are witness to human folly.

A dam built across a great river is impressive.

In the countryside where I was born, and where I live, I have seen the night illuminated, and the kitchens warmed, and the homes heated, where once the cheerless night and the ceaseless cold held sway. And all this happened because electricity came to our area along the humming wires of the REA.[2] Electrification of the countryside—yes, that, too, is impressive.

A rich harvest in a hungry land is impressive.

The sight of healthy children in a classroom is impressive.

These—not mighty arms—are the achievements which the American Nation believes to be impressive.

And, if we are steadfast, the time may come when all other nations will also find it so.

Every night before I turn out the lights to sleep I ask myself this question: Have I done everything that I can do to unite this country? Have I done everything I can to help unite the world, to try to bring peace and hope to all the peoples of the world? Have I done enough?

Ask yourselves that question in your homes—and in this hall tonight. Have we, each of us, all done all we could? Have we done enough?

We may well be living in the time foretold many years ago when it was said: "I call heaven and earth to record this day against you, that I have set before you life and death, blessing and cursing: therefore choose life, that both thou and thy seed may live."

This generation of the world must choose: destroy or build, kill or aid, hate or understand.

We can do all these things on a scale never dreamed of before.

## DOCUMENT 11. THE DECISION TO ESCALATE—1965

Like Presidents Truman, Kennedy, and Eisenhower before him, Johnson initially tried to prevent a communist takeover of Vietnam without a major commitment of U.S. troops. By the spring of 1965, however, the military and political situation in South Vietnam had so deteriorated that General William Westmoreland, the commanding U.S. military officer in Saigon, warned LBJ that South Vietnam would fall without an immediate and massive escalation of American military power.

In July 1965, Johnson convened his top military and civilian advisers to consider Westmoreland's request. The following selection from the transcript of those meetings, kept by Assistant to the President Jack Valenti, reveals the assumptions of key policymakers and the reasons for Johnson's fateful decision to escalate the war.

---

[2] The Rural Electrification Administration (REA) was a New Deal agency responsible for bringing electricity to rural America. For Johnson's role in bringing REA power to Texas, see Chapter 1, pages 20–22.

# JACK VALENTI
# From *A Very Human President*
## July 1965

Initially at the meeting of July 21 [, 1965] were Robert McNamara, secretary of defense; Dean Rusk, secretary of state; Cyrus Vance, deputy secretary of defense; McGeorge Bundy, special assistant to the president for national security affairs; General Earle Wheeler, chairman of the joint chiefs of staff; George Ball, under secretary of state; William Bundy, assistant secretary of state and brother of McGeorge Bundy; Henry Cabot Lodge, ambassador to Vietnam, and Jack Valenti, special assistant to the president, among others.

McNamara: They [the GVN, or government of South Vietnam] are trying to increase [their own forces] by 10,000 per month. Our country team is optimistic. But I am not. The desertion rate is high. . . . We did not find any threat of discontent among our own troops. U.S. morale is of the highest order. . . . [The enemy] are suffering heavy losses. They are well supplied with ammunition. I suspect much of the inflow of supplies is water-borne. . . . But even if we did have tight control, it would make little difference in the next six to nine months.

[The President entered the room.]

Johnson: Would you please begin, Bob. [McNamara summarized the Pentagon recommendation to plan to support 200,000 troops in Vietnam by the first of 1966 by calling up the same number of reserves. By mid-1966 approximately 600,000 additional men would be available.]

Ball: Isn't it possible that the VC will do what they did against the French—stay away from confrontation and not accommodate us?

Wheeler: Yes, that is possible, but by constantly harassing them, they will have to fight somewhere. . . .

Ball: Mr. President, I can foresee a perilous voyage, very dangerous. I have great and grave apprehensions that we can win under these conditions. But let me be clear. If the decision is to go ahead, I am committed.

Jack Valenti, *A Very Human President* (New York: Pocket Books, 1975), 322–53, as excerpted and reprinted in William Appleman Williams et al., eds., *America in Vietnam: A Documentary History* (New York: W. W. Norton and Co., 1989), 249–53.

JOHNSON: But, George, is there another course in the national interest, some course that is better than the one McNamara proposes? We know it is dangerous and perilous, but the big question is, can it be avoided? . . .

BALL: Take what precautions we can, Mr. President. Take our losses, let their government fall apart, negotiate, discuss, knowing full well there will be a probable take-over by the Communists. This is disagreeable, I know.

JOHNSON: I can take disagreeable decisions. But I want to know can we make a case for your thoughts? Can you discuss it fully? . . .

RUSK: What we have done since 1954 to 1961 has not been good enough. We should have probably committed ourselves heavier in 1961. . . .

LODGE: There is not a tradition of a national government in Saigon. There are no roots in the country. Not until there is tranquility can you have any stability. I don't think we ought to take this government seriously. There is simply no one who can do anything. We have to do what we think we ought to do regardless of what the Saigon government does. . . . [McNamara and Wheeler then returned to the Pentagon recommendation for more men to be sent to Vietnam. These men would give the South Vietnamese army a breathing space. No more than 100,000 would be sent at this time.]

JOHNSON: It seems to me that you will lose a greater number of men. I don't like that.

WHEELER: Not precisely true, Mr. President. The more men we have there the greater the likelihood of smaller losses.

JOHNSON: Tell me this. What will happen if we put in 100,000 more men and then two, three years later you tell me you need 500,000 more? How would you expect me to respond to that? And what makes you think if we put in 100,000 men, Ho Chi Minh won't put in another 100,000, and match us every bit of the way.

WHEELER (smiling): This means greater bodies of men from North Vietnam, which will allow us to cream them.

JOHNSON: But what are the chances of more North Vietnamese soldiers coming in?

WHEELER: About a fifty-fifty chance. The North would be foolhardy to put one-quarter of their forces in SVN. It would expose them too greatly in the North. . . .

[The meeting reconvened at 2:30 P.M.]

BALL: We cannot win, Mr. President. This war will be long and protracted. The most we can hope for is a messy conclusion. There remains a great danger of intrusion by the Chinese. But the biggest problem is the problem of the long war. . . . As casualties increase, the pressure to strike at the very jugular of North Vietnam will become very great. I am concerned about world opinion. . . . If the war is long and protracted, as I believe it will be, then we will suffer because the world's greatest power cannot defeat guerrillas. Then there is the problem of national politics. Every great captain in history was not afraid to make a tactical withdrawal if conditions were unfavorable to him. The enemy cannot even be seen in Vietnam. He is indigenous to the country. I truly have serious doubt that an army of westerners can successfully fight orientals in an Asian jungle. . . . The least harmful way to cut losses in SVN is to let the government decide it doesn't want us to stay there. Therefore, we should put such proposals to the SVN that they can't accept. Then, it would move to a neutralist position. I have no illusions that after we were asked to leave South Vietnam, that country would soon come under Hanoi control. . . . If we wanted to make a stand in Thailand, we might be able to make it. . . . Between a long war and cutting our losses, the Japanese would go for the latter. . . .

JOHNSON: But George, wouldn't all these countries say that Uncle Sam was a paper tiger, wouldn't we lose credibility breaking the word of three presidents. . . .

BALL: The worse blow would be that the mightiest power on earth is unable to defeat a handful of guerrillas. . . .

JOHNSON: There are two basic troublings within me. First, that westerners can ever win a war in Asia. Second, I don't see how you can fight a war under direction of other people whose government changes every month. . . .

RUSK: If the Communist world finds out we will not pursue our commitment to the end, I don't know where they will stay their hand. I have to say I am more optimistic than some of my colleagues. I don't believe the VC have made large advances among the Vietnamese people. It is difficult to worry about massive casualties when we say we can't find the enemy. I feel strongly that one man dead is a massive casualty, but in the sense that we are talking, I don't see large casualties unless the Chinese come in.

LODGE: I feel there is a greater threat to start World War III if we don't go. Can't we see the similarity to our own indolence at Munich [the Munich conference of 1938 when Hitler, with the acquiescence of the West, seized part of Czechoslovakia]. I simply can't be as pessimistic as

Ball. We have great seaports in Vietnam. We don't need to fight on roads. We have the sea. Let us visualize meeting the VC on our own terms. We don't have to spend all our time in the jungles. If we can secure our bases, the Vietnamese can secure, in time, a political movement to, one, apprehend the terrorist, and two, give intelligence to the government. . . . The Vietnamese have been dealt more casualties than, per capita, we suffered in the Civil War. The Vietnamese soldier is an uncomplaining soldier. He has ideas he will die for.

## Conference of July 22 with Pentagon Officials on Committing Large Numbers of Troops to Vietnam

At the meeting were the President; McNamara; Vance; General Wheeler; General Harold K. Johnson, chief of staff of the Army; General John P. McConnell, Air Force chief of staff; Admiral D. L. McDonald, chief of Naval Operations; General Wallace M. Greene, Jr., commandant of the Marine Corps; Secretary of the Air Force Harold Brown; Secretary of the Navy Paul Nitze; Bundy; and Valenti, among others.

JOHNSON: The options open to us are: one, leave the country, with as little loss as possible; two, maintain present force and lose slowly; three, add 100,000 men, recognizing that may not be enough and adding more next year. The disadvantages of number three option are the risk of escalation, casualties high, and the prospect of a long war without victory. . . .

McDONALD: I agree with McNamara that we are committed to the extent that we can't move out. If we continue the way we are now, it will be a slow, sure victory for the other side. By putting more men in it will turn the tide and let us know what further we need to do. I wish we had done this long before.

JOHNSON: But you don't know if 100,000 men will be enough. What makes you conclude that if you don't know where we are going—and what will happen—we shouldn't pause and find this out?

McDONALD: Sooner or later we will force them to the conference table.

JOHNSON: But if we put in 100,000 men won't they put in an equal number, and then where will we be?

McDONALD: No, if we step up our bombing. . . .

JOHNSON: Is this a chance we want to take?

McDONALD: Yes, sir, when I view the alternatives. Get out now or pour in more men. . . . I think our allies will lose faith in us.

JOHNSON: We have few allies really helping us now.

McNAMARA: The current plan is to introduce 100,000 men with the possibility of a second 100,000 by the first of the year. . . .

JOHNSON: Why wouldn't North Vietnam pour in more men? Also, why wouldn't they call on volunteers from China and Russia?

WHEELER: First, they may decide they can't win by putting in force they can't afford. At most they would put in two more divisions. Beyond that, they strip their country and invite a countermove on our part. Second, on volunteers—the one thing all North Vietnam fears is the Chinese. For them to invite Chinese volunteers is to invite China taking over North Vietnam. The weight of judgment is that North Vietnam may reinforce their troops, but they can't match us on a buildup. From a military viewpoint, we can handle, if we are determined to do so, China and North Vietnam.

McDONALD: . . . First, supply the forces Westmoreland has asked for. Second, prepare to furnish more men, 100,000, in 1966. Third, commence building in air and naval forces, and step up air attacks on North Vietnam. Fourth, bring in needed reserves and draft calls.

JOHNSON: Do you have any ideas of what this will cost?

McNAMARA: Yes, sir, twelve billion dollars in 1966. . . . It would not require wage and price controls in my judgment.

McCONNELL: If you put in these requested forces and increase air and sea effort, we can at least turn the tide to where we are not losing anymore. We need to be sure we get the best we can out of the South Vietnamese. We need to bomb all military targets available to us in North Vietnam. As to whether we can come to a satisfactory solution with these forces, I don't know. . . .

JOHNSON: Doesn't it really mean that if we follow Westmoreland's requests we are in a new war? Isn't this going off the diving board?

McNAMARA: If we carry forward all these recommendations, it would be a change in our policy. We have relied on the South to carry the brunt. Now we would be responsible for satisfactory military outcome. . . .

JOHNSON: But I don't know how we are going to get the job done. There are millions of Chinese. I think they are going to put their stack in. Is this the best place to do it? We don't have the allies we had in Korea. Can we get our allies to cut off supplying the North?

McNAMARA: No, sir, we can't prevent Japan, Britain, and the others from chartering ships to Haiphong [the North Vietnamese port].

JOHNSON: Are we starting something that in two or three years we simply can't finish?

BROWN: It is costly to us to strangle slowly. But the chances of losing are less if we move in. . . .

## DOCUMENT 12. WE CAN WIN IN VIETNAM: HAWKS CRITICIZE LBJ'S STRATEGY

Johnson's strategy in Southeast Asia provoked criticism both from opponents of the war, the so-called doves who agitated for immediate withdrawal from Vietnam, and from hard-line anticommunists, "hawks" who believed Johnson was not prosecuting the war vigorously enough. Hawks focused their criticism on Johnson's refusal to risk intervention by the Chinese, particularly his reluctance to bomb targets near North Vietnam's borders with China, to mine Haiphong and other North Vietnamese harbors, or to deploy tactical nuclear weapons. The hawk argument that LBJ hamstrung the American military gained currency during the 1970s and 1980s as an explanation for the defeat in Vietnam.

In the selection that follows, James Burnham, a columnist for the conservative magazine *National Review*, forcefully states the hawk position in June 1966. Burnham, a one-time socialist who became an ardent cold warrior during the 1950s, recommends pulling out all the stops in the battle against communist aggression.

## JAMES BURNHAM
## *What Is the President Waiting For?*
### *June 28, 1966*

Defense Secretary McNamara has just announced commitment of 18,000 more troops to the Vietnam war; the total figure is expected to be close to 400,000 by the end of the year. U.S. casualties are now running above 1,000 weekly, more than 100 of them killed. Admitted U.S. plane losses to enemy action are nearing 300. Money costs are said to be at an annual rate of $18 billion and rising. As nonwars go, this is getting rather impressive.

The President's repeated explanations of why U.S. troops are fighting in Vietnam have not been notably persuasive—mostly because they are compounded of irrelevant Liberal abstractions. But he and his aides at least attempt *some* sort of explanation. As to why he continues, in a conflict that has reached this level, to impose such a multitude of restrictions on weapons, tactics and strategy, neither he nor any of his spokes-

James Burnham, "What Is the President Waiting For?," *National Review*, June 28, 1966, 612.

men has had anything at all to say for a long while. It is time to demand, on this crucial point, an accounting. In truth, the problem can be put in moral terms—a mode much favored in the Presidential rhetoric. By what moral right does the President order hundreds of thousands of young citizens into a distant and most alien land, under conditions that mean death or grievous injury for many thousands of them and hardship for nearly all, and at the same time forbid them to use the most effective available weapons and methods against the enemy.

Those of us who approve firm action in Southeast Asia find ourselves awkwardly placed. We hesitate to criticize the President, because we know this tends to play into the hands of the Vietniks and appeasers; and, in fact, we do wholeheartedly support the President as against the appeasers. Moreover, we realize, or should realize, that in the face of the massive international as well as domestic appeasement pressures, Lyndon Johnson has proved almost incredibly resolute. Criticism thus seems ungrateful as well as inexpedient. But as the war goes on and intensifies, continuing silence from the firm side has the relative effect of multiplying the sounds from the soft. The President's political problem must appear to him to be that of coming to terms with the appeasers—including the appeasers within his official family of making sufficient concessions to them to patch up his consensus. The hard critics he can take for granted.

Prior to the Korean War it would have been assumed that if we (or any other nation) started fighting against an enemy in the field, the objective would be to defeat the enemy force. Besides using the most suitable military, economic and political weapons, suitably employed, in direct relation to the enemy force, this meant shutting off—so far, at any rate, as feasible—the lines of support, supply and recruitment, and excluding any notion of a privileged sanctuary.

## Korea and After

These rules are plain common sense. They were junked in the Korean War—in particular by the failure to use nuclear weapons or to bomb the Chinese bases and airfields beyond the Yalu. Though the Korean restrictions were vigorously defended at the time, I have read no subsequent analysis of the Korean War that considers them justified, and many that consider them to have been catastrophically mistaken. The same restrictions plus a number of others are currently imposed in the Vietnam war. To what conceivable purpose?

So far as I know, two and only two reasons have been publicly stated: first, that the war might otherwise escalate to a level involving direct

Chinese intervention or general nuclear exchange; second, that the lower key gives a better chance of negotiating a satisfactory settlement with Hanoi. This second argument is ridiculous on its face, and besides has been disproven by experience. Naturally, the strongest inducement for Hanoi to come to terms would be Hanoi's knowledge that it is being badly hurt and was going to hurt much more badly. As for nuclear escalation, it is absurd to think that the Kremlin would hazard Moscow for Southeast Asia. If Peking were irrational enough to try to use one of its half-dozen nuclear bombs against a U.S. carrier or base, that would merely complete the case for wiping out China's nuclear installations. In fact, the U.S. has not had since the Korean War—which was the perfect moment, since at that time the enemy didn't even possess a nuclear arsenal—a better occasion for using nuclear weapons.

## Professionals to the Rescue

A nuclear strike or two on a Vietcong concentration or in North Vietnam would be the best guarantee that Chinese troops would *not* intervene. However, Chinese mass intervention is in any case most improbable. The logistics problem would be all but insuperable. China is totally vulnerable to U.S. air attack. Her nuclear installations are at this stage more a hostage than a threat. Many military strategists would add: so much the better if China *did* come in; the Chinese challenge will have to be met some day, and it won't be easier when she has a functioning nuclear weapons system; let her at least be shown that, if she is going to expand, it will have to be in Siberia.

Our inhibited Vietnam strategy does not seem to express the President's own Texan instincts (though it may be in accord with the wheeler-dealer side of his complex nature); it is most certainly counter to the judgment of our professional military leadership. Perhaps the President ought to consider returning to our traditional command structure, under which the Commander-in-Chief sets the prime objectives of combat, and assigns to the professionals the conduct of operations.

## DOCUMENT 13. THE STUDENT LEFT OPPOSES LBJ

The following selection documents radical protest against the war in Vietnam. Centered on the nation's college campuses and spearheaded by growing discontent with Lyndon Johnson in particular and liberal reform in general, antiwar protest mounted throughout the 1960s. In the spring of

1965, Paul Potter, president of the Students for a Democratic Society (SDS), the principal organization for New Left protest, addressed an antiwar rally in Washington, D.C. The war in Vietnam, Potter told his audience, had exposed the hypocrisy of American policy and the emptiness of Johnson's solemn words about freedom and democracy (see Document 12). Potter indicted the entire system, which wrongly "persists in calling itself free and persists in finding itself fit to police the world." The antiwar movement's task, he asserted, was to "name that system," to understand it and change it.

## PAUL POTTER

## *"The Incredible War"*: Speech at the *Washington Antiwar March*

### *April 17, 1965*

The incredible war in Vietnam has provided the razor, the terrifying sharp cutting edge that has finally severed the last vestiges of illusion that morality and democracy are the guiding principles of American foreign policy. The saccharine, self-righteous moralism that promises the Vietnamese a billion dollars of economic aid at the very moment we are delivering billions for economic and social destruction and political repression is rapidly losing what power it might ever have had to reassure us about the decency of our foreign policy. The further we explore the reality of what this country is doing and planning in Vietnam the more we are driven toward the conclusion of Senator Morse[3] that the U.S. may well be the greatest threat to peace in the world today. . . .

The President says that we are defending freedom in Vietnam. Whose freedom? Not the freedom of the Vietnamese. The first act of the first dictator (Diem) the U.S. installed in Vietnam was to systematically begin the persecution of all political opposition, non-Communist as well as Communist. . . .

---

[3] U.S. Senator Wayne Morse of Oregon, one of only two congressional opponents of the Gulf of Tonkin Resolution in 1964 and a critic of U.S. intervention in Vietnam.

---

Paul Potter, "The Incredible War": Speech at Washington Antiwar March, April 17, 1965, from Massimo Teodori, ed., *The New Left: A Documentary History* (New York: Bobbs-Merrill, 1968), 246–48.

The pattern of repression and destruction that we have developed and justified in the war is so thorough that it can only be called "cultural genocide." I am not simply talking about napalm or gas or crop destruction or torture hurled indiscriminantly on women and children, insurgent and neutral, upon the first suspicion of rebel activity. That in itself is horrendous and incredible beyond belief. But it is only part of a large pattern of destruction to the very fabric of the country. We have uprooted the people from the land and imprisoned them in concentration camps called "sunrise villages." Through conscription and direct political intervention and control we have broken or destroyed local customs and traditions, trampled upon those things of value which give dignity and purpose to life. . . .

Not even the President can say that this is war to defend the freedom of the Vietnamese people. Perhaps what the President means when he speaks of freedom is the freedom of the Americans.

What in fact has the war done for freedom in America? It has led to even more vigorous governmental efforts to control information, manipulate the press and pressure and persuade the public through distorted or downright dishonest documents such as the White Paper[4] on Vietnam. . . .

In many ways this is an unusual march, because the large majority of the people here are not involved in a peace movement as their primary basis of concern. What is exciting about the participants in this march is that so many of us view ourselves consciously as participants as well in a movement to build a more decent society. There are students here who have been involved in protest over the quality and kind of education they are receiving in growingly bureaucratized, depersonalized institutions called universities; there are Negroes from Mississippi and Alabama who are struggling against the tyranny and repression of those states; there are poor people here—Negro and white—from Northern urban areas who are attempting to build movements that abolish poverty and secure democracy; there are faculty who are beginning to question the relevance of their institutions to the critical problems facing the society. . . .

The President mocks freedom if he insists that the war in Vietnam is a defense of American freedom. Perhaps the only freedom that this war protects is the freedom of the warhawks in the Pentagon and the State Department to "experiment" with "counter-insurgency" and guerrilla warfare in Vietnam. Vietnam, we may say, is a "laboratory" run by a new breed of gamesmen who approach war as a kind of rational exercise in international power politics. . . .

[4] An official statement of government policy.

Thus far the war in Vietnam has only dramatized the demand of ordinary people to have some opportunity to make their own lives, and of their unwillingness, even under incredible odds, to give up the struggle against external domination. We are told however that that struggle can be legitimately suppressed since it might lead to the development of a Communist system—and before that menace, all criticism is supposed to melt.

This is a critical point and there are several things that must be said here—not by way of celebration, but because I think they are the truth. First, if this country were serious about giving the people of Vietnam some alternative to a Communist social revolution, that opportunity was sacrificed in 1954 when we helped to install Diem and his repression of non-Communist movements. There is no indication that we were serious about that goal—that we were ever willing to contemplate the risks of allowing the Vietnamese to choose their own destinies. Second, those people who insist now that Vietnam can be neutralized are for the most part looking for a sugar coating to cover the bitter pill. We must accept the consequences that calling for an end of the war in Vietnam is in fact allowing for the likelihood that a Vietnam without war will be a self-styled Communist Vietnam. Third, this country must come to understand that the creation of a Communist country in the world today is not an ultimate defeat. If people are given the opportunity to choose their own lives it is likely that some of them will choose what we have called "Communist systems." . . . And yet the war that we are creating and escalating in Southeast Asia is rapidly eroding the base of independence of North Vietnam as it is forced to turn to China and the Soviet Union.

But the war goes on; the freedom to conduct that war depends on the dehumanization not only of Vietnamese people but of Americans as well; it depends on the construction of a system of premises and thinking that insulates the President and his advisers thoroughly and completely from the human consequences of the decisions they make. I do not believe that the President or Mr. Rusk or Mr. McNamara or even McGeorge Bundy are particularly evil men. If asked to throw napalm on the back of a 10-year-old child they would shrink in horror—but their decisions have led to mutilation and death of thousands and thousands of people.

What kind of system is it that allows "good" men to make those kinds of decisions? What kind of system is it that justifies the U.S. or any country seizing the destinies of the Vietnamese people and using them callously for our own purpose? What kind of system is it that disenfranchises people in the South, leaves millions upon millions of people throughout the country impoverished and excluded from the mainstream and promise of American society, that creates faceless and terrible bureaucracies and makes those the place where people spend their lives and do their work, that consistently puts material values before human values—and still persists in calling itself free and still persists in finding itself fit to police the world? . . .

We must name that system. We must name it, describe it, analyze it, understand it and change it. For it is only when that system is changed and brought under control that there can be any hope for stopping the forces that create a war in Vietnam today or a murder in the South tomorrow. . . .

If the people of this country are to end the war in Vietnam, and to change the institutions which create it, then, the people of this country must create a massive social movement—and if that can be built around the issue of Vietnam, then that is what we must do. . . .

But that means that we build a movement that works not simply in Washington but in communities and with the problems that face people throughout the society. That means that we build a movement that understands Vietnam, in all its horror, as but a symptom of a deeper malaise, that we build a movement that makes possible the implementation of the values that would have prevented Vietnam, a movement based on the integrity of man and a belief in man's capacity to determine his own life; a movement that does not exclude people because they are too poor or have been held down; a movement that has the capacity to tolerate all of the formulations of society that men may choose to strive for; a movement that will build on the new and creative forms of protest that are beginning to emerge, such as the teach-in, and extend their efforts and intensify them; a movement that will not tolerate the escalation or prolongation of this war but will, if necessary, respond to the Administration war effort with massive civil disobedience all over the country that will wrench the country into a confrontation with the issues of the war; a movement that must of necessity reach out to all those people in Vietnam or elsewhere who are struggling to find decency and control for their lives.

For in a strange way the people of Vietnam and the people on this demonstration are united in much more than a common concern that the war be ended. In both countries there are people struggling to build a movement that has the power to change their condition. The system that frustrates these movements is the same. All our lives, our destinies, our very hopes to live depend on our ability to overcome that system. . . .

# 11

# The End of Liberalism

## DOCUMENT 14. LBJ INSISTS ON GUNS AND BUTTER

Many analysts, from LBJ's closest confidants to his most vociferous critics, agree that Johnson's most egregious error was promising both guns and butter—simultaneously waging war in Southeast Asia and building the Great Society—without a tax increase. That decision exacerbated inflation and other economic woes, weakened Johnson's influence in Congress, harmed his credibility when he finally reversed course and asked for a tax increase, and eroded his political constituency.

Nonetheless, Johnson and his top advisers maintained throughout his presidency that the war in Asia need not cause economic hardship or compromise the war on poverty. As late as 1967, Secretary of Defense Robert McNamara told a congressional committee that Johnson's policies imposed no undue strain on the nation's economy. The national economy, most experts agree, could have afforded both guns and butter, but the federal government could not—unless new taxes transferred wealth from the private sector into the Treasury. Johnson was initially unwilling and eventually unable to raise taxes and alert the American people to the true costs of his two-front war. In the selection here, from Johnson's 1966 State of the Union Address, LBJ offered a vigorous defense of his policy, assuring the Congress and his television audience that the nation was mighty enough to battle communism abroad and build a Great Society at home without much sacrifice from the American people.

# LYNDON B. JOHNSON

## Annual Message to the Congress on the State of the Union

### January 12, 1966

*Mr. Speaker, Mr. President, Members of the House and the Senate, my fellow Americans:*

Our Nation tonight is engaged in a brutal and bitter conflict in Vietnam. Later on I want to discuss that struggle in some detail with you. It just must be the center of our concerns.

But we will not permit those who fire upon us in Vietnam to win a victory over the desires and the intentions of all the American people. This Nation is mighty enough, its society is healthy enough, its people are strong enough, to pursue our goals in the rest of the world while still building a Great Society here at home. . . .

Because of Vietnam we cannot do all that we should, or all that we would like to do.

We will ruthlessly attack waste and inefficiency. We will make sure that every dollar is spent with the thrift and with the commonsense which recognizes how hard the taxpayer worked in order to earn it.

We will continue to meet the needs of our people by continuing to develop the Great Society. . . .

Tonight the cup of peril is full in Vietnam.

That conflict is not an isolated episode, but another great event in the policy that we have followed with strong consistency since World War II.

The touchstone of that policy is the interest of the United States—the welfare and the freedom of the people of the United States. But nations sink when they see that interest only through a narrow glass.

In a world that has grown small and dangerous, pursuit of narrow aims could bring decay and even disaster.

An America that is mighty beyond description—yet living in a hostile or despairing world—would be neither safe nor free to build a civilization to liberate the spirit of man. . . .

---

Annual Message to the Congress on the State of the Union, January 12, 1966, *Public Papers of the Presidents of the United States: Lyndon B. Johnson, 1966,* Book 1 (Washington, D.C.: Government Printing Office, 1966), 3–7.

# DOCUMENT 15. THE LIBERAL COALITION BREAKS UP

As the opposition drove LBJ and the Democratic party from the White House, astute observers noted the fraying of the liberal electoral coalition that FDR had assembled in 1936 and LBJ had triumphantly reunited in 1964. In 1969, journalist Peter Schrag explained the collapse of Johnson's vaunted consensus, the ways the events of the 1960s alienated the constituencies at the core of the New Deal coalition and helped to usher in two decades of conservative politics. In the essay that follows, Schrag profiles the "Forgotten American," the once solidly Democratic urban ethnic who largely rejected Lyndon Johnson, his party, and his liberal policies in the 1970s and 1980s.

## PETER SCHRAG
### *The Forgotten American*
#### *August 1969*

There is hardly a language to describe him, or even a set of social statistics. Just names: racist-bigot-redneck-ethnic-Irish-Italian-Pole-Hunkie-Yahoo. The lower middle class. A blank. The man under whose hat lies the great American desert. Who watches the tube, plays the horses, and keeps the niggers out of his union and his neighborhood. Who might vote for Wallace[1] (but didn't). Who cheers when the cops beat up on demonstrators. Who is free, white, and twenty-one, has a job, a home, a family, and is up to his eyeballs in credit. In the guise of the working class—or the American yeoman or John Smith—he was once the hero of the civics books, the man that Andrew Jackson called "the bone and sinew of the country." Now he is "the forgotten man," perhaps the most alienated person in America.

Nothing quite fits, except perhaps omission and semi-invisibility. America is supposed to be divided between affluence and poverty, between slums and suburbs. John Kenneth Galbraith begins the foreword to *The*

---

[1] George C. Wallace, segregationist governor of Alabama and candidate for president of the United States in 1964, 1968, and 1972. See pages 76–77, 109.

Peter Schrag, "The Forgotten American," *Harper's*, August 1969, 27–34.

*Affluent Society*[2] with the phrase, "Since I sailed for Switzerland in the early summer of 1955 to begin work on this book. . . . " But *between* slums and suburbs, between Scarsdale and Harlem, between Wellesley and Roxbury, between Shaker Heights and Hough, there are some eighty million people (depending on how you count them) who didn't sail for Switzerland in the summer of 1955, or at any other time, and who never expect to go. Between slums and suburbs: South Boston and South San Francisco, Bell and Parma, Astoria and Bay Ridge, Newark, Cicero, Downey, Daly City, Charlestown, Flatbush. Union halls, American Legion posts, neighborhood bars, and bowling leagues, the Ukranian Club and the Holy Name. Main Street. To try to describe all this is like trying to describe America itself. If you look for it, you find it everywhere: the rows of frame houses overlooking the belching steel mills in Bethlehem, Pennsylvania; two-family brick houses in Canarsie (where the most common slogan, even in the middle of a political campaign, is "curb your dog"); the Fords and Chevies with a decal American flag on the rear window (usually a cut-out from the *Reader's Digest*, and displayed in counter-protest against peaceniks and "those bastards who carry Vietcong flags in demonstrations"); the bunting on the porch rail with the inscription, "Welcome Home, Pete." The gold star in the window.

When he was Under Secretary of Housing and Urban Development, Robert C. Wood tried a definition. It is not good, but it's the best we have:

> He is a white employed male . . . earning between $5,000 and $10,000. He works regularly, steadily, dependably, wearing a blue collar or white collar. Yet the frontiers of his career expectations have been fixed since he reached the age of thirty-five, when he found that he had too many obligations, too much family, and too few skills to match opportunities with aspirations.
>
> This definition of the "working American" involves almost 23 million American families.
>
> The working American lives in the gray area fringes of a central city or in a close-in or very far-out cheaper suburban subdivision of a large metropolitan area. He is likely to own a home and a car, especially as his income begins to rise. Of those earning between $6,000 and $7,500, 70 percent own their own homes and 94 percent drive their own cars.
>
> 94 percent have no education beyond high school and 43 percent have only completed the eighth grade.

[2]*The Affluent Society* was an influential 1958 book by Harvard University Professor John Kenneth Galbraith, one of the nation's leading economists and an adviser to President John F. Kennedy.

He does all the right things, obeys the law, goes to church and insists—usually—that his kids get a better education than he had. But the right things don't seem to be paying off. While he is making more than he ever made—perhaps more than he'd ever dreamed—he's still struggling while a lot of others—"them" (on welfare, in demonstrations, in the ghettos) are getting most of the attention. "I'm working my ass off," a guy tells you on a stoop in South Boston. "My kids don't have a place to swim, my parks are full of glass, and I'm supposed to bleed for a bunch of people on relief." In New York a man who drives a Post Office trailer truck at night (4:00 P.M. to midnight) and a cab during the day (7:00 A.M. to 2:00 P.M.), and who hustles radios for his Post Office buddies on the side, is ready, as he says, to "knock somebody's ass." "The colored guys work when they feel like it. Sometimes they show up and sometimes they don't. One guy tore up all the time cards. I'd like to see a white guy do that and get away with it." . . .

## What Counts

The reaction is directed at almost every visible target: at integration and welfare, taxes and sex education, at the rich and the poor, the foundations and students, at the "smart people in the suburbs." In New York State the legislature cuts the welfare budget; in Los Angeles, the voters reelect Yorty[3] after a whispered racial campaign against the Negro favorite. In Minneapolis a police detective named Charles Stenvig, promising "to take the handcuffs off the police," wins by a margin stunning even to his supporters: in Massachusetts the voters mail tea bags to their representatives in protest against new taxes, and in state after state legislatures are passing bills to punish student demonstrators. ("We keep talking about permissiveness in training kids," said a Los Angeles labor official, "but we forget that these are our kids.")

And yet all these things are side manifestations of a malaise that lacks a language. Whatever law and order means, for example, to a man who feels his wife is unsafe on the street after dark or in the park at any time, or whose kids get shaken down in the school yard, it also means something like normality—the demand that everybody play it by the book, that cultural and social standards be somehow restored to their civics-book simplicity, that things shouldn't be as they are but as they were supposed to be. If there is a revolution in this country—a revolt in manners,

---

[3] Sam Yorty, mayor of Los Angeles during the Watts riots and a strong advocate of "law and order." He unsuccessfully sought the Democratic presidential nomination in 1968 and 1972.

standards of dress and obscenity, and, more importantly, in our official sense of what America is—there is also a counter-revolt. Sometimes it is inarticulate, and sometimes (perhaps most of the time) people are either too confused or apathetic—or simply too polite and too decent—to declare themselves. In Astoria, Queens, a white working-class district of New York, people who make $7,000 or $8,000 a year (sometimes in two jobs) call themselves affluent, even though the Bureau of Labor Statistics regards an income of less than $9,500 in New York inadequate to a moderate standard of living. And in a similar neighborhood in Brooklyn a truck driver who earns $151 a week tells you he's doing well, living in a two-story frame house separated by a narrow driveway from similar houses, thousands of them in block after block. This year, for the first time, he will go on a cruise—he and his wife and two other couples—two weeks in the Caribbean. He went to work after World War II ($57 a week) and he has lived in the same house for twenty years, accumulating two television sets, wall-to-wall carpeting in a small living room, and a basement that he recently remodeled into a recreation room with the help of two moonlighting firemen. "We get fairly good salaries, and this is a good neighborhood, one of the few good ones left. We have no smoked Irishmen around."

Stability is what counts, stability in job and home and neighborhood, stability in the church and in friends. At night you watch television and sometimes on a weekend you go to a nice place—maybe a downtown hotel—for dinner with another couple. (Or maybe your sister, or maybe bowling, or maybe, if you're defeated, a night at the track.) The wife has the necessary appliances, often still being paid off, and the money you save goes for your daughter's orthodontist, and later for her wedding. The smoked Irishmen—the colored (no one says black; few even say Negro)—represent change and instability, kids who cause trouble in school, who get treatment that your kids never got, that you never got. ("Those fucking kids," they tell you in South Boston, "raising hell, and not one of 'em paying his own way. Their fucking mothers are all on welfare.") The black kids mean a change in the rules, a double standard in grades and discipline, and—vaguely—a challenge to all you believed right. Law and order is the stability and predictability of established ways. Law and order is equal treatment—in school, in jobs, in the courts—even if you're cheating a little yourself. The Forgotten Man is Jackson's man. He is the vestigial American democrat of 1840: "They all know that their success depends upon their own industry and economy and that they must not expect to become suddenly rich by the fruits of their toil." He is also

Franklin Roosevelt's man—the man whose vote (or whose father's vote) sustained the New Deal. . . .

## At the Bottom of the Well

American culture? Wealth is visible, and so, now, is poverty. Both have become intimidating clichés. But the rest? A vast, complex, and disregarded world that was once—in belief, and in fact—the American middle: Greyhound and Trailways bus terminals in little cities at midnight, each of them with its neon lights and its cardboard hamburgers; acres of tar-paper beach bungalows in places like Revere and Rockaway; the hair curlers in the supermarket on Saturday, and the little girls in the communion dresses the next morning; pinball machines and the *Daily News,* the *Reader's Digest* and Ed Sullivan; houses with tiny front lawns (or even large ones) adorned with statues of the Virgin or of Sambo welcomin' de folks home; Clint Eastwood or Julie Andrews at the Palace; the trotting tracks and the dog tracks—Aurora Downs, Connaught Park, Roosevelt, Yonkers, Rockingham, and forty others—where gray men come not for sport and beauty, but to read numbers, to study and dope. (If you win you have figured something, have in a small way controlled your world, have surmounted your impotence. If you lose, bad luck, shit. "I'll break his goddamned head.") Baseball is not the national pastime; racing is. For every man who goes to a major-league baseball game there are four who go to the track and probably four more who go to the candy store or the barbershop to make their bets. (Total track attendance in 1965: 62 million plus another 10 million who went to the dogs.)

There are places, and styles, and attitudes. If there are neighborhoods of aspiration, suburban enclaves for the mobile young executive and the aspiring worker, there are also places of limited expectation and dead-end districts where mobility is finished. But even there you can often find, however vestigial, a sense of place, the roots of old ethnic loyalties, and a passionate, if often futile, battle against intrusion and change. "Everybody around here," you are told, "pays his own way." In this world the problems are not the ABM[4] or air pollution (have they heard of Biafra?[5]) or

[4] Acronym for antiballistic missile, a missile designed to attack and destroy incoming missiles. In 1972, the United States and the Soviet Union concluded a treaty limiting the development and deployment of these weapons.

[5] A region of the West African nation of Nigeria that attempted to separate from Nigeria during the 1960s. Civil war erupted and world attention focused on the plight of the Biafran people, particularly on widespread malnutrition and starvation in the region.

the international population crisis; the problem is to get your street cleaned, your garbage collected, to get your husband home from Vietnam alive; to negotiate installment payments and to keep the schools orderly. Ask anyone in Scarsdale or Winnetka about the schools and they'll tell you about new programs, or about how many are getting into Harvard, or about the teachers; ask in Oakland or the North Side of Chicago, and they'll tell you that they have (or haven't) had trouble. Somewhere in his gut the man in those communities knows that mobility and choice in this society are limited. He cannot imagine any major change for the better; but he can imagine change for the worse. And yet for a decade he is the one who has been asked to carry the burden of social reform, to integrate his schools and his neighborhood, has been asked by comfortable people to pay the social debts due to the poor and the black. In Boston, in San Francisco, in Chicago (not to mention Newark or Oakland) he has been telling the reformers to go to hell. The Jewish schoolteachers of New York and the Irish parents of Dorchester have asked the same question: "What the hell did Lindsay[6] (or the Beacon Hill Establishment) ever do for us?"

The ambiguities and changes in American life that occupy discussions in university seminars and policy debates in Washington, and that form the backbone of contemporary popular sociology, become increasingly the conditions of trauma and frustration in the middle. Although the New Frontier and Great Society contained some programs for those not already on the rolls of social pathology—federal aid for higher education, for example—the public priorities and the rhetoric contained little. The emphasis, properly, was on the poor, on the inner cities (e.g., Negroes) and the unemployed. But in Chicago a widow with three children who earns $7,000 a year can't get them college loans because she makes too much; the money is reserved for people on relief. New schools are built in the ghetto but not in the white working-class neighborhoods where they are just as dilapidated. In Newark the head of a white vigilante group (now a city councilman) runs, among other things, on a platform opposing pro-Negro discrimination. "When pools are being built in the Central Ward—don't they think white kids have got frustration? The white can't get a job; we have to hire Negroes first." The middle class, said Congressman Roman Pucinski of Illinois, who represents a lot of it, "is in revolt. Everyone has been generous in supporting anti-poverty. Now the middle-class American is disqualified from most of the programs."

[6]John V. Lindsay, Republican mayor of New York City. In the early 1970s, this liberal Republican changed parties and campaigned for the 1972 Democratic presidential nomination.

## "Somebody has to say no . . . "

The frustrated middle. The liberal wisdom about welfare, ghettos, student revolt, and Vietnam has only a marginal place, if any, for the values and life of the working man. It flies in the face of most of what he was taught to cherish and respect: hard work, order, authority, self-reliance. He fought, either alone or through labor organizations, to establish the precincts he now considers his own. Union seniority, the civil-service bureaucracy, and the petty professionalism established by the merit system in the public schools become sinecures of particular ethnic groups or of those who have learned to negotiate and master the system. A man who worked all his life to accumulate the points and grades and paraphernalia to become an assistant school principal (no matter how silly the requirements) is not likely to relinquish his position with equanimity. Nor is a dock worker whose only estate is his longshoreman's card. The job, the points, the credits become property:

> Some men leave their sons money [wrote a union member to the *New York Times*], some large investments, some business connections, and some a profession. I have only one worthwhile thing to give: my trade. I hope to follow a centuries-old tradition and sponsor my sons for an apprenticeship. For this simple father's wish it is said that I discriminate against Negroes. Don't all of us discriminate? Which of us . . . will not choose a son over all others?

Suddenly the rules are changing—all the rules. If you protect your job for your own you may be called a bigot. At the same time it's perfectly acceptable to shout black power and to endorse it. What does it take to be a good American? *Give the black man a position because he is black, not because he necessarily works harder or does the job better.* What does it take to be a good American? Dress nicely, hold a job, be clean-cut, don't judge a man by the color of his skin or the country of his origin. What about the demands of Negroes, the long hair of the students, the dirty movies, the people who burn drafts cards and American flags? Do you have to go out in the street with picket signs, do you have to burn the place down to get what you want? What does it take to be a good American? *This is a sick society, a racist society, we are fighting an immoral war.* ("I'm against the Vietnam war, too," says the truck driver in Brooklyn. "I see a good kid come home with half an arm and a leg in a brace up to here, and what's it all for? I was glad to see *my kid* flunk the Army physical. Still, somebody has to say no to these demonstrators and enforce the law.") What does it take to be a good American?

The conditions of trauma and frustration in the middle. What does it take to be a good American? Suddenly there are demands for Italian power and Polish power and Ukrainian power. In Cleveland the Poles demand a seat on the school board, and get it, and in Pittsburg John Pankuch, the seventy-three-year-old president of the National Slovak Society, demands "action, plenty of it to make up for lost time." Black power is supposed to be nothing but emulation of the ways in which other ethnic groups made it. But have they made it? In Reardon's Bar on East Eighth Street in South Boston, where the workmen come for their fish-chowder lunch and for their rye and ginger, they still identify themselves as Galway men and Kilkenny men; in the newsstand in Astoria you can buy *Il Progresso, El Tiempo,* the *Staats-Zeitung,* the *Irish World,* plus papers in Greek, Hungarian, and Polish. At the parish of Our Lady of Mount Carmel the priests hear confession in English, Italian, and Spanish and, nearby, the biggest attraction is not the stickball game, but the *bocce* court. Some of the poorest people in America are white, native, and have lived all of their lives in the same place as their fathers and grandfathers. The problems that were presumably solved in some distant past, in that prehistoric era before the textbooks were written—problems of assimilation, of upward mobility—now turn out to be very much unsolved. The melting pot and all: millions made it, millions moved to the affluent suburbs; several million—no one knows how many—did not. The median income in Irish South Boston is $5100 a year but the community-action workers have a hard time convincing the local citizens that any white man who is not stupid or irresponsible can be poor. Pride still keeps them from applying for income supplements or Medicaid, but it does not keep them from resenting those who do. In Pittsburgh, where the members of Polish-American organizations earn an estimated $5,000 to $6,000 (and some fall below the poverty line), the Poverty Programs are nonetheless directed primarily to Negroes, and almost everywhere the thing called urban backlash associates itself in some fashion with ethnic groups whose members have themselves only a precarious hold on the security of affluence. Almost everywhere in the old cities, tribal neighborhoods and their styles are under assault by masscult. The Italian grocery gives way to the supermarket, the ma-and-pa store and the walk-up are attacked by urban renewal. And almost everywhere, that assault tends to depersonalize and to alienate. It has always been this way, but with time the brave new world that replaces the old patterns becomes increasingly bureaucratized, distant, and hard to control.

Yet beyond the problems of ethnic identity, beyond the problems of Poles and Irishmen left behind, there are others more pervasive and more dangerous. For every Greek or Hungarian there are a dozen American Americans who are past ethnic consciousness and who are as alienated, as confused, and as angry as the rest. The obvious manifestations are the same everywhere—race, taxes, welfare, students—but the threat seems invariably more cultural and psychological than economic or social. What upset the police at the Chicago convention most was not so much the politics of the demonstrators as their manners and their hair. (The barbershops in their neighborhoods don't advertise Beatle Cuts but the Flat Top and the Chicago Box.) The affront comes from middle-class people—and their children—who had been cast in the role of social exemplars (and from those cast as unfortunates worthy of public charity) who offend all the things on which working class identity is built: "hippies [said a San Francisco longshoreman] who fart around the streets and don't work"; welfare recipients who strike and march for better treatment; "all those [said a California labor official] who challenge the precepts that these people live on." If ethnic groups are beginning to organize to get theirs, so are others: police and firemen ("The cop is the new nigger"); schoolteachers; lower-middle-class housewives fighting sex education and bussing; small property owners who have no ethnic communion but a passionate interest in lower taxes, more policemen, and stiffer penalties for criminals. In San Francisco the Teamsters, who had never been known for such interests before, recently demonstrated in support of the police and law enforcement and, on another occasion, joined a group called Mothers Support Neighborhood Schools at a school-board meeting to oppose—with their presence and later, apparently, with their fists—a proposal to integrate the schools through bussing. ("These people," someone said at the meeting, "do not look like mothers.") . . .

## Can the Common Man Come Back?

Beneath it all there is a more fundamental ambivalence, not only about the young, but about institutions—the schools, the churches, the Establishment—and about the future itself. In the major cities of the East (though perhaps not in the West) there is a sense that time is against you, that one is living "in one of the few decent neighborhoods left," that "if I can get $125 a week upstate (or downstate) I'll move." The institutions that were supposed to mediate social change and which, more than ever, are becoming priesthoods of information and conglomerates of social engineers, are increasingly suspect. To attack the Ford Foundation (as Wright Patman[7] has done) is not only to fan the embers of historic

[7] Democratic representative from Texas.

populism against concentrations of wealth and power, but also to arouse those who feel that they are trapped by an alliance of upper-class Wasps and lower-class Negroes. If the foundations have done anything for the blue-collar worker he doesn't seem to be aware of it. At the same time the distrust of professional educators that characterizes the black militants is becoming increasingly prevalent among a minority of lower-middle-class whites who are beginning to discover that the schools aren't working for them either. ("Are all those new programs just a cover-up for failure?") And if the Catholic Church is under attack from its liberal members (on birth control, for example) it is also alienating the traditionalists who liked their minor saints (even if they didn't actually exist) and were perfectly content with the Latin Mass. For the alienated Catholic liberal there are other places to go; for the lower-middle-class parishioner in Chicago or Boston there are none.

Perhaps, in some measure, it has always been this way. Perhaps none of this is new. And perhaps it is also true that the American lower middle has never had it so good. And yet surely there is a difference, and that is that the common man has lost his visibility and, somehow, his claim on public attention. There are old liberals and socialists—men like Michael Harrington[8]—who believe that a new alliance can be forged for progressive social action:

> From Marx to Mills,[9] the Left has regarded the middle class as a stratum of hypocritical, vacillating rear-guarders. There was often sound reason for this contempt. But is it not possible that a new class is coming into being? It is not the old middle class of small property owners and entrepreneurs, nor the new middle class of managers. It is composed of scientists, technicians, teachers, and professionals in the public sector of the society. By education and work experience it is predisposed toward planning. It could be an ally of the poor and the organized workers—or their sophisticated enemy. In other words, an unprecedented social and political variable seems to be taking shape in America.
>
> The American worker, even when he waits on a table or holds open a door, is not servile; he does not carry himself like an inferior. The openness, frankness, and democratic manner which Tocqueville de-

---

[8] America's most prominent Democratic Socialist and the author of *The Other America* (New York: Macmillan, 1962), the 1962 book that inspired President Kennedy to investigate the problem of poverty in the United States. See pages 70–71.

[9] C. Wright Mills: sociologist and author of *White Collar* (New York: Oxford University Press, 1957) and *The Power Elite* (New York: Oxford University Press, 1956). Mills's radical critique of American politics and American society inspired and informed the student radicals of the 1960s New Left.

scribed in the last century persists to this very day. They have been a source of rudeness, contemptuous ignorance, violence—and of a creative self-confidence among great masses of people. It was in this latter spirit that the CIO was organized and the black freedom movement marched.

There are recent indications that the white lower middle class is coming back on the roster of public priorities. Pucinski tells you that liberals in Congress are privately discussing the pressure from the middle class. There are proposals now to increase personal income-tax exemptions from $600 to $1,000 (or $1,200) for each dependent, to protect all Americans with a national insurance system covering catastrophic medical expenses, and to put a floor under all incomes. Yet these things by themselves are insufficient. Nothing is sufficient without a national sense of restoration. What Pucinski means by the middle class has, in some measure, always been represented. A physician earning $75,000 a year is also a working man but he is hardly a victim of the welfare system. Nor, by and large, are the stockholders of the Standard Oil Company or U.S. Steel. The fact that American ideals have often been corrupted in the cause of self-aggrandizement does not make them any less important for the cause of social reform and justice. "As a movement with the conviction that there is more to people than greed and fear," Harrington said, "the Left must . . . also speak in the name of the historic idealism of the United States."

The issue, finally, is not *the program* but the vision, the angle of view. A huge constituency may be coming up for grabs, and there is considerable evidence that its political mobility is more sensitive than anyone can imagine, that all the sociological determinants are not as significant as the simple facts of concern and leadership. When Robert Kennedy was killed last year, thousands of working-class people who had expected to vote for him—if not hundreds of thousands—shifted their loyalties to Wallace. A man who can change from a progressive democrat into a bigot overnight deserves attention.

# An LBJ Chronology
# (1908–1975)

## 1908
Lyndon Baines Johnson is born on August 27 near Stonewall, Texas, on the Pedernales River in central Texas.

## 1924
Lyndon graduates from high school and drives west with a carload of friends. He spends the next year in California.

## 1927
Johnson enrolls at Southwest Texas State Teachers College in San Marcos, Texas.

## 1928–29
While interrupting his studies at San Marcos, Johnson serves as teacher and principal at Welhausen Elementary School in Cotulla Texas.

## 1929
The Great Depression begins.

## 1930
**July:** Johnson makes his first political speech at a rally in Henly, Texas, impressing state legislator Welly Hopkins, who hires Johnson to manage his campaign for state senate.

**August:** Johnson receives his B.S. in education and history from Southwest Texas State Teachers College.

## 1931
Texas Representative Richard Kleberg hires Johnson as his congressional secretary in Washington.

## 1933
President Franklin D. Roosevelt launches the New Deal.

## 1934
Johnson meets and marries Claudia Alta ("Lady Bird") Taylor.

## 1935
Johnson becomes Texas state director of the National Youth Administration.

## 1937
Johnson wins special election to fill vacant congressional seat for central Texas.

## 1939
Germany invades Poland. World War II begins.

## 1941
**April:**   Johnson opens his campaign for a seat in the U.S. Senate.

**June:**   In an election famous for fraud and irregularities, Governor W. Lee ("Pappy") O'Daniel narrowly defeats Johnson in race for seat in the U.S. Senate.

**December:**   Japanese aircraft attack the U.S. fleet at Pearl Harbor, and the United States enters World War II. Johnson goes on active duty in the U.S. Navy.

## 1942
**June:**   On an inspection tour in the Pacific, Johnson joins the crew of the B-26 bomber *Heckling Hare* on a dangerous raid over Lae, New Guinea. Johnson is awarded the Silver Star.

**July:**   Johnson leaves active duty and returns to the House of Representatives.

## 1945
**April:**   President Franklin D. Roosevelt dies. He is succeeded by Harry S. Truman.

**August:**   U.S. warplanes drop atomic bombs on Hiroshima and Nagasaki. Japan surrenders, ending World War II.

**September:**   Ho Chi Minh proclaims Vietnam's independence from French rule.

## 1948
In a close, contested election, Johnson wins the runoff against Coke Stevenson for a seat in the U.S. Senate by just eighty-seven votes, earning him the nickname "Landslide Lyndon."

## 1950

**February:**   Senator Joseph McCarthy claims that communist agents have infiltrated the U.S. Department of State.

**June:**   The United States, fighting with United Nations forces, goes to war in Korea.

## 1951

Johnson is elected majority whip of the U.S. Senate.

## 1953

**January:**   Johnson's Democratic colleagues elect him to the post of minority leader.

**July:**   The Korean War ends.

## 1954

**April:**   Vietnamese rebels defeat the French at Dien Bien Phu. President Eisenhower introduces the *domino theory.*

**May:**   The United States Supreme Court declares segregated schools unconstitutional in *Brown v. Board of Education.*

**July:**   Johnson's landslide victory in the state Democratic primary ensures his reelection.

**December:**   The U.S. Senate censures Joseph McCarthy.

## 1955

**January:**   Johnson is elevated to the post of majority leader.

**July:**   Johnson suffers a heart attack.

## 1957

**August:**   Congress approves the Civil Rights Act of 1957.

**October:**   The Soviets launch *Sputnik I.*

## 1960

**July:**   John F. Kennedy wins the Democratic presidential nomination and invites LBJ to be his running mate.

**November:**   Kennedy and Johnson win.

## 1961

**March:**   President Kennedy establishes the President's Committee on Equal Employment Opportunity. Vice President Johnson is appointed chairman of the committee.

**May:**   Johnson travels to Vietnam, India, and Pakistan.

**August:**   After the erection of the Berlin Wall, President Kennedy sends Johnson to Berlin to reiterate the United States's commitment to the defense of West Berlin.

**November:**   Kennedy approves a memorandum committing the United States to "preventing the fall of South Vietnam to the communists" and recognizing that "U.S. forces may be necessary to achieve this objective."

## 1963

**April:**   Racial turmoil begins in Birmingham, Alabama.

**August:**   The March on Washington takes place.

**November 7:**   Vietnamese President Ngo Dinh Diem is assassinated in Saigon.

**November 22:**   Kennedy is assassinated in Dallas. Johnson is sworn in as the thirty-sixth president of the United States.

## 1964

**January:**   In his first State of the Union Address, President Johnson declares "unconditional war on poverty."

**May:**   Johnson introduces the Great Society in a graduation day address at the University of Michigan.

**July:**   Johnson signs the Civil Rights Act of 1964.

**August 20:**   Johnson signs the Economic Opportunity Act, formally launching the war on poverty programs.

**August 24–27:**   At the Democratic National Convention in Atlantic City, the Mississippi Freedom Democratic Party challenges the credentials of the all-white Mississippi delegation. The convention nominates Lyndon Johnson and Hubert Humphrey as the party's standard-bearers for the fall elections.

**November:**   Johnson defeats Barry Goldwater in the presidential election.

## 1965

**February:**   Vietnamese guerrillas attack a U.S. military barracks in Pleiku, killing eight American servicemen. Johnson orders immediate reprisals and soon adopts a strategy of continuing air attacks against North Vietnam.

**March 7:**   In response to the murder of civil rights activist Jimmie Lee Jackson, protesters march from Selma toward the Alabama State Capitol in Montgomery. As the marchers cross the Edmund Pettas Bridge outside Selma, state troopers set upon them with clubs and tear gas. Reports of "Bloody Sunday" spark national outrage.

**March 15:**   President Johnson appears before a joint session of Congress to demand action on voting rights for black southerners.

**April 7:** At Johns Hopkins University, Johnson lays out U.S. war aims in Vietnam, a program he calls "Peace Without Conquest."

**April 11:** LBJ signs the Elementary and Secondary Education Act in Johnson City, Texas.

**June:** Johnson delivers the commencement address at Howard University, promising to seek "equality as a fact and result" for black Americans.

**July:** Johnson makes the decision to escalate the war in Vietnam.

**August 6:** Johnson signs the Voting Rights Act.

**August 12:** Racial unrest erupts in Watts.

## 1966

**January:** In his State of the Union Address, Johnson pledges to pursue both the Great Society at home and the war in Vietnam.

**November:** Liberal Democrats suffer heavy losses in the midterm congressional elections.

## 1967

**July:** Major race riots erupt in Newark and Detroit.

**August:** Johnson sends a tax bill to Congress, proposing an income tax surcharge to restrain inflation and finance the war in Vietnam.

## 1968

**January:** Vietcong forces launch the Tet offensive.

**March 12:** Johnson wins the Democratic presidential primary in New Hampshire, but Minnesota Senator Eugene McCarthy, a strong opponent of the Vietnam War, captures 42 percent of the vote.

**March 16:** New York Senator Robert Kennedy challenges President Johnson for the Democratic presidential nomination.

**March 31:** Johnson announces his decision to de-escalate the war in Vietnam and withdraw from the 1968 presidential campaign.

**April 4:** Martin Luther King, Jr., is assassinated in Memphis, Tennessee.

**April 11:** Johnson signs the Civil Rights Act of 1968.

**June 5:** Robert F. Kennedy is assassinated in Los Angeles.

**August:** Amidst massive demonstrations by antiwar protesters and violent confrontations between demonstrators and Chicago police, the Democratic National Convention nominates Hubert H. Humphrey as the party's presidential candidate.

**November:** Richard Nixon narrowly defeats Hubert Humphrey in the presidential election.

## 1969

Johnson retires to the LBJ Ranch.

## 1973

**January 22:**   Johnson suffers a fatal heart attack and dies at the LBJ Ranch.

**January 23:**   President Nixon announces a peace treaty, ending the war in Vietnam.

## 1975

**May:**   The National Liberation Front and North Vietnamese troops complete their takeover of South Vietnam. They raise their flag over Saigon, renaming it Ho Chi Minh City, as the last American officials flee in helicopters.

# Suggestions for Further Reading

Lyndon Johnson's *The Vantage Point* (New York: Popular Library, 1971), reads more like a carefully wrought defense brief for his policies, especially the war in Vietnam, than a personal memoir, but it offers his personal account of many of the pivotal events of his presidency. *Quotations from Chairman LBJ* (New York: Simon and Schuster, 1968), an irreverent collection of Johnson's speeches and aphorisms modeled on Mao's *Little Red Book*, offers a less ponderous introduction to LBJ's words and deeds. More revealing than either of these is *A White House Diary* (New York: Holt, Rinehart, and Winston, 1970), Lady Bird Johnson's journal entries for the presidential years.

Lyndon Johnson made a strong impression on the people around him so it is not surprising that many of his associates have published colorful and occasionally insightful reminiscences about him. Princeton historian Eric F. Goldman served as LBJ's liaison to the nation's intellectuals, and his memoir, *The Tragedy of Lyndon Johnson* (New York: Dell, 1969), details Johnson's intellectual strengths and insecurities. Special Assistant Jack Valenti paints a flawed but generally heroic portrait of his one-time boss in *A Very Human President* (New York: Pocket Books, 1977). Domestic policy chief Joseph A. Califano, Jr.'s account, *The Triumph and Tragedy of Lyndon Johnson* (New York: Simon and Schuster, 1991), offers a particularly insightful and vivid analysis of policies and personalities in the Johnson White House. In *Lyndon: An Oral Biography* (New York: Ballantine, 1980), Merle Miller collects the testimony of numerous Johnson friends and colleagues to construct a narrative of LBJ's career.

Two White House aides have produced odd but compelling hybrid books. Press Secretary George Reedy's *The Twilight of the Presidency* (New York: Mentor, 1970) draws on his experiences with LBJ to fashion a critique of the modern presidency, while Doris Kearns blends accounts of her collaboration with Johnson on his memoirs, biography, and psychohistory in her engrossing study, *Lyndon Johnson and the American Dream* (New York: Signet, 1976).

The richest sources of information on Johnson are (and probably will continue to be) the massive research biographies by Robert Dallek and Robert A. Caro. Dallek's *Lone Star Rising* (New York: Oxford University Press, 1991), the first of a projected two-volume study of Johnson's life and times, is a work of prodigious research and erudition. It covers Johnson's progress from the Hill Country to the vice presidency. While critical of LBJ's opportunism and ruthlessness, Dallek nonetheless admires Johnson as a successful politician and credits him for the maintenance and development of liberal nationalism in the 1940s and 1950s. In Robert A. Caro's detailed and dramatic *The Years of Lyndon Johnson*, the first two volumes, *The Path to Power* (New York: Alfred A. Knopf, 1982) and *Means of Ascent* (New York: Alfred A. Knopf, 1990), chart the Johnson family's history from the arrival of LBJ's ancestors in the Hill Country until LBJ's election to the Senate in 1948. With considerable verve and relentless dedication, Caro exposes the young Johnson's greed, unscrupulousness, and ambition. Unlike Dallek, Caro uncovers little worth celebrating in LBJ's character or legacy.

Neither of the major research biographies reaches beyond 1960, but Paul Conkin has briefly chronicled Johnson's entire career in *Big Daddy from the Pedernales* (Boston: Twayne, 1986), and Vaughn Bornet has focused on the 1960s in his entry in the Kansas history of the presidency series, *The Presidency of Lyndon B. Johnson* (Lawrence: University Press of Kansas, 1983). In *The Politician* (New York: W. W. Norton, 1982), Texas journalist Ronnie Dugger has produced an insightful analysis of Johnson's early years and the growth of "predatory politics" in the 1940s and 1950s.

Several journalists essayed Johnson's character and achievements during his presidency. They range from William S. White's *The Professional* (New York: Crest Books, 1964), a glowing assessment by one of Johnson's friends in the press corps, to Robert Sherrill's *The Accidental President* (New York: Pyramid Books, 1967), a damning indictment of LBJ. The two most balanced and revealing of these contemporary accounts are *Lyndon B. Johnson: The Exercise of Power* (New York: Signet Books, 1966) by syndicated columnists Rowland Evans and Robert Novak and *JFK and LBJ* (Baltimore: Pelican Books, 1969) by *New York Times* reporter Tom Wicker.

The great issues of Johnson's presidency—civil rights, the Great Society, Vietnam—have each spawned voluminous scholarly literature. Hugh Davis Graham's *The Civil Rights Era* (New York: Oxford University Press, 1990) offers a comprehensive analysis of the development of civil rights policy during the 1960s. An abridged paperback version, *Civil Rights and the Presidency*, was published by Oxford in 1992. J. Harvie Wilkinson's *From Brown to Bakke* (New York: Oxford University Press, 1979) and Richard Kluger's *Simple Justice* (New York: Vintage, 1975) detail the legal history of the battle against segregation. Specialized studies of various aspects of the civil rights struggle, the experiences of particular communities, and the biographies of key individuals are too numerous to list here. Useful surveys of the movement include Aldon Morris, *The Origins of the Civil Rights Movement* (New York: Free Press, 1984); Clayborne Carson, *In Struggle* (Cambridge: Harvard University Press, 1981); Robert Weisbrot, *Freedom Bound* (New York: W. W. Norton, 1990); Harvard Sitkoff, *The Struggle for Black Equality, 1954–1980* (New York: Hill and Wang, 1981); and Steven Lawson, *Running for Freedom* (New York: McGraw-Hill, 1991). The Kerner Commission report on the racial disturbances of the 1960s is available as the *Report of the National*

*Advisory Commission on Civil Disorders* (New York: Bantam, 1968). Clayborne Carson et al., eds., *Eyes on the Prize: A Reader and Guide* (New York: Penguin, 1987), collect a large number of primary source documents. In *The Great Society Reader* (New York: Vintage, 1967), editors Marvin E. Gettleman and David Mermelstein assemble a broad variety of contemporary viewpoints on Johnson's domestic programs. In *Maximum Feasible Misunderstanding* (New York: The Free Press, 1969), Daniel Patrick Moynihan offers an insider's analysis of what went wrong with the Community Action Program.

Since LBJ's death, numerous scholars have debated the legacy of his War on Poverty. Prominent defenders of the Great Society include John E. Schwarz in *America's Hidden Success* (New York: W. W. Norton, 1983); Sar A. Levitan in *The Great Society's Poor Law* (Baltimore: Johns Hopkins University Press, 1969); *Beyond The Safety Net* (Cambridge: Ballinger, 1984), and, with Martin Rein and David Marwick, *Work and Welfare Go Together* (Baltimore: Johns Hopkins University Press, 1972). Critics have assailed Johnson's social programs from all points on the ideological landscape. Frances Fox Piven and Richard A. Cloward advance a radical critique in *Regulating the Poor* (New York: Vintage, 1971). From the center-right, neoconservative Nathan Glazer offers a sobering assessment in *The Limits of Social Policy* (Cambridge: Harvard University Press, 1988). Most prominently, Charles Murray's *Losing Ground* (New York: Basic Books, 1984) attacks from the Reaganite right, insisting that Johnson-era social programs not only failed to eliminate poverty and unemployment but actually exacerbated those problems. To celebrate the twentieth anniversary of the Great Society, the Johnson School of Public Affairs invited a number of scholars and poverty warriors to a conference in Austin. Their reflections are assembled in *The Great Society: A Twenty-Year Critique,* edited by Barbara Jordan and Elspeth Rostow (Austin: LBJ Library, 1986). For an overview of the history of the battle against economic deprivation, see James T. Patterson's *America's Struggle Against Poverty, 1900–1980* (Cambridge: Harvard University Press, 1981). Editors Sheldon H. Danziger and Daniel H. Weinberg anthologize recent social science assessments of poverty and welfare in *Fighting Poverty* (Cambridge: Harvard University Press, 1986).

The war in Vietnam, as many observers have noted, was the American cataclysm, an event that profoundly altered the ways Americans conceived of themselves, their nation, and the world. Not surprisingly, the books on the war and its impact would alone fill a small library. The best single-volume history of the conflict is George Herring's nuanced and balanced *America's Longest War,* 2nd ed. (New York: Alfred A. Knopf, 1986). *America in Vietnam: A Documentary History,* edited by William Appleman Williams et al. (New York: W. W. Norton, 1989), and the *New York Times* edition of *The Pentagon Papers* (New York: Bantam, 1971) assemble the essential policy documents, while Larry Engelmann's moving oral history, *Tears Before the Rain* (New York: Oxford University Press, 1990), offers personal testimony on the fall of South Vietnam. Johnson's stewardship of the war is detailed in

Brian VanDeMark's *Into the Quagmire* (New York: Oxford University Press, 1991) and in two volumes by Larry Berman, *Planning a Tragedy* (New York: W. W. Norton, 1982) and *Lyndon Johnson's War* (New York: W. W. Norton, 1989). Among Johnson's aides, George Ball and Townsend Hoopes have produced noteworthy accounts of wartime policymaking. See Townsend Hoopes's *The Limits of Intervention*, rev. ed. (New York: W. W. Norton, 1987), and George Ball's *The Past Has Another Pattern* (New York: W. W. Norton, 1982).

Many American journalists and military personnel have offered personal reminiscences of their years in Vietnam. Among these, Tim O'Brien's *If I Die in a Combat Zone* (New York: Dell, 1987) deserves particular attention. On the experiences of returned veterans, see psychologist Robert Lifton's disturbing study, *Home From the War* (New York: Simon and Schuster, 1973).

In *Backfire* (New York: Ballantine, 1985), Loren Baritz probes the links between the war in Vietnam and American culture. A June 1967 report of the Center for Strategic Studies at Georgetown University analyzes "The Economic Impact of the Vietnam War" (Washington: Center for Strategic Studies, 1967), while in *The Draft* (Chicago: University of Chicago Press, 1967), editor Sol Tax collects wartime perspectives on the selective service system. Kathleen J. Turner assesses the "Credibility Gap" in *Lyndon Johnson's Dual War: Vietnam and the Press* (Chicago: University of Chicago Press, 1985). On the antiwar movement, consult Todd Gitlin's *The Sixties* (New York: Bantam, 1987) and James Miller's *Democracy Is in the Streets* (New York: Simon and Schuster, 1987).

For a general history of the Johnson era, especially the rise and fall of American liberalism, see Godfrey Hodgson's *America in Our Time* (New York: Vintage, 1976), Allen J. Matusow's *The Unraveling of America* (New York: Harper and Row, 1984), John Morton Blum's *Years of Discord* (New York: W. W. Norton, 1991), and Alonzo Hamby's *Liberalism and Its Challengers*, 2nd ed. (New York: Oxford University Press, 1992). Especially insightful is the anthology edited by Steve Fraser and Gary Gerstle, *The Rise and Fall of the New Deal Order* (Princeton: Princeton University Press, 1989). In *From Cotton Belt to Sunbelt* (New York: Oxford University Press, 1991), Bruce J. Schulman examines the ties between the fate of Johnson's native region and the odyssey of American liberalism. The evolution of postwar liberalism and LBJ's crucial role in shaping that development receive outstanding treatment in Laura Kalman's magisterial biography, *Abe Fortas: A Biography* (New Haven: Yale University Press, 1990), a study of Johnson's confidant and appointee to the Supreme Court. The collapse of the liberal coalition is deftly analyzed in *Chain Reaction*, by Thomas Edsall with Mary Edsall (New York: W. W. Norton, 1991); *Why Americans Hate Politics*, by E. J. Dionne, Jr. (New York: Touchstone, 1991); and *Canarsie: The Jews and Italians of Brooklyn against Liberalism*, by Jonathan Rieder (Cambridge: Harvard University Press, 1985).

*(Acknowledgments continued from page iv)*

Allen J. Matusow. Reprinted by permission of the LBJ School of Public Affairs and by permission of the author.

Paul Potter. Reprinted with the permission of Macmillan Publishing company from *The New Left: A Documentary History* by Massimo Teodori. Copyright © 1968 by Massimo Teodori.

Peter Schrag. Repinted by permission of the author.

Jack Valenti. Reprinted from *A Very Human President* by Jack Valenti with the permission of W. W. Norton & Company, Inc. Copyright © 1975 by Jack Valenti.

ILLUSTRATIONS

*Pages 18, 54, 66, 69, 72, 78, 142:* UPI/Bettmann.
*Pages 44:* LBJ Library photo by Y. R. Okamoto.
*Page 128:* From *Herblock: A Cartoonist's Life* (Lisa Drew Books/Macmillan, 1993).

# Index

*Pages with illustrations are indicated by italics.*

Dallek, Robert, on LBJ and politics, 2
Dams
    LBJ's support for, 20
    LBJ's support for on Mekong River,
        61, 136
Da Nang, Marine Corps sent to, 135
Debate team, LBJ coaches, 10
de Gaulle, Charles, on LBJ, 165
Democracy, new liberal views of, 37
Democratic Congressional Campaign
    Committee, LBJ heads, 24–25
Democratic National Convention (1964),
    106
    civil rights disputes during, 105–06
    conflict over Mississippi delegates, 106
Dewey, Thomas E., loses to Truman, 34
Diem, Premier. *See* Ngo Dinh Diem
Dien Bien Phu, 130
Dies, Martin, 25
Dignity of man, LBJ on, 194
Diplomacy, LBJ's weakness in, 126
Dirksen, Everett, civil rights bill and, 74,
    110
Discrimination laws, LBJ on, 195
Dodge Hotel, LBJ moves into, 11
Dominican Republic, marines sent to, 134
Douglas, Paul, 35
Dugger, J. Ronnie, on LBJ and Brown
    and Root, 24

Economic Opportunity Act, 98
Economic woes, LBJ's, 157–58
Economics, LBJ and, 156–59
Education
    Great Society and, 179, 181
    James Farmer on community programs
        for, 199
    JFK's problems with aid to, 62
    laws, 5
    LBJ on, 5
    LBJ on African American, 203
    regional views of aid to, 62–63
Eisenhower, Dwight D., 35
    and the domino theory, 130
    and Vietnam, 130
    attitude toward Ho Chi Minh, 130
    LBJ as opponent of, 47
    meets with LBJ, 47
Election of 1941, 26
Election of 1960, 58–59
Election of 1964, 76–79
Electrification, rural, 21
Elementary and Secondary Education
    Act, 181, 186–87

implementation of, 94
LBJ signs, 5, 89
provisions of, 89
English, LBJ on importance of teaching, 9
Environment
    government regulation of, 91–92
    Great Society and the, 179
Equal Employment Opportunity Commis-
    sion (EEOC)
    and group-based rights, 120
    and LBJ's civil rights policies, 121
    and Moynihan report, 120
    expanded powers of, 120
    problems of, 119–20
Equal opportunity, LBJ on, 202
Equal rights, LBJ on denial of, 193
Ethnic identity, 242–43
Evans, Rowland, and Robert Novak
    coin term "The Treatment," 43
    on Moynihan report, 117

Families, breakdown of African American,
    206
Farmer, James
    on black militancy, 198–200
    on Civil Rights acts, 200
    on community and political organization,
        200
    on Great Society programs, 199–200
Federal Communications Commission
    (FCC), LBJ and, 39
Federal law, Great Society's use of, 182,
    183
Filibuster, southern mastery of, 52
Foreign affairs, LBJ on, 70
Foreign policy
    LBJ's abilities for, 125–26
    LBJ's support for bipartisan, 47
"Forgotten man," Peter Schrag on, 235–
    45
Fortas, Abe
    advises LBJ on Coke Stevenson chal-
        lenge, 32
    as southern liberal, 17
    builds links to business, 85
    drafts antidiscrimination bill, 59
    founds law firm, 39
    public power and, 20
Four freedoms, 12
France
    defeat at Dien Bien Phu, 130
    relationship to Vietnam, 129
Freedom, LBJ on, 202